NATIVE
AMERICAN CULTURE

THE NATIVE AMERICAN SOURCEBOOK

NATIVE AMERICAN CULTURE

EDITED BY KATHLEEN KUIPER, MANAGER, ARTS AND CULTURE

Britannica®
Educational Publishing

IN ASSOCIATION WITH

ROSEN
EDUCATIONAL SERVICES

First Edition

Britannica Educational Publishing
Michael I. Levy: Executive Editor
J.E. Luebering: Senior Manager
Marilyn L. Barton: Senior Coordinator, Production Control
Steven Bosco: Director, Editorial Technologies
Lisa S. Braucher: Senior Producer and Data Editor
Yvette Charboneau: Senior Copy Editor
Kathy Nakamura: Manager, Media Acquisition
Kathleen Kuiper: Manager, Arts and Culture

Rosen Educational Services
Jeanne Nagle: Senior Editor
Nelson Sá: Art Director
Cindy Reiman: Photography Manager
Matthew Cauli: Designer, Cover Design
Introduction by David Nagle

Library of Congress Cataloging-in-Publication Data

Native American culture / edited by Kathleen Kuiper. — 1st ed.
    p. cm. -- (The Native American sourcebook)
"In association with Britannica Educational Publishing, Rosen Educational Services."
Includes bibliographical references and index.
ISBN 978-1-61530-138-6 (library binding)
1. Indians of North America—Social life and customs. 2. Indians of North America—Social
conditions. 3. Indians of North America—History. I. Kuiper, Kathleen.
E98.S7N38 2011
970.004'97—dc22

2010010369

Manufactured in the United States of America

On the cover: Dancer in traditional regalia at a Virginia powwow in 2005. *Stan Honda/ AFP/Getty Images*

Pages 17, 21, 45, 74, 98, 137, 175, 202, 223: *Rich Reid/National Geographic Image Collection/ Getty Images*

CONTENTS

43

50

53

67

72

78

128

144

150

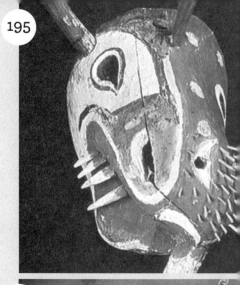

195

197

212

229

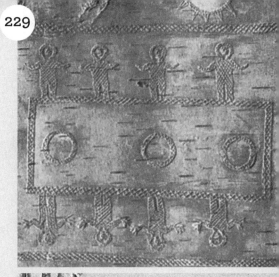

232

INTRODUCTION

Perhaps the greatest mistake one could make when considering Native American culture would be to assume that there existed only one such homogeneous culture among the indigenous peoples of North America. Rather, there is an assortment of distinct and diverse cultural aspects that, when bound together, make a whole. This book will show that there isn't just a group of American "Indians," but rather individual societies with marked differences—and similarities—that form what is called Native American culture.

The "first peoples" of North America are believed to have arrived on the continent as the result of Asiatic migrations over what is today known as the Bering Strait. Though some recent evidence disputes this theory, these peoples are supposed to have traveled over a land bridge that existed during the time of these migrations, between 20,000 and 60,000 years before the present era. The land bridge was most likely caused by glacial activity that lowered ocean levels to such an extent that groups of Stone-Age hunters were able to travel on foot from present-day Russia to what is now Alaska. Once across, these groups split up in a broad fashion spreading throughout the continent and beyond: from Greenland and today's eastern United States seaboard to the east, to the tip of South America to the south, and extending past the Arctic Circle in the north.

As a generally recognized point of reference, Christopher Columbus's arrival in the New World begins a natural curiosity by Europeans about this amazing frontier. It is believed that in 1492 there existed a population of between 600,000 and 2 million indigenous peoples living in the areas now known as Canada and the United States. This population segment and its descendants are the focus of this book.

Since the turn of the 20th century, one tool anthropologists use in their studies is defining culture areas, which are geographic regions where similar cultural traits co-occur. There are 10 commonly defined culture areas for Native Americans. The Arctic is comprised of the northernmost North America and Greenland, while the Subarctic encompasses the Alaskan and Canadian region south of the Arctic, not including the Maritime Provinces. The Northwest culture area is defined by a narrow strip of Pacific coast land and islands from the southern border of Alaska to northwest Canada. Roughly all of present-day California and the northern section of Baja California (northern Mexico) make up the aptly named California culture area. The Plateau region lies between the Rocky Mountains and the Pacific Coast mountain system. The Great Basin culture area encompasses almost all of present-day Utah and Nevada, as well as parts of Oregon, Idaho, Wyoming, Colorado,

A man in dance regalia at the United Tribes Powwow in Bismarck, N.D. © MedioImages/ Getty Image

Arizona, Montana, and California. The Southwest culture area involves the southwestern United States. Indigenous people living in the grasslands bounded by the Mississippi River, the Rocky Mountains, the present-day provinces of Saskatchewan and Alberta, and parts of Texas are part of the Plains culture area. The Northeast culture area encompasses a wide swath of the United States bounded by the Atlantic Ocean and the Mississippi River, arced from the North Carolina coast northwest to the Ohio River, and back southwest to the Mississippi. Finally, the Southeast culture area is made up of parts or all of several American states—Florida, Georgia, Alabama, Mississippi, Louisiana, Tennessee, the Carolinas, Virginia, and Arkansas.

Within each of these areas are several traits that define particularly strong aspects of Native American culture, and chief among them is language. The fluidity in language development is evident throughout each of these groups, as can be seen clearly in the example of peoples living in the Arctic and subarctic. Arctic people, commonly known as Eskimos, consist mainly of two widely dispersed groups: the Inuit and the Yupik. The Inuit possess a common language with many variant dialects, while the Yupik speak no fewer than five different languages. Another Arctic people, the Aleuts, have one language with two distinct dialects, showing influences from Russian fur traders who were common visitors to that area.

It has been estimated that approximately 300 different Native American languages were spoken throughout North America. At one time, there were more languages in use among the peoples of the California culture area than in all of Europe. Major language groups and subgroups have existed throughout the Native American population, among them, Hokan and Uto-Aztecan in the Great Basin and Southwest (e.g., Paiute, Shoshone); Athabaskan in the western subarctic and Southwest (e.g., Navajo, Carrier, Apache); Algonquian in the eastern Subarctic, Plains, and Northeast (e.g., Cree, Ojibwa, Cheyenne); and Iroquoian in the Northeast and Southeast (e.g., Cherokee, Seneca, Mohawk).

A common assumption might be that although there are many languages, there may have been a common language or two brought over the land bridge many thousands of years ago that, through dispersion, had fragmented into numerous variations of the origin language. However, linguists have found no commonality among the major language groups that would support this theory.

Social hierarchies are another defining trait. How people interact with each other in social groups speaks to their experience and their values. Native American social groups—immediate kin, extended family, and other members—varied greatly in how they were set up. The overriding causal circumstances were geography and availability of food. In those culture areas where food was relatively scarce, a great deal depended on where animals were located to be hunted for sustenance. In the case of the Arctic, Eskimos were extremely dependent on reindeer for not only food but clothing and tools. Great barren spaces resulted in natural migratory patterns for reindeer, and the people followed the animals on which their survival depended. Temporary lodging could be provided by igloos as the people followed these massive herds.

In the subarctic, the people depended upon reindeer as well. However, in a more forested, brushy area, they were able to herd these animals. This resulted in a social style that could be described as more sedentary and group-defined than that of their migratory northern neighbours. It's easy to see where this diversification might cause more of a dependence on, and development of, the self over the group for the Inuit and Yupik, while the Aleuts and similarly positioned groups would develop stronger patterns of group reliance. People adapt to their surrounding conditions, and all culture areas were affected by their physical place in the world.

In general, areas with abundant food that was easily obtained had a more complex and stratified social system. Where people remained in the same place, they developed stronger political systems due to their need to share resources. These systems could be depended upon as a foundation for resolving differences between members of the group. The Northwest area is a prime example of this evolution. Salmon and other seafood was plentiful, so the people held a common title to these resources. While elites existed, commoners were considered full members of the group and were always allowed to speak in public during most group discussions. Even slaves, mostly members of other groups who had been captured in war, could eventually rise to become full-fledged members of a tribe.

Similar arrangements existed in other areas where food was plentiful, with exceptions. This arrangement is in stark contrast to those culture areas that developed in places where food/water might be scarce. These areas more generally consisted of smaller, migratory bands of people existing in "tribelets," whose fluidity required more self-reliance and a more decentralized form of political structure.

To some extent, all Native American culture areas had strong, extended-family bonds that were defined by maternal or paternal lineage, or both. These familial connections tended to result in the formation of bands or clans. These smaller groups came together to form tribes, which, in turn, may have formed strong cohesive bonds with one another for the common good. A prime example of this situation is the Iroquois Confederacy, an alliance of five tribes that forestalled European attempts at dominance in North America during the 17th and 18th centuries. All Native American cultures have strong and readily defined similarities to one another in their sense of spirituality and their religious ceremonies. While there existed many differences in what was celebrated and when, there were a number of common central beliefs that were shared by most cultures, including animism, shamanism, vision quests, and spirits.

Animism is the belief that souls or spirits exist not only in humans, but in animals, rocks, trees—essentially all natural phenomena. Specific animals had certain defined characteristics; some tribes even believed that animals existed before humankind and established on Earth the various rules and guidelines that humans were meant to follow. Many ceremonies, therefore, were prescribed and held as "perfect" as they were handed down to people eons ago. Whether it was the Salmon Ceremony in the Northwest, the Green Corn Dance in the Southeast, the False Face Ceremony of the Iroquois, or the Sun Dance Ceremony in the Plains, nature was to be celebrated, thanked, and maybe appeased for the gifts that had been bestowed on a tribe.

Shamanism is a system of beliefs and practices designed to facilitate communication with the spirit world. Many objects, ceremonies, songs, and dances are believed to hold sacred properties, and it is the shaman's responsibility to relay this information to the group members. A shaman, then, can be seen as a sort of priest or practitioner through whom various spirits let themselves be known to humans. Shamans as healers,

psychopomps (conductors of souls who accompany the dead to the other world), and prophets play an important role in social cohesiveness.

The concept of vision quests is essentially an extended and personalized acknowledgement of the overriding belief in all things, all spirits. Almost every culture area has a version of vision quest, in which someone—many times a boy entering puberty—is to walk his own path in the spirit/dream world to help uncover his path in this life. This activity reflects the strong belief in "soul dualism," where each person is given two souls, one for the physical world and one for the spirit world, and everyone has a distinct path to follow. All things—including people—are capable of doing good or evil; the vision quest helps one to know what his or her place is in the world. Dreams also were considered portals into the spirit world, and special importance was attached to what was revealed in them.

Most groups also held to the belief that there was a "Great Spirit," a main deity that was recognized as the overseer of life on Earth. Whether known as Kitchi-Manitou, as the Algonquian-speaking peoples of North America knew this Great Spirit, or by another appellation, the master deity existed in the physical and spirit worlds, along with the tricksters, heroes, monsters, giants, and spirits that made up many a Native American's worldview.

It's important to understand that, in the Native American world, all objects associated with ceremonies, dances, and other sacred activities were a reflection of their spiritual belief in the sacredness of the natural and spirit worlds. While created objects might have a utilitarian purpose, they also had a greater purpose— to honour and please the deity present in all things. Singing and dancing were natural expressions of joy, fear, or hope in which all members of the group were involved. Dances had specific meanings and were tied to important celebrations. There were songs connected to certain dances, each replete with tonalities, choral arrangements, and instrumentation that varied among the various culture areas.

As the whole of the art, dance, and song aspects of Native American culture are brought together toward this volume's end, the premise with which the book began is reinforced and clarified. While they share a deeply spiritual outlook, Native American culture is composed of an amalgam of many different types of people, ideas, and beliefs that, when examined as a whole, present a fascinating story of the North American continent's indigenous peoples.

CHAPTER 1

OVERVIEW

For many years the American Indians of both the United States and Canada were perceived as vanishing peoples—unfortunate, but inevitable, victims of Western civilization's march toward perfection. Today this sense of their teetering on the brink of cultural or physical extinction has largely disappeared. In fact, many members of U.S. Indian tribes and Canada's First Nations actively engage in cultural nurturing and revitalization, including new emphasis on tribal government, identification of stable sources for group economic well-being, and encouragement of the use of indigenous languages. There is also increased concern about the preservation of sacred sites and the repatriation of sacred objects.

NORTH AMERICAN INDIAN HERITAGE

The date of the arrival in North America of the initial wave of peoples from whom the American Indians (or Native Americans) emerged is still a matter of considerable uncertainty. It is relatively certain that they were Asiatic peoples who originated in northeastern Siberia and crossed the Bering Strait (perhaps when it was a land bridge) into Alaska and then gradually dispersed throughout the Americas. The glaciations of the Pleistocene Epoch (1.6 million to 10,000 years ago) coincided with the evolution of modern humans, and ice sheets blocked ingress into North America for extended periods of time. It was only during the interglacial periods that people ventured into this unpopulated land.

ACCULTURATION AND ASSIMILATION

The effects of culture contact are generally characterized under the rubric of acculturation, a term encompassing the changes in artifacts, customs, and beliefs that result from cross-cultural interaction. Voluntary acculturation, often referred to as incorporation or amalgamation, involves the free borrowing of traits or ideas from another culture. Forced acculturation can also occur, as when one group is conquered by another and must abide by the stronger group's customs.

Assimilation is the process whereby individuals or groups of differing ethnicity blend into the dominant culture of a society and may also be either voluntary or forced. In the 19th- and early 20th-century United States, millions of European immigrants became assimilated within two or three generations through means that were for the most part voluntary. Homogenizing factors included attendance at elementary schools (either public or private) and churches, as well as unionization. During the same period, however, the United States and Canada had policies designed to force the assimilation of Native American and First Nations peoples, most notably by mandating that indigenous children attend residential or boarding schools.

Assimilation is rarely complete. Most groups retain at least some preference for the religion, food, or other cultural features of their predecessors.

Some scholars claim an arrival before the last (Wisconsin) glacial advance, about 60,000 years ago. The latest possible date now seems to be 20,000 years ago, with some pioneers filtering in during a recession in the Wisconsin glaciation.

These prehistoric invaders were Stone Age hunters who led a nomadic life, a pattern that many retained until the coming of Europeans. As they worked their way southward from a narrow, ice-free corridor in what is now the state of Alaska into the broad expanse of the continent—between what are now Florida and California—the various communities tended to fan out, hunting and foraging in comparative isolation. Until they converged in the narrows of southern Mexico

and the confined spaces of Central America, there was little of the fierce competition or the close interaction among groups that might have stimulated cultural inventiveness.

The size of the pre-Columbian aboriginal population of North America remains uncertain, since the widely divergent estimates have been based on inadequate data. The pre-Columbian population of what is now the United States and Canada, with its more widely scattered societies, has been variously estimated at somewhere between 600,000 and 2 million. By that time, the Indians there had not yet adopted intensive agriculture or an urban way of life, although the cultivation of corn, beans,

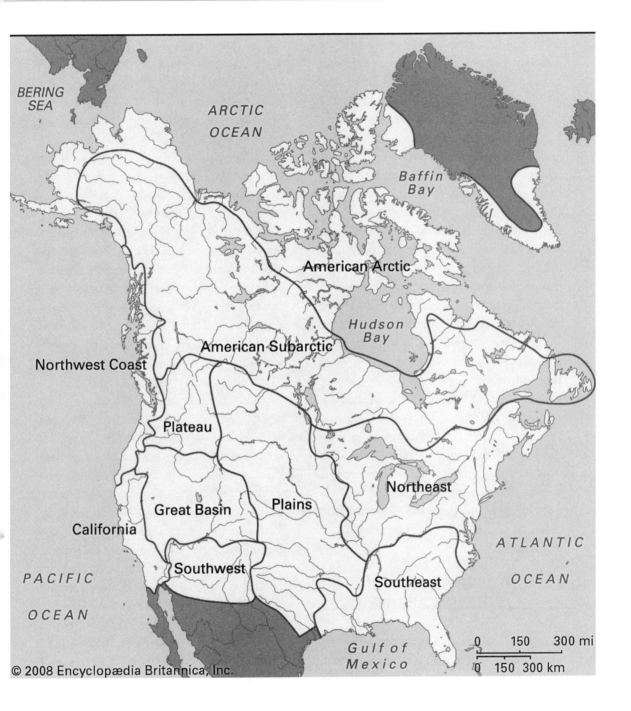

Culture areas of North American Indians.

and squash supplemented hunting and fishing throughout the Mississippi and Ohio river valleys and in the Great Lakes–St. Lawrence river region, as well as along the Gulf of Mexico and Atlantic Coastal Plain. In those areas, semisedentary peoples had established villages, and among the Iroquois and the Cherokee, powerful federations of tribes had been formed. Elsewhere, however, on the Great Plains, the Canadian Shield, the northern Appalachians, the Cordilleras, the Great Basin, and the Pacific Coast, hunting, fishing, and gathering constituted the basic economic activity; and, in most instances, extensive territories were needed to feed and support small groups.

The history of the entire aboriginal population of North America after the Spanish conquest has been one of unmitigated tragedy. The combination of susceptibility to Old World diseases, loss of land, and the disruption of cultural and economic patterns caused a drastic reduction in numbers—indeed, the extinction of many communities. It is only since about 1900 that the numbers of some Indian peoples have begun to rebound.

NATIVE AMERICAN CULTURE AREAS

Comparative studies are an essential component of all scholarly analyses, whether the topic under study is human society, fine art, paleontology, or chemistry. The similarities and differences found in the entities under consideration help to organize and direct research programs and exegeses. The comparative study of cultures falls largely in the domain of anthropology, which often uses a typology known as the culture area approach to organize comparisons across cultures.

The culture area approach was delineated at the turn of the 20th century and continued to frame discussions of peoples and cultures into the 21st century. A culture area is a geographic region where certain cultural traits have generally co-occurred. For instance, in North America between the 16th and 19th centuries, the Northwest Coast Native American culture area was characterized by traits such as salmon fishing, woodworking, large villages or towns, and hierarchical social organization.

The specific number of culture areas delineated for Native America has been somewhat variable because regions are sometimes subdivided or conjoined. The 10 culture areas discussed in this volume are among the most commonly used—the Arctic, the subarctic, the Northeast, the Southeast, the Plains, the Southwest, the Great Basin, California, the Northwest Coast, and the Plateau. Notably, some scholars prefer to combine the Northeast and Southeast into one Eastern Woodlands culture area, or the Plateau and Great Basin into a single Intermontane culture area. Discussion of each culture area considers the location, climate, environment, languages, tribes, and common cultural characteristics of the area before it was heavily colonized.

CHAPTER 2

THE AMERICAN ARCTIC AND SUBARCTIC CULTURES

The three major environmental zones of forest, tundra, and coast, and the transitions between them, establish the range of conditions to which the ways of life of the circumpolar peoples are adapted. Broadly speaking, four types of adaptation are found. The first is entirely confined within the forest and is based on the exploitation of its fairly diverse resources of land animals, birds, and fish. Local groups tend to be small and widely scattered, each exploiting a range of territory around a fixed, central location.

The second kind of adaptation spans the transition between forest and tundra. It is characterized by a heavy, year-round dependence on herds of reindeer or caribou, whose annual migrations from the forest to the tundra in spring and from the tundra back to the forest in autumn are matched by the lengthy nomadic movements of the associated human groups. In North America, these are hunters, who aim to intercept the herds on their migrations, rather than herders, as in Eurasia.

The third kind of adaptation, most common among Inuit (Eskimo) groups, involves a seasonal movement in the reverse direction, between the hunting of sea mammals on the coast in winter and spring and the hunting of caribou and fishing on the inland tundra in summer and autumn.

Fourth, typical of cultures of the northern Pacific coast is an exclusively maritime adaptation. People live year-round in relatively large, coastal settlements, hunting the rich resources of marine mammals from boats in summer and from the ice in winter.

In northern North America the forest and forest-tundra modes of subsistence are practiced only by Indian peoples, while coastal and coastal-tundra adaptations are the exclusive preserve of the Inuit and of the Aleut of the northern Pacific islands. Indian cultures are thus essentially tied to the forest, whereas Inuit and Aleut cultures are entirely independent of the forest and tied rather to the coast. Conventionally, this contrast has been taken to mark the distinction between peoples of the subarctic and those of the Arctic.

PEOPLES OF THE AMERICAN ARCTIC

Scholarly custom separates the American Arctic peoples from other American Indians, from whom they are distinguished by various linguistic, physiological, and cultural differences. Because of their close social, genetic, and linguistic relations to Yupik speakers in Alaska, the Yupik-speaking peoples living near the Bering Sea in Siberia are sometimes discussed with these groups.

LINGUISTIC COMPOSITION

Various outside relationships for the Eskimo-Aleut language stock have been suggested, but in the absence of conclusive evidence the stock must be considered to be isolated. Internally, it falls into two related divisions, Eskimo and Aleut.

The Eskimo division is further subdivided into Inuit and Yupik. Inuit, or Eastern Eskimo (in Greenland called Greenlandic or Kalaaleq; in Canada, Inuktitut; in Alaska, Inupiaq), is a single language formed of a series of intergrading dialects that extend thousands of miles, from eastern Greenland to northern Alaska and around the Seward Peninsula to Norton Sound; there it adjoins Yupik, or Western Eskimo. The Yupik section, on the other hand, consists of five separate languages that were not mutually intelligible. Three of these are Siberian: Sirenikski is now virtually extinct, Naukanski is restricted to the easternmost Chukchi Peninsula, and Chaplinski is spoken on Alaska's St. Lawrence Island, on the southern end of the Chukchi Peninsula, and near the mouth of the Anadyr River in the south and on Wrangel Island in the north. In Alaska, Central Alaskan Yupik includes dialects that covered the Bering Sea coast from Norton Sound to the Alaska Peninsula, where it met Pacific Yupik (known also as Sugpiaq or Alutiiq). Pacific Yupik comprises three dialects: that of the Kodiak Island group, that of the south shore of the Kenai Peninsula, and that of Prince William Sound.

Aleut now includes only a single language of two dialects. Yet before the disruption that followed the 18th-century arrival of Russian fur hunters, it included several dialects, if not separate languages, spoken from about longitude 158° W on the Alaska Peninsula, throughout the Aleutian Islands, and westward to Attu, the westernmost island of the Aleutian chain. The Russians transplanted some Aleuts to formerly unoccupied islands of the Commander group, west of the Aleutians, and to those of the Pribilofs, in the Bering Sea.

ETHNIC GROUPS

In general, American Eskimo peoples did not organize their societies into units such as clans or tribes. Identification of group membership was traditionally made by place of residence, with the suffix -miut ("people of") applied in a nesting set of labels to people of any specifiable place—from the home of a family or two to a broad region with many residents. Among the largest of the customary -miut designators are those coinciding at least roughly with the limits of a dialect or sub-dialect, the speakers of which tended to seek spouses from within that group; such groups might range in size from 200 to as many as 1,000 people.

Historically, each individual's identity was defined on the basis of connections such as kinship and marriage in addition to place and language. All of these continued to be important to Arctic self-identity in the 20th and 21st centuries, although native peoples in the region have also formed large—and in some cases pan-Arctic—organizations in order to facilitate their representation in legal and political affairs.

Ethnographies, historical accounts, and documents from before the late 20th century typically used geographic nomenclature to refer to groups that shared similar dialects, customs, and material cultures. For instance, in reference to groups residing on the North Atlantic and Arctic coasts, these texts might discuss the East Greenland Eskimo, West Greenland Eskimo, and Polar Eskimo, although only the last territorial division corresponded to a single self-contained, in-marrying (endogamous) group. The peoples of Canada's North Atlantic and eastern Hudson Bay were referred to as the Labrador Eskimo and the Eskimo of Quebec. These were often described as whole units, although each comprises a number of separate societies. The Baffinland Eskimo were often included in the Central Eskimo, a grouping that otherwise included the Caribou Eskimo of the barrens west of Hudson Bay and the Iglulik, Netsilik, Copper, and Mackenzie Eskimo, all of whom live on or near the Arctic Ocean in northern Canada. The Mackenzie Eskimo, however, are also set apart from other Canadians as speakers of the western, or Inupiaq, dialect of the Inuit (Eastern Eskimo) language. Descriptions of these Alaskan Arctic peoples have tended to be along linguistic rather than geographic lines and include the Inupiaq-speaking Inupiat, who live on or near the Arctic Ocean and as far south as the Bering Strait. All of the groups noted thus far reside near open water that freezes solid in winter, speak dialects of the Inuit language, and are commonly referred to in aggregate as Inuit (meaning "the people").

The other American Arctic groups live farther south, where open water is less likely to freeze solid for greatly extended periods. The Bering Sea Eskimo and St. Lawrence Island Eskimo live around the Bering Sea, where resources include migrating sea mammals and, in the mainland rivers, seasonal runs of salmon and other fish. The Pacific Eskimo, on the other hand, live on the shores of the North Pacific itself, around Kodiak Island and Prince William Sound, where the Alaska Current prevents open water from freezing at all. Each of these three groups speaks a distinct form of Yupik; together they are commonly referred to as Yupik Eskimo or as Yupiit ("the people").

In the Gulf of Alaska, ethnic distinctions were blurred by Russian colonizers who used the term Aleut to refer not only to people of the Aleutian Islands but also to the culturally distinct groups residing on Kodiak Island and the neighbouring areas of the mainland. As a result, many modern native people from Kodiak, the Alaska Peninsula, and Prince William Sound identify themselves as Aleuts, although only those from the tip of the peninsula and the Aleutian Islands are descended from people who spoke what linguists refer to as the Aleut language; these latter refer to themselves as Unangan ("people"). The groups from Kodiak Island and the neighbouring

areas traditionally spoke the form of Yupik called Pacific Yupik, Sugpiaq, or Alutiiq and refer to themselves as Alutiiq (singular) or Alutiit (plural).

TRADITIONAL CULTURE

The traditional cultures of the Arctic are generally discussed in terms of two broad divisions: seasonally migratory peoples living on or near winter-frozen coastlines (the northern Yupiit and the Inuit) and more-sedentary groups living on or near the open-water regions of the Pacific coast (the southern Yupiit and Aleuts).

SEASONALLY MIGRATORY PEOPLES: THE NORTHERN YUPIIT AND THE INUIT

The seasonally organized economy of these peoples derived from that of their Thule ancestors and focused on the exploitation of both sea and land resources. Traditional peoples generally followed the Thule subsistence pattern, in which summers were spent in pursuit of caribou and fish and other seasons were devoted to the pursuit of sea mammals, especially seals. Food was also stored for consumption during the deepest part of winter.

There were exceptions to this pattern, however. People of the Bering Strait islands, for instance, depended almost entirely on sea mammals, walrus being very important. In the specialized Alaskan whaling villages between the Seward Peninsula and Point Barrow, caribou and

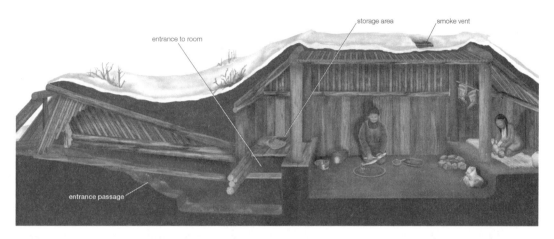

Cross section of a traditional semisubterranean dwelling of the North American Arctic and sub-arctic peoples. © Encyclopædia Britannica, Inc.; adapted using information from the Field Museum, Chicago

seals were outweighed as food resources by bowhead whales *(Baleana mysticetus)*. In the Brooks Range of northern Alaska, some people were year-round caribou hunters who also depended on traded sea-mammal oil as a condiment and for heat. In the Barren Grounds, west of Hudson Bay, some groups used no sea products at all, illuminating their snow houses with burning caribou fat and heating these homes with twig fires.

Most shelter in winter was in substantial semisubterranean houses of stone or sod over wooden or whalebone frameworks. In Alaska, save for the far north, heat was provided by a central wood fire that was placed beneath a smoke hole; throughout the north and in Greenland, a large sea-mammal oil lamp served the same purpose. In 19th-century Siberia and on St. Lawrence Island, the older semisubterranean house was given up for a yurt-like structure with sod walls and a walrus-hide roof.

The people nearest the Arctic Ocean relied on the snow house in winter, with most groups moving onto fresh ice fields in search of seals during that season. Caribou hunters and lake and river fishermen used the snow house on land. The caribou specialists of northern Alaska often lived through the winter in double-layered dome-shaped tents, heated like the coastal snow houses with an oil lamp; these dwellings commonly housed an extended family. In East and West Greenland, communal dwellings were built of stone, housed as many as 50 people from different kin groups, and were arranged such that each nuclear family had its own interior space and oil lamp. Communities in the far north of Greenland chose to use smaller stone houses designed to shelter nuclear families.

Among the Yupiit a special large semisubterranean house, called a *kashim* by the Russians, was used for public and ceremonial occasions and as a men's residence. The *kashim* was the place where men built their boats, repaired their equipment, took sweat baths, educated young boys, and hosted community dances. Women had their own homes in which they worked and cared for their children. In many cases the women's homes were connected to one another and to the *kashim* by a system of tunnels, not all of them generally known; a number of folktales tell how canny women saved their families from raids by directing them to hidden tunnels that opened far away from the village.

The institution of the *kashim* was stronger to the south of the Bering Strait than to its north. *Kashims* did not exist on St. Lawrence Island or in Siberia, nor were they found east of Point Barrow until the late 19th or early 20th century, when they began to be used by Inuit living near the Mackenzie River.

Both the single-cockpit kayak and the larger open umiak were virtually universal, although they were not used the same way everywhere. The kayak was generally used as a seal-hunting craft, but, in the places where open-water sealing was limited, it was used to intercept migrating caribou as they crossed lakes and rivers. The umiak was usually a freight vessel, often rowed by women facing backward, but in whaling and walrus-hunting regions it was used as a hunting boat and paddled by a male crew facing forward. Winter transport was by sled, pulled by dogs or by both dogs and people. In most regions the number of sled dogs—which ate the same food as humans and thus were a burden in times of want—was limited, an exception being the few areas in which relative plenty was provided by whales or migrating salmon.

The bow and arrow were the standard tools of land hunters. Seals and walrus were taken from shore with a thrown harpoon tipped with a toggling head—an asymmetrical point with a line affixed, shaped to twist sidewise in the wound as the detachable shaft pulled loose. Kayak-based seal hunters used specialized harpoons with fixed barbs rather than toggling heads; these were often cast with the spear-thrower or throwing board, a flat trough of wood that cradled the butt of the dart and formed an extension of the thrower's arm, increasing the velocity of the thrown projectile. The whaling umiak was manned by a professional crew; it was directed by the boat's owner, or *umialik*, and a marksman who wielded a heavy harpoon with a detachable toggling head and line attached to sealskin floats. In Quebec, whales were harpooned from kayaks or run aground in shallow bays.

The flexibility of movement required by the seasonally varied subsistence quest was supported by the flexible organization of society. Individuals obtained psychological and material support from their kindred and tended to avoid people who were not kin, but there were devices for creating kinlike relationships that could extend the social and territorial sphere in which an individual could move in safety and comfort. These included a variety of institutionalized relationships. People bearing the same name as a relative might be treated as if they held the same relation, and trading partners, song partners, meat-sharing partners, and partners created by the temporary exchange of spouses might also be treated approximately as relatives.

Generally, American Eskimo recognized kin on both the paternal and maternal sides of the family to about the degree of second cousin. Marriage with cousins was frowned upon by most groups, although permitted by some. Certain groups also emphasized paternal kin over maternal. On St. Lawrence Island and in Siberia, however, there were patrilineal clans—named groups of all people related in the male line. In Siberia marriage could not be contracted by two members of the same clan, although on St. Lawrence such a rule was not enforced. There the walrus- and whale-hunting crews were composed of clansmen, the senior male became clan chief, and the chief of the strongest local clan acted as the village chief.

Among other groups there was no formal position of chief, the closest to an exception being the *umialik* of the Inupiat. In addition to owning the boat used for whaling, the *umialik* was the employer of a whaling crew, recruiting his men for their professional ability and acting as benefactor to them and their families. In many villages each *umialik* and his crew controlled a *kashim*. The title of *umialik* was also used in some villages not devoted to whaling, especially in the northern Alaskan interior, where the *umialik* was the organizer of a caribou-hunting team. The position of *umialik* was not inherited but was gained by skilled entrepreneurs, and it brought no control over anyone but the *umialik*'s own crew (and then only to the extent that an individual chose to remain a crew member). South of the Bering Strait the title was rarely used.

Religious beliefs were based on animism; all things—animate or otherwise—were believed to have a living essence. Thus, all humans, animals, plants, and objects had souls or spirits, which might be related to one another in a hereafter, details of the location of which varied from group to group. Courtesies given to freshly killed animals promoted their reincarnation as new animals of the same species. The souls of humans were subject to interference from other spirits, and soul loss meant illness or even death. There also were ideas of human reincarnation. The name of a deceased person was given to a child who "became" that person by being addressed with kinship terms appropriate to the deceased.

Traditionally, all people were in contact with the spirit world. They carried amulets of traditional or individual potency, experienced dreams, devised songs or other words of power, and

Kinugumiut Yupik incised walrus ivory shaman's figure, c. 1890; in the National Museum of the American Indian, George Gustav Heye Center, Smithsonian Institution, New York City. Courtesy of the Museum of the American Indian, Heye Foundation, New York

achieved special relationships with particular spirit-beings. Men and women who were especially adept at such contact became shamans. They were called on to cure the sick by recovering lost soul-stuff, to foretell the future, to determine the location of game, and so forth—all with the help of powerful spirit familiars.

Shamans were also expected to contact a few more strongly personified spirit-beings, such as the female being (whose name and attributes varied from group to group) who governed important land or sea mammals. When game was scarce, the shaman might cajole her into providing more bounty. In Greenland the shaman was also an entertainer whose séances, escape tricks, and noisy spirit helpers could enliven a long winter's night in the communal house.

SEDENTARY PEOPLES: THE SOUTHERN YUPIIT AND THE ALEUTS

These groups made use of the sod-covered and semisubterranean house, the skin-covered kayak and the umiak, and fishing and hunting apparatus similar to those of the northern Yupiit and the Inuit. Yet, like many neighbouring Northwest Coast Indians, they focused almost exclusively on aquatic resources and had a hierarchical society comprising formal chiefs (apparently inherited in the male line), other elites, commoners, and a class of slaves that was generally composed of war captives. Although the Yupik-speaking people of the Kodiak region maintained *kashims* that seem to

IGLOO

The igloo, also called aputiak, *is the temporary winter home or hunting-ground dwelling of Canadian and Greenland Inuit (Eskimos). The term* igloo *(also spelled* iglu*), from the Eskimo word* igdlu *(meaning "house"), is related to Iglulik, a town, and Iglulirmiut, an Inuit people, both on an island of the same name. Usually made from blocks of snow and dome-shaped, the igloo is used only in the area between the Mackenzie River delta and Labrador where, in the summer, Inuit live in sealskin or, more recently, cloth tents.*

To build the igloo, the builder takes a deep snowdrift of fine-grained, compact snow and cuts it into blocks with a snow knife, a swordlike instrument originally made of bone but now usually of metal. Each block is a rectangle measuring about 2 feet by 4 feet (60 centimetres by 120 centimetres) and 8 inches (20 cm) thick. After a first row of these blocks has been laid out in a circle on a flat stretch of snow, the top surfaces of the blocks are shaved off in a sloping angle to form the first rung of a spiral. Additional blocks are added to the spiral to draw it inward until the dome is completed except for a hole left at the top for ventilation.

Joints and crevices are filled with loose snow. A clear piece of ice or seal intestine is inserted for a window. A narrow, semicylindrical passageway about 10 feet (3 metres) long, with vaults for storing supplies, leads into the igloo. Drafts are kept from the main room by a sealskin flap hung over the exterior entrance to the passageway and by a low, semicircular retaining wall that is sometimes built out a few feet from the end of the tube. The major furnishings are a shallow saucer to burn seal blubber for heat and light and a low sleeping platform of snow covered with willow twigs topped by caribou furs.

The dimensions of igloos vary, but they generally accommodate only one family. An experienced Inuit can build a snow igloo in between one and two hours. Sod, stone, and wood have also been used to construct igloos.

have functioned generally like those of the north and were said to be "owned" by local chiefs, the Aleut-speaking groups had no similar structure. Unfortunately, the region's conquest by Russian fur hunters eradicated many details of indigenous life before they could be thoroughly recorded.

HISTORICAL DEVELOPMENTS

The European colonization of the American Arctic flowed inland from the coasts of Greenland, southern and southwestern Alaska, and the Arctic Ocean and Hudson Bay. The discussions below consider these major areas of colonization in turn.

GREENLAND

Erik the Red founded a small Norse colony on Greenland in AD 986, although the Norse and the Thule people seem not to have interacted until the 13th century. The Norse colony was abandoned in the early 15th century, a time when a general climatic cooling trend probably made subsistence farming unsustainable there. European fishermen built seasonally used base camps on Greenland's southern coasts during the 16th and 17th centuries. During the periods of European absence, Inuit peoples sometimes burned the seemingly abandoned buildings in order to simplify the collection of iron nails and metal fittings; these were easily transformed into implements that proved more durable than traditional stone tools. This destruction of fishing camps created tensions between the Europeans and the Inuit. The groups sometimes fought, but there were apparently no attempts at political domination.

In 1721 a permanent Danish-Norwegian colony was founded on Greenland. Its goals were missionization and trade. Unusually, the region's indigenous peoples were from the first treated as full citizens of the kingdom. Epidemics of European diseases struck almost immediately, killing as many as a third of the people on the island. In 1776 the Danish government granted a trade monopoly to the Royal Greenlandic Trading Company. With the restriction of contact with outsiders, losses to epidemic disease were greatly reduced. Denmark retained a trading monopoly with Greenland until 1951.

Indigenous languages remained in general use after colonization. Because missionaries often learned Inuit while residing in Nuuk (now the capital city) and then left for more-distant locales,

the Nuuk dialect came into common use throughout Greenland. This helped create a sense of ethnic unity among indigenous Greenlanders, and that unity continued to grow with the 1861 publication of the first Inuit-language newspaper, *Atuagagdliutit* (an invented word originally meaning "distributed reading matter" or "free newspaper"). By the late 19th century, Greenland's native peoples had created a significant and growing vernacular literature and a name for their shared identity, Kalaaleq ("Greenland Inuk"). Inuk is the local ethnonym for someone who is a member of an Inuit-speaking group.

In 1862 Greenland was granted limited local self-government. In the period from 1905 to 1929, its residents shifted from a traditional subsistence economy to sheep breeding and cod fishing (although hunting remained important in the early 21st century); schools also began to teach Danish. In 1953, after more than 200 years as a colony, Greenland became an integral part of Denmark and gained representation in the national legislative assembly; in 1979 it achieved complete home rule.

The Inuit Institute, Greenland's first institution of higher education, was formed in 1983. In 1989 it was reorganized as a university, Ilisimatusarfik, and became one of the few institutions dedicated to the study of Kalaaleq traditional cultures and languages. Within Greenland, university training in other subjects is still limited; as younger Kalaaleq commonly speak Danish as a second language, many enroll in Danish universities.

SOUTHERN AND SOUTHWESTERN ALASKA

In 1728 the Russian tsar Peter I (the Great) supported an expedition to the northern Pacific. Led by Vitus Bering, the expedition set out to determine whether Siberia and North America were connected and, if not, whether there was a navigable sea route connecting the commercial centres of western Russia to China. Although poor visibility limited the results of this voyage, subsequent Russian journeys determined that the Pacific coast of North America was home to a seemingly inexhaustible population of sea otters. Russian entrepreneurs quickly seized on the opportunity to garner sea otter pelts, known for their lush feel and superior insulating qualities, as these were at the time almost the only items for which the Chinese were willing to engage in trade with Russia.

Russian rule was established in the region quickly and often brutally. Perhaps the worst atrocities occurred in 1745, when a large party of Russian and Siberian hunters overwintered in the Aleutian Islands. Members of the party engaged in such wholesale murder and sexual assault that they were later charged in the Russian courts and punished. Similar incidents of violent conquest occurred throughout the region, and over the next several decades the indigenous population was forced into virtual slavery. Russian administrators recognized native expertise in capturing sea otters and so negotiated with the hunters during the first part of the colonial era (albeit on an unequal basis given the colonizers' imposing firepower). However, these more or less voluntary levels of fur production proved inadequate for commercial trading.

By 1761 the Russians had instituted a village-based quota system. They remained unsatisfied with the results and soon took entire villages hostage as a way to ensure the docility of Aleut and Yupik men, nearly all of whom were impressed into service as hunters. This created intense hardship for the elders, women, and children left behind. Hunting had provided most of their subsistence, and, with the hunters away or exhausted, many communities suffered from malnourishment or starvation in addition to the epidemic diseases that characterized European conquest throughout the Americas. Within a century of initial contact, the Aleut-speaking population had declined to no more than 2,000; at least 80 percent of their original number was gone. Around Kodiak Island and the Pacific coast, the decrease in roughly the same period was to about 3,000, a loss of about two-thirds. On the Bering Sea, where the fur trade was less intense, the loss was limited to about one-third or one-half of the population, all of it coming in the 19th century.

In 1799 the Russian-American Company was granted what amounted to governance of the Russian colonies in the

North Pacific. The company undertook a period of expansion and eventually ruled thousands of miles of coast, from the Bering Sea to northern California. Russian Orthodox missionaries arrived at about the same time. They observed the brutalities committed against indigenous peoples, reported these to the tsar, and worked to ameliorate the horrendous conditions in the hostage villages. Although protective language was placed in the company's second charter, enforcement was haphazard. Nonetheless, and perhaps because the priests were clearly their advocates, many Aleuts and Yupiit converted to Orthodox Christianity.

The U.S. government purchased Russian America in 1867 and subsequently imposed its assimilationist policies on Native Alaskans. Various forms of pressure were applied to ensure that native communities shifted from subsistence to wage labour, from the use of their own languages to English, and from Russian Orthodox traditions to mainline Protestantism, among other things.

As elsewhere in the United States, these policies undermined indigenous traditions and generally caused local economies to shift from self-sufficiency and sustainability to a reliance on outside capital. As the sea otter neared extinction, some Yupik and Aleut communities shifted to the hunting of other fur-bearing mammals, such as seals and Arctic foxes. As among the neighbouring Northwest Coast Indians, other groups used their knowledge of local fisheries to ensure employment. These strategies met with various levels of success, but the native communities often faced circumstantial difficulties. Demand for furs collapsed during the Great Depression of the 1930s, and fishermen had to cope with natural cycles in the population levels of various kinds of fish, the vagaries of consumer taste, and competition from better-equipped Euro-Americans.

By the mid-20th century, international politics had also affected large numbers of indigenous Alaskans. World War II saw the removal of whole Native Alaskan communities under the aegis of protection and national defense. After the war, having in some cases endured years of difficult "temporary" conditions, those who returned to their homes found them in disrepair and in some cases ransacked. The Cold War ensured that the military presence in Alaska would continue to grow until the late 20th century. New facilities were often placed on property that indigenous groups used and regarded as their own, creating further hardships.

CANADA AND NORTHERN ALASKA

The region from the Bering Strait northward and east to the Mackenzie River was untouched by Russians, but after the mid-19th century, it was visited by great numbers of European and Euro-American whalers, who imported both disease and alcohol. The native population declined by two-thirds or more between 1850 and 1910. In far northern Canada the impact was lessened somewhat, for contact was limited and the thinly distributed populations more easily avoided the spread of disease. Nevertheless, European whalers active in Hudson Bay and elsewhere were a source of disease and disruption that resulted in a significant decline in native population in the 19th century.

Intensive whaling, and later the hunting of walruses, depleted some of the major food sources of far northern communities and in some cases created localized hardship. However, whalers often recognized the technical skills of the northern Yupiit and the Inuit and arranged for various kinds of partnership; a Euro-American might reside with a local family for a winter, gaining food, shelter, and company while the family would gain labour-saving technology, such as metal knives, steel needles, and rifles.

Widespread difficulties arose with the imposition of assimilationist policies by the United States and Canada and later, after the discovery of gold, oil, and mineral resources in the region. By the late 19th century, church-sponsored experiments in reindeer herding were promoting assimilation in northern Alaska. These ventures generally failed due to their incompatibility with the local culture; people were accustomed to moving widely across the landscape but also had the habit of returning frequently to their home communities, a practice that quickly caused overgrazing near settlements. In addition, Euro-American entrepreneurs generally had enough capital to crowd out native reindeer operations. Gold strikes on Canada's Klondike River in 1896 and near Nome, Alaska, in 1898 shifted attention away from indigenous economic development, incidentally providing many northern Native Alaskans with a welcome opportunity to return to traditional modes of subsistence.

As in western and southwestern Alaska, the northern parts of Alaska and Canada saw an increase in military facilities during and after World War II. By the 1950s and '60s, concerns about environmental degradation and land seizures caused Native Alaskans to file lawsuits to halt the development of oil and other resources. These suits eventually led to the Alaska Native Claims Settlement Act of 1971, in which the United States agreed to provide to Alaskan natives some $962.5 million and 44 million acres of land, all to be administered through native-run corporations. For administrative purposes and to encourage local development, the state was divided among 12 regional native corporations (seven of them Inuit or Yupik, one Aleut, and the rest Indian), each including a series of village corporations in which individual natives were sole shareholders. A 13th corporation serves Native Alaskans who reside outside the state. The corporations have promoted housing, local schools, satellite communications facilities, medical facilities, and programs directed at alcohol abuse and have provided a training ground for native politicians active in state government, where they represent an increasingly sophisticated native citizenry.

Canada did not seek direct rule over the northern coastal region until the early 20th century, and the Canadian Inuit have had the same opportunities to vote and hold office as other Canadians only since about 1960—a time that coincides with the creation of increasingly stable settlements, the extension of social welfare, a decline in the importance of the traditional hunting economy, and the beginnings of native organizations that seek the recognition of the Inuit as a distinct people with rights of self-governance and to lands and traditional culture.

Canada's Inuit proved quite adept at effecting political change. In the mid-1970s the province of Quebec took from the dominion government all political responsibility for relationships with Inuit residing there. Inuit communities soon organized into village corporations with defined rights to land and resources. At about the same time, the Northwest Territories elected people of aboriginal descent to a majority of the 15 seats then in the territorial legislative assembly; in 1979 the first Inuit was elected to one of the two Northwest Territories seats in the national House of Commons. A proposal to divide the Northwest Territories into two parts, the eastern to include the major Inuit territory, was submitted to a plebiscite in 1982. The proposal won heavily in the east but only narrowly overall. It eventually passed, and what had been the eastern part of the Northwest Territories became the territory of Nunavut in 1999.

CONTEMPORARY DEVELOPMENTS

During the 20th century, indigenous populations throughout the American Arctic were regenerating. After World War II, national health systems reduced both chronic and acute infections, and populations doubled between 1950 and 1980. Early 21st-century population estimates indicated that the total population of persons self-identified as Inuit, Yupik, or Aleut stood at about 130,000 individuals in Canada and the United States, with approximately 45,000 additional individuals in Greenland.

For native peoples throughout the Arctic, a key development from the late 20th century onward has been their sophisticated activism and increasing transnationalism. They were heavily involved in the broad global push for indigenous, or "Fourth World," rights that had begun by the late 1960s and was encouraged by the civil rights movements of the so-called First World and the new independence of the formerly colonized Third World. In 1977 the Inuit Circumpolar Conference was formed by the Inuit peoples of Greenland, Canada, and Alaska; in 1983 it was recognized officially by the United Nations. By the early 21st century it represented some 150,000 individuals of Inuit and Yupik heritage, including those of Siberia. The Aleut International Association, a sister group, formed in 1998. These organizations are particularly active in promoting the preservation of indigenous cultures and languages and in protecting the northern environment from global warming and resource exploitation. They are two of the six indigenous associations and eight member states with permanent membership status in the Arctic Council, an international forum for intergovernmental research, cooperation, and advocacy that works frequently with the United Nations.

AMERICAN SUBARCTIC PEOPLES

The Native American peoples whose traditional area of residence is the subarctic region of Alaska and of Canada are referred to differently. Those from Alaska are often referred to in aggregate as Native Alaskans, while in Canada they are known as First Nations peoples.

The subarctic is dominated by the taiga, or boreal forest, an ecosystem of coniferous forest and large marshes. Subarctic peoples traditionally used a variety of technologies to cope with the cold northern winters and were adept in the production of well-insulated homes, fur garments, toboggans, ice chisels, and snowshoes. The traditional diet included game animals such as moose, caribou, bison (in the southern locales), beaver, and fish, as well as wild plant foods such as berries, roots, and sap. Food resources were distributed quite thinly over the subarctic landscape, and starvation was always a potential problem.

By the 1600s European fur traders had recognized that the taiga provided an optimal climate for the production of dense pelts. These traders decisively influenced the region's indigenous peoples, as did Christian missionaries. The fur trade had an especially strong impact on traditional economies, as time spent trapping furs could not be spent on direct subsistence activities. This caused a rather rapid increase in the use of purchased food items such as flour and sugar, which were substituted for wild fare. Despite much pressure to change, however, the relative isolation of the region has facilitated the persistence of many traditional beliefs, hunting customs, kinship relations, and the like.

The American subarctic culture area contains two relatively distinct zones. The eastern subarctic is inhabited by speakers of Algonquian languages, including the Innu (formerly Montagnais and Naskapi) of northern Quebec, the Cree, and several groups of Ojibwa who, after the beginning of the fur trade, displaced the Cree from what are now west-central Ontario and eastern Manitoba. The western subarctic is largely home to Athabaskan speakers, whose territories extend from Canada into Alaska. Cultural differences among the Athabaskans justify the delineation of the western subarctic into two subareas. The first, drained mostly by the northward-flowing Mackenzie River system, is inhabited by the Chipewyan, Beaver, Slave, and Kaska nations. Their cultures were generally more mobile and less socially stratified than that of the second subarea, where salmon streams that drain into the Pacific Ocean provide a reliable food resource and natural gathering places. Its groups include the Carrier, part of the Gwich'in (Kutchin), the Tanaina, and the Deg Xinag (Ingalik).

Northward the Algonquians and Athabaskans border on the Inuit (Canadian Eskimo). To the west the Canadian Athabaskans encounter the Tlingit, Tsimshian, and other Northwest Coast Indians, while the Alaskan groups abut Yupik/Yupiit (American Eskimo) lands.

ETHOS

Given the difficult environmental conditions of the region, it is perhaps not surprising that most of its cultures traditionally placed a high value on personal autonomy and responsibility, conceived of the world as a generally dangerous place, and emphasized concrete, current realities rather than future possibilities. In anticipation of potential scarcity, subarctic cultural concepts included not only personal competence but also an acknowledgement of the individual's need to rely upon others, and to place the well-being of the group ahead of personal gain.

Many subarctic cultures cultivated personality traits such as reticence, emotionally undemonstrative interaction styles, deference to others, strong individual control of aggressive impulses, and the ability to bear up stoically to deprivation. Although hostility was not absent from traditional culture, most groups preferred that it be only indirectly revealed through such outlets as sorcery or gossip. Subarctic individuals' ease with long silences and preference for subdued emotional responses have sometimes been a source of cross-cultural misunderstanding with individuals from outside the region, who are often less taciturn.

TERRITORIAL ORGANIZATION

Before contact with Europeans, the subarctic peoples were subsistence hunters and gatherers. Although their specific economic strategies and technologies were highly adapted to the northern environment, many of their other cultural practices were typical of traditional hunting and gathering cultures worldwide. Most northern societies were organized around nuclear, or sometimes three-generation, families. The next level of social organization, the band, comprised a few related couples, their dependent children, and their dependent elders. Bands generally included no more than 20 to 30 individuals, who lived, hunted, and traveled together.

Although eastern subarctic peoples traditionally identified with a particular geographic territory, they generally chose not to organize politically beyond the level of the band; instead, they identified themselves as members of the same tribe or nation based on linguistic and kinship affinities they shared with neighbouring bands. Seasonal gatherings of several bands often occurred at good fishing lakes or near rich hunting grounds for periods that were as intensely sociable as they were abundantly provided with fish or game. The fur trade period created a new type of territorial group among these peoples, known as the home guard or trading-post band, usually named for the settlement in which its members traded. These new groups amalgamated the smaller bands and notably expanded the population in which marriage occurred.

In the Pacific drainage area, sedentary villages were the preferred form of geopolitical organization, each with an associated territory for hunting and gathering. On the lower Yukon and upper Kuskokwim rivers, Deg Xinag village life centred on the *kashim*, or men's house, where a council of male elders met to hear disputes and where elaborate seasonal ceremonies were performed.

Whether organized in bands or villages, individual leadership and authority derived primarily from the combination of eloquence, wisdom, experience, healing or magical power, generosity, and a capacity for hard work.

SETTLEMENT AND HOUSING

In pursuit of a livelihood, families and local bands shifted their location as the seasons changed. In northwest Canada, groups scattered in early winter to hunt caribou in the mountains. Elsewhere, autumn drew people to the shorelines of lakes and bays where large numbers of ducks and geese could be taken for the winter larder. At other times people gathered around lakes to fish. In late winter the Deg Xinag quit their villages and headed for spring camps, as much for a change of scenery as for the good fishing.

As dependence on fur trapping became heavier, the Cree, Slave, Kaska, and many other groups developed a two-part annual cycle. In winter the family lived on its trapline. In summer the family brought its furs to the trading post and camped there until fall, enjoying abundant social interaction. The warm months with their long daylight became a time for visiting and often included dances (often to fiddle music), marriages, and appearances by the region's Anglican or Roman Catholic bishop.

Despite much movement, shelters were not always portable. The Deg Xinag spent winters in houses excavated in the soil, roofed with beams and poles, hung with mats, and provided with an entry. Other groups, such as the Cree and Ojibwa, built conical winter lodges durably roofed with boughs, earth, and snow. On the trail, however, people put up skin or brush shelters, simple lean-tos, or camped in the open facing a fire.

PRODUCTION AND TECHNOLOGY

Everywhere in the subarctic a large and varied set of weapons, traps, and other ingenious appliances played a vital role in traditional subsistence activities. Important devices included the bow and arrow, with stone or bone tips for different kinds of game; lances; the spear-thrower (or atlatl) and spear; weirs and basket traps for fish; nets of willow bark and of other substances; snares for small game such as rabbits; deadfalls (traps with logs or other weights that fall on game and kill them); pit traps; and decoys for birds. Vehicles were also vital, as people depended heavily on mobility for survival; these included bark canoes, hardwood toboggans, and travel aids such as large sinew-netted snowshoes to run down big game, a smaller variety to break trail for the toboggan, and snow goggles to use against the glare of the spring sun.

Because dog teams require large quantities of meat, they were not kept to pull toboggans until the fur trade period, when people began to supplement their diets with European staples; after that point, dog teams became increasingly important in transporting furs to market. An idea of the extent to which people depended on game and of the labour involved in obtaining adequate amounts of food can be gained from food-consumption figures obtained in the mid-20th century. In the relatively poor country west of James Bay, 400 Cree men, women, and children in the course of a fall, winter, and spring (nine months) consumed about 128,000 pounds (58,000 kg) of meat and fish in addition to staples from the store, especially flour, lard, and sugar.

Subarctic peoples augmented their technical resourcefulness and skill in hunting with magic and divination. A noteworthy form of divination used in locating game required heating a large animal's shoulder blade over fire until it cracked. Hunters then went in the direction of the crack. The random element in the method increased the chances that they would go to a fresh, relatively undisturbed piece of ground.

Across the subarctic, people preserved meat by drying and pounding it together with fat and berries to make pemmican. The Pacific-drainage Athabaskans also preserved salmon by smoking. Other widely distributed technical skills included complicated chemical processes, as in using animal brains or human urine to tan caribou and moose skins. These were then sewn into garments with the help of bone needles and animal sinew. Women also plaited rabbit skins into ropes and wove roots to form watertight baskets.

PROPERTY AND SOCIAL STRATIFICATION

In traditional subarctic cultures, land and water, the sources of food, were not considered to be either individual or group property, yet nobody would usurp the privilege of a group that was currently exploiting a berry patch, beaver creek, or hunting range. Clothing, the contents of food caches, and other portable goods were recognized as having individual owners. When in need, a group could borrow from another's food cache, provided the food was replaced and the owners told of the act as soon as possible.

Legally inalienable family trapping territories came into being with the fur trade and in many places have been registered by the federal or dominion government. Sharing game was always important economically, while gifts other than food were bestowed primarily for ceremonial purposes.

Although social stratification was not customary across the entire subarctic, the Deg Xinag informally recognized three classes of families. Usually at least three-quarters of a Deg Xinag village comprised common people. Rich families, which accumulated surplus food thanks to members' industry or superior hunting and fishing abilities, constituted about 5 percent of the community. They took the lead in the community's ceremonial life. The rest of the people did little and lived off the others; consequently, they enjoyed so little respect that they had a hard time finding spouses.

FAMILY AND KINSHIP RELATIONS

Within the local band, the two- or three-generation family of husband, wife, children—frequently including adopted children—and (in some cases) dependent elders constituted the traditional unit of economic activity and emotional security. The intense importance of the family, especially during childhood, is revealed in folklore about the unhappy lot of cruelly treated orphans; children with neither parents nor grandparents suffered the worst.

Kinship in the subarctic traditionally included some categories that are common in traditional cultures but less commonly observed in the 21st century. Parallel cousins, the children of one's mother's sisters or father's brothers, were usually called by the same kinship term as one's siblings and treated as such. In contrast, cross-cousins, the children of one's father's sisters or mother's brothers, were often seen as the best pool from which to draw a mate. Northern peoples held strong prohibitions against incest, which was traditionally defined as sexual contact between siblings (including parallel cousins), between parents and children, and between adjacent generations of in-laws (e.g., mothers-in-law and sons-in-law, fathers-in-law and daughters-in-law).

Kin relations among subarctic peoples often involved a sort of emotional division of labour. Supportive, teasing, or joking relationships occurred with one group of relatives, while authoritative, circumspect, or avoidance relationships were the norm with another group of kin. In many cases, and probably in support of the incest prohibition, the appropriate form of interaction was based on generational proximity. Grandparents and grandchildren would tease, joke, hug, and cuddle, while interaction between adjacent generations (parent-child, sibling-sibling, parents-in-law and children-in-law) would be more reserved. In other cases the relationships were based on lineage; casual interactions tended to be more common with relatives from the mother's line and avoidance relations more common with those from the father's line. Some groups combined both generational and lineal forms.

In following these customs, siblings of the opposite sex who had reached puberty generally conducted themselves circumspectly in each other's presence and even tended to practice polite avoidance, as did fathers and their grown daughters. Ceremonial avoidance also governed the relationship of a man and his mother-in-law, contrasting with the camaraderie linking brothers-in-law, which was one of the warmest of all relationships between grown men. Among the Kaska, for instance, a group that could joke freely, and even engage in sexual ribaldry, comprised a woman, her husband's brother, and her sister's husband (or alternatively, a man, his wife's sister, and his brother's wife).

Marriages in the subarctic were traditionally founded upon an agreement between the parents of a potential bride and groom. The preferences of those to wed were taken into account, but obedience to parental choices was expected. The value placed on both women's and men's contributions in the difficult environment meant that a marriage usually entailed one of two kinds of social and economic exchange. Most typically, the groom would provide services to the bride's family for a period of time. The couple's residence with the wife's family provided emotional support as well as time to evaluate the husband's hunting

prowess and ensured the wife's female kin were available to assist her in at least her first pregnancy and childbirth. Less often, two young women would exchange places, with a daughter from each family becoming daughter-in-law to the other family.

Although households were primarily monogamous, some marriages included one husband shared by two wives. This could happen, for example, when a man engaged in the levirate, a custom in which he espoused his dead brother's widow and took on the responsibility of providing for her and her children.

Socialization of Children

Traditional subarctic cultures included a variety of pregnancy taboos and postnatal observances to ensure the well-being of mother and child. Birth took place at home, in a special birth structure or, according to early travelers among neighbouring Mi'kmaq, in the woods. One or more knowledgeable women assisted the mother in giving birth and in caring for the delivered child. Swaddled babies were diapered with moss and carried on the mother's back in an ornamented skin bag or a cradleboard.

Family members and other relatives played the major role in the informal process of childhood education. A child had considerable scope to learn through copying others. Thus, a Kaska parent might say "Make tea!" and a small girl would try to reconstruct what she had often observed her mother and older sisters doing but what she had never been formally instructed to do. Parents did not neglect disciplining and even chastising a disobedient child for such offenses as stealing and rebelliousness. More important for the formation of personalities is the fact that parental treatment subtly but firmly encouraged children to become independent and self-reliant.

Several "firsts," including the first tooth, the first game killed by a boy, and a girl's first menstruation (menarche), were ceremonially recognized, sometimes by a small feast. Menarche was recognized by an elaborate series of ritual observances that were undertaken to protect the girl and her family from the powerful forces that were effecting the changes in her body. Athabaskan peoples paid the greatest ritual attention to menarche, with Gwich'in girls moving to a special shelter constructed some distance from the family camp and staying there for up to a year. At the menarche camp a girl wore a pointed hood that caused her to look down toward the ground. Other ceremonial precautions included a rattle of bone that was supposed to prevent her from hearing anything, a special stick to use if she wanted to scratch her head, and a special cup that should not touch her lips. Subsequent menstruation involved only a short period of seclusion.

RELIGIOUS BELIEFS

Subarctic peoples traditionally had a highly individualistic relationship with the supernatural: Most men and women undertook a vision quest in their youth and relied heavily upon one or more guardian spirits for protection and guidance. In Kaska terms the vision occurred by "dreaming of animals in a lonely place" or hearing "somebody sing," perhaps a moose in the guise of a person. Dreams notified an individual of impending events and might advise one how to behave in order to achieve success or avoid misfortune.

Among many subarctic peoples there was a widespread belief that hunting success depended upon treating prey animals and their remains with reverence. This involved various practices such as disposing of the animals' bones carefully so that dogs could not chew them. Respect was particularly evident in the use of polite circumlocutions to refer to bears. Many groups undertook several ceremonial observances in bear hunting, including a purifying sweat bath before departing on the hunt and an offer of tobacco to a bear that had been killed. Afterward the people feasted and danced in its honour.

Two important concepts of the Innu and other Algonquian groups were manitou and the "big man" (a concept quite different from the "big men" of Melanesian cultures, who are local leaders). Manitou represents a pervasive power in the world that individuals can learn to use on their own behalf. The term Great Manitou, designating a personal god, probably represents a missionary-inspired adaptation of an older idea. A person's big man is an intimate spirit-being who confers wisdom, competence, skill, and strength in the food quest as well as in other areas of life, including magic. Maintaining a relationship with this being requires ethically good conduct. Animal-spirit "bosses" who control the supply of caribou, fish, and other creatures are another traditional belief shared by Algonquian and certain Athabaskan groups.

Three of the most popular characters in Algonquian folklore are Witiko (Windigo), a terrifying cannibalistic giant apt to be encountered in the forest; Tcikapis, a kindly, powerful young hero and the subject of many myths; and Wiskijan (Whiskeyjack), an amusing trickster. "Witiko psychosis" refers to a condition in which an individual would be seized by the obsessive idea that he was turning into a cannibal with a compulsive craving for human flesh.

Shamanism was an important feature of traditional subarctic culture. The shaman, who could be male or female, served as a specialist curer and diviner in addition to his or her routine adult responsibilities. It was thought that occasionally shamans became evil and behaved malignantly. Shamanistic ability came to an individual from dreaming of animals who taught the dreamer to work with their aid; such ability had to be validated through successful performance.

The Deg Xinag conceived of humans as comprising body, soul, and "speech," the latter an element surviving after death but, unlike the soul, not reincarnated. Hazards to life came from the soul always being menaced by various supernatural figures that were the primary enemies of human survival and by the souls of powerful evil shamans acting on behalf of these supernatural figures. In contrast, spirit-beings associated with animals and berries supported human survival. Animal songs and amulets created good relations with helpful animal spirits. Elaborate ceremonies in the men's house, to which the spirit-beings were invited, protected the food supply.

CULTURAL CONTINUITY AND CHANGE

By the late 19th century, Canada and the United States had established their dominance over all American subarctic peoples. In contrast to many European colonial powers, which often promoted racial segregation, the United States and Canada promoted Indian assimilation, a policy that attempted to replace indigenous lifeways with those of the dominant culture. Both countries used mechanisms such as compulsory education at boarding schools and the elimination of separate legal status for aboriginal peoples to implement their assimilationist goals.

During the 20th century subarctic peoples encountered profound local economic changes in addition to assimilationist policies. Well into the first third of the century, the northern subsistence

Yellowknife, the capital of the Northwest Territories (Can.), was founded in 1935 on the north shore of the Great Slave Lake. George Hunter

economy continued to depend heavily upon hunting, while the cash economy derived almost entirely from the fur trade. During the Great Depression of the 1930s, demand for pelts drastically decreased, decimating the region's cash economy; following World War II, new governmental restrictions on subsistence hunting and on trapping slowed economic recovery. In response to the increasing need for wage-based income, many indigenous families relocated from the forests and trading centres to established northern cities such as Fairbanks (Alaska), Whitehorse (Yukon), and Churchill (Manitoba), as well as to new towns, such as Schefferville (Quebec), Yellowknife (Northwest Territories), and Inuvik (Northwest Territories). These towns offered employment in industries such as commercial fishing, construction, mining, and defense. Expanding economic opportunities in the north also drew families from southern Canada, and for the first time fairly large numbers of indigenous subarctic peoples and Euro-Americans interacted.

By the close of the 20th century, many subarctic peoples had become involved in cultural preservation or revitalization movements, and a portion of those chose to remain in or relocate to smaller trading-post settlements to foster a more traditional lifestyle. Whether in rural or urban areas, many First Nations peoples and Native Alaskans began to view an intact forest landscape as an intrinsic part of their heritage. They became increasingly concerned about the economic development of the north and used a variety of means, from protest through land claims and other legal actions, to prevent or ameliorate the effects of such development. Many of their efforts have proved successful, most notably those resulting in the Alaskan Native Claim Settlement Act (U.S., 1971) and associated legislation and the creation of Nunavut (Canada, 1999), a province with a predominantly aboriginal government.

CHAPTER 3

NORTHWEST COAST AND CALIFORNIA CULTURE AREAS

The Northwest Coast was the most sharply delimited culture area of native North America. It covered a long narrow arc of Pacific coast and offshore islands from Yakutat Bay in the northeastern Gulf of Alaska south to Cape Mendocino in present-day California. Its eastern limits were the crest of the Coast Ranges from the north down to Puget Sound, the Cascades south to the Columbia River, and the coastal hills of what is now Oregon and northwestern California. Although the sea and various mountain ranges provide the region with distinct boundaries to the east, north, and west, the transition from the Northwest Coast to the California culture area is gradual, and some scholars classify the southernmost tribes discussed in this chapter as California Indians.

The California culture area corresponds roughly to the present states of California (U.S.) and northern Baja California (Mex.). The peoples living in the California culture area at the time of first European contact in the 16th century were only generally circumscribed by the present state boundaries. Some were culturally intimate with peoples from neighbouring areas. For instance, California groups living in the Colorado River valley, such as the Mojave and Quechan (Yuma), shared traditions with the Southwest Indians, while those of the Sierra Nevada, such as the Washoe, shared traditions with the Great Basin Indians, and many northern California groups shared traditions with the Northwest Coast Indians.

NORTHWEST COAST INDIAN PEOPLES

The Kuroshio, a Pacific Ocean current, warms the region; temperatures are rarely hot and seldom drop below freezing. The offshore current also deluges the region with rain; although it falls rather unevenly across the region, annual precipitation averages more than 160 inches (406 cm) in many areas and rarely drops below 30 inches (76 cm) in even the driest climatic zones. The northern Coast Range averages an elevation of about 3,300 feet (1,000 m) above sea level, with some peaks and ridges rising to more than 6,600 feet (2,000 m). In most of the Northwest, the land rises steeply from the sea and is cut by a myriad of narrow channels and fjords. The shores of Puget Sound, southwestern Washington, and the Oregon coast hills are lower and less rugged.

In general, traditional Northwest Coast economies were oriented toward aquatic resources. The region's coastal forests—dense and predominantly coniferous, with spruces, Douglas fir, hemlock, red and yellow cedar, and, in the south, coast redwood—supported abundant fauna and a wide variety of wild plant foods.

LINGUISTIC AND TERRITORIAL ORGANIZATION

The peoples of the Northwest Coast spoke a number of North American Indian languages. From north to south the following linguistic divisions occurred: Tlingit, Haida, Tsimshian, northern Kwakiutl, Bella Coola, southern Kwakiutl, Nuu-chah-nulth (Nootka), Coast Salish, Quileute-Chimakum, Kwalhioqua, and Chinook. Along the Oregon coast and in northwestern California, a series of smaller divisions occurred: Tillamook, Alsea, Siuslaw, Umpqua, Coos, Tututni-Tolowa, Yurok, Wiyot, Karok, and Hupa.

Northwest Coast groups can be classified into four units or "provinces." The northern province included speakers of Tlingit, Haida, Tsimshian, and the Tsimshian-influenced Haisla (northernmost Heiltsuq or Kwakiutl). The Wakashan province included all other Kwakiutl, the Bella Coola, and the Nuu-chah-nulth. The Coast Salish–Chinook province extended south to the central coast of Oregon and included the Makah, Chinook, Tillamook, Siuslaw, and others. The northwestern California province included the Athabaskan-speaking Tututni-Tolowa as well as the Karok, Yurok, Wiyot, and Hupa.

The Northwest Coast was densely populated when Europeans first made landfall in the 18th century. Estimates of density in terms of persons per square mile mean little in a region where long stretches of coast consist of uninhabitable cliffs rising from the sea. However, early historic sources indicate that many winter villages had hundreds of inhabitants.

STRATIFICATION AND SOCIAL STRUCTURE

The Northwest Coast was the outstanding exception to the anthropological truism that hunting and gathering cultures—or, in this case, fishing and gathering cultures—are characterized by simple technologies, sparse possessions, and small egalitarian bands. In this region food was plentiful. Less work was required to meet the subsistence needs of the population than in farming societies of comparable size, and, as with agricultural societies, the food surpluses of the Northwest encouraged the development of social stratification. The region's traditional cultures typically had a ruling elite that controlled use rights to corporately held or communal property, with a "house society" form of social organization. The best analogues for such cultures are generally agreed to be the medieval societies of Europe, China, and Japan, with their so-called noble houses.

In house societies the key social and productive unit was a flexible group of a few dozen to 100 or more people who considered themselves to be related (sometimes only distantly), who were coresident in houses or estates for at least part of the year, and who held common title to important resources; in the Northwest those resources included sites for fishing, berry picking, hunting, and habitation. House groups also held a variety of less-tangible privileges, including the exclusive use of particular names, songs, dances, and, especially in the north, totemic representations or crests.

Within a house group, each member had a social rank that was valued according to the individual's degree of relatedness to a founding ancestor. Although social stratification in Northwest Coast communities is frequently described as including three divisions—chiefly elites, commoners, and slaves or war captives—each person in fact had a particular hereditary status that placed him within the group as though he occupied one step on a long staircase of statuses, with the eldest of the senior line on the highest step and the most remotely related at the bottom. Strictly speaking, each person was in a class by himself.

The highest in rank invariably held a special title that in each language was translated into English as "chief." This person administered the group's properties. Usually a man or the widow of a past chief, this leader determined many of the patterns of daily life—when to move to the salmon-fishing station, when to build weirs and traps, when to make the first catch, when and where to perform the rite propitiating the first salmon of the season, which other groups should be invited to feasts, and so on. A chief had many prerogatives and sumptuary privileges and in turn was expected to administer efficiently and to tend to the social and ritual affairs that ensured the general welfare and prestige of the group.

Notionally those of high rank had vast authoritarian powers. However, within the group all mature persons other than slaves could voice their opinions on group affairs, for a house group's property was held in common. Most leaders refrained from abusing other members of the house and community—not only were they kin, but the chief also needed their cooperation to accomplish even the most basic tasks. For example, many strong arms and sturdy backs were needed to obtain, assemble, and position the heavy materials required to build or repair a house, to construct fish weirs and traps, and to launch and paddle the chief's huge dugout canoe. Many singers, dancers, and attendants were necessary to stage important ceremonies properly, and many bold warriors were needed to defend the group against foes. Leaders were also aware that there was enough flexibility in the social structure that those of low rank could abandon an abusive situation and move in with kindred elsewhere.

Slaves, however, had few or no rights of participation in house group decisions. They usually had been captured in childhood and taken or traded so far from their original homes that they had little hope of finding their way back. They were chattels who might be treated well or ill, traded off, slain, married, or freed at their owner's whim; a typical house group owned at least one slave but rarely more

than a dozen. Their duties generally included boring, repetitive, and messy work such as stocking the house with firewood and water. In some groups, slaves could achieve better social standing by displaying an unusual talent, such as luck in gambling, which made them eligible for marriage to a person of higher status.

In many cases, insignia or other devices were used to signal personal status. Chiefly people often wore robes of sea otter fur, as otter pelts were quite valuable in the fur trade; the quality and level of decoration on clothing marked other statuses as well. Head flattening was considered a beautifying process from the northern Kwakiutl region to the central Oregon coast, as well as among some of the neighbouring Plateau Indians. This painless, gradual procedure involved binding a newborn child's head to a cradleboard in such a way as to produce a long subconical form, a strong slope from the eyebrows back, or a distinctive wedge shape in which the back of the skull was flattened. In the Northwest Coast culture area, head flattening was practiced only on relatively high-status infants, although the capture and enslavement of children from neighbouring tribes that also undertook this modification meant that a shapely head was no guarantee of an individual's current status.

The status of each member of a house group was hereditary but was not automatically assumed at birth. Such things had to be formally and publicly announced at a potlatch, an event sponsored by each group north of the Columbia River. The term comes from the trade jargon used throughout the region and means "to give." A potlatch always involved the invitation of another house (or houses), whose members were received with great formality as guests and witnesses of the event. The potlatch reached its most elaborate development among the southern Kwakiutl from 1849 to 1925.

Potlatches were used to mark a wide variety of transitions, including marriages, the building of a house, chiefly funerals, and the bestowal of adult names, noble titles, crests, and ceremonial rights. Trivial events were used just as often, because the main purpose of a potlatch was not the occasion itself but the validation of claims to social rank. The potlatch was also used as a face-saving device by individuals who had suffered public embarrassment and as a means of competition between rivals in social rank.

Having witnessed the proceedings, potlatch guests were given gifts and served prodigious amounts of food with the expectation that what was left uneaten would be taken home. The social statuses of the guests were recognized and reified through the potlatch, for gifts were distributed in rank order and the more splendid gifts were given to the guests of highest status. Whether hosting or acting as guests at a potlatch, all members of a house usually participated in the proceedings, a process that served to strengthen their identification with the group.

Although potlatches shared some fundamental characteristics across cultures, there were also regional variations. In the northern province, for example, a major potlatch was part of the cycle of mortuary observances after the death of a chief, at which his heir formally assumed chiefly status; in the Wakashan and Salish regions, a chief gave a potlatch before his own demise in order to bestow office on his successor.

Some early anthropologists argued that the potlatch was an economic enterprise in which the giver expected to recover a profit on the goods he had distributed when, in turn, his guests became potlatch hosts. However, this was an impossibility because only a few guests of highest rank would ever stage such affairs and invite their former hosts; those of intermediate and low rank could not afford to do so, yet the value of the gifts bestowed on them was considerable. Indeed, before the fur trade made great quantities of manufactured goods available, potlatches were few, whereas feasts, though also formal but not occasions for bestowing titles and gifts, were very frequent.

SUBSISTENCE, SETTLEMENT PATTERNS, AND HOUSING

The traditional Northwest Coast economy was a complex whole. One of its most important distinctions was the highly efficient use of natural resources. Aquatic resources were especially bountiful and included herring, oil-rich candlefish (eulachon), smelt, cod, halibut, mollusks, five species of salmon, and gray whales.

However, the fisheries were scattered across the region and not equally easy to exploit. Certain species of salmon, for example, traveled upriver from the sea to spawn each year, but only in certain rivers and only at particular times of the year.

Generally, the important species for preservation for winter stores were the pink and the chum salmon. Because these species ceased to feed for some time before entering fresh water, their flesh had less fat and when smoked and dried would keep for a long period of time.

Other salmon species, such as sockeye, coho, and the flavoursome chinook or king salmon, were eaten immediately or dried and kept for a short period, but their high fat content caused the meat to spoil relatively quickly even when dried. Therefore, the principal fishing sites were those along rivers and streams in which pink or chum salmon ran in the fall. In the spring other sorts of fish became available in tremendous schools. Herring came in to spawn in coves, candlefish entered certain rivers, and, farther south,

Yurok man with canoe on the Trinity River in California, photograph by Edward S. Curtis, c. 1923. Edward S. Curtis Collection/Library of Congress, Washington, D.C. (neg. no. LC-USZ62-118588)

smelt spawned on sandy beaches in summer. People also went to sea to hunt marine mammals and to fish for offshore species such as halibut.

Water transport was highly important in the region for subsistence purposes and as a way to effect trade between tribes and later with fur traders. All groups made efficient dugout canoes. Northern groups, as well as the Kwakiutl and Salish down to Puget Sound, made dugouts with vertical cutwaters, or projecting bow and stern pieces, as well as those with rounded sterns and hulls. The Nuu-chah-nulth and some of their neighbours made vessels with curving cutwaters at the bow, vertical sterns, and angular flat bottoms. Northwestern California dugouts had upturned rounded ends, rounded hulls, carved seats, and foot braces for the steersman. Watercraft were made in different proportions for different purposes; for instance, large reinforced vessels were used to move people and cargo, while shorter, narrower craft were used for sea mammal hunting.

Summer was a time for hard work; food had to be caught or gathered and processed for winter consumption. Usually homesites and settlements were limited to narrow beaches or terraces because the land fell so steeply to the shore or riverbank. Between the limited number of building sites and the uneven distribution of natural resources, it was most efficient for a house group to have several bases of operation. In summer they dispersed into small groups that moved among fishing and berry-picking sites and other established but minor residential areas as their resources became available.

Most people spent the winter in villages with several sizable houses (each with its associated group), as well as at least one very large structure in which the highest-ranking group lived and where the village could hold a large potlatch. During winter people of higher status rarely worked at day-to-day activities (leaving that to slaves), instead using the time to create two- and three-dimensional art and conduct potlatches, dances, and sacred ceremonies that brought people together to socialize, trade, and negotiate relationships within and between communities. For instance, from Tlingit country in the north to at least as far south as Puget Sound and perhaps farther, several house groups would typically pass the winter together at a site in a sheltered cove that was protected from winter winds. During this period the relative prestige of each group and individual was factored into all interactions. These assemblages of multiple house groups at winter village sites are often called "tribes," but it must be noted that such units were not politically integrated, for each of the component houses retained its economic and political autonomy.

As structures, Northwest Coast houses shared a few significant traits. All were rectilinear in floor plan, with plank walls and a plank roof, and all but those of northwestern California were large. In the north, most houses were built on a nearly square plan, reaching sizes as large as 50 feet wide by 55 feet long (15.25 by 16.75 m). They were typically constructed around a deep central pit, with vertical plank walls and a gabled roof intermeshed for stability. To the south, in the Wakashan province, houses were typically rectangular and reached sizes of approximately 40 feet by 60 to 100 feet (12 m by 18.25 to 30.5 m). Huge cedar posts with side beams and ridgepoles constituted a permanent framework to which were attached wall planks and roof planks that could be taken down, loaded onto canoes, and transported from one site to another.

Some peoples in the Coast Salish–Chinook province also built houses of permanent frameworks with detachable siding and roofing, although they generally used a shed roof system with one slope instead of a peaked roof. Along the lower Columbia River, the typical house was built over a large rectangular pit that was fairly deep and lined with planks, as the earth provided excellent insulation against the cold and damp; only the gabled roof and its end supports showed above ground. At the southernmost limit of the culture area, the northwestern California house type was designed for single-family use. These homes were constructed over a central pit, with low side walls of redwood planks and a three-pitch roof somewhat reminiscent of a pyramid. The peoples of northwestern California also built a combined clubhouse and sweat house that was the focus of male activity; these multipurpose structures were common to many California Indian groups.

TECHNOLOGY AND THE VISUAL ARTS

The indigenous peoples of the Northwest Coast drew from the heavily wooded environment for much of their technology. Woodworking was facilitated by the abundance of easily worked species of trees, especially the giant arborvitae (*Thuja plicata*, also known as red cedar) and the redwood (*Sequoia sempervirens*). The trunks of these trees could be split into planks or hollowed out into canoes, containers, and other useful objects.

The peoples of this region were noted for their artistic skill, and many everyday items were decorated in some way. More than most other groups in North America, Northwest Coast visual arts emphasized symmetry, neatness of finish, and embellishment through carving and painting. Traditional carving implements included adzes, mauls, wedges, chisels, drills, and curved knives, all made of stone; sharkskin was used for sanding or polishing wooden items.

As far south as the Columbia River, wooden boxes were made of red cedar boards that were kerfed—cut nearly through transversely. The wood was steamed at these points until it was flexible enough to shape into the form of a box. Dishes often were hollowed out of pieces of wood, sometimes plain, sometimes in the form of animals or monsters. Other items made of wood included spoons and ladles, canoe bailers, trinket boxes, chamber pots, masks and rattles used in ceremonies, magnificent memorial

Haida headdress, painted wood, swan's down, and abalone, c. 1870; in the Denver Art Museum. Courtesy of the Denver Art Museum, Colorado

or totem poles and interior house posts, housefronts and screens, halibut hooks, and even the triggers of animal traps. Sometimes items were made from the horns of mountain goats, bighorn sheep, or elk, which were carved by essentially the same methods as wood. Occasionally sculptures were carved from stone.

Artists in the northern province emphasized low-relief carving accented by painting. Their motifs were the hereditary crests of the clans or parts of the crests. Different groups in the northern province expressed themselves in

somewhat different styles. Haida art, for instance, tended to be massive and to comprise highly conventionalized balanced elements. In Tsimshian carving and painting, there was an effort to leave no open space in or between the conventionalized motifs. Filler elements such as eye designs and miniature figures were used intensively. Tlingit art was slightly less conventionalized, with relatively little use of filler elements.

In the Wakashan province, representative art was frankly sculptural, impressionistic, and bold. There was

Totem Pole

Totem poles are carved and painted logs, mounted vertically, that are constructed by the Indians of the Northwest Coast of the United States and Canada. There are seven principal kinds of totem pole: memorial, or heraldic, poles, erected when a house changes hands to commemorate the past owner and to identify the present one; grave markers (tombstones); house posts, which support the roof; portal poles, which have a hole through which a person enters the house; welcoming poles, placed at the edge of a body of water to identify the owner of the waterfront; mortuary poles, in which the remains of the deceased are placed; and ridicule poles, on which an important individual who had failed in some way had his likeness carved upside down.

The carving on totem poles separates and emphasizes the flat, painted surfaces of the symbolic animals and spirits depicted on them. Each pole generally has from one (as with a grave

Tlingit totem pole and community house in Totem Bight State Park, Ketchikan, Alaska. Bob and Ira Spring

marker) to many (as with a family legend) animal images on it, all following standardized forms that are familiar to all Indians of the Northwest Coast. Beavers, for example, always include cross-hatched tails, and eagles show downward curved beaks.

The word totem *refers to a guardian or ancestral being, usually supernatural, that is revered and respected, but not always worshipped. The significance of the real or mythological animal carved on a totem pole is its identification with the lineage of the head of the household. The animal is displayed as a type of family crest, much as an Englishman might have a lion on his crest or a rancher a bull on his brand.*

More widely known, but in fact far less common, are the elaborately carved tall totem poles that relate an entire family legend in the form of a pictograph. This legend is not something that can be read in the usual sense of the word; only with an understanding of what the symbols mean to the Indians and a knowledge of the history and customs of the clan involved can the pole be interpreted. Each animal or spirit carved on the pole has meaning, and when combined on the pole in sequence, each figure is an important symbol constituent of a story or myth. An exact interpretation of any set of symbols, however, would be almost impossible without the help of a knowledgeable narrator from the family.

The totem pole was also a sign of the owner's affluence, for hiring an artist to make a pole was an expensive proposition. The carving of totem poles reached its peak in the early and middle 19th century, when the introduction of good metal tools and the wealth gained from the fur trade made it possible for many chiefs to afford these displays. Few examples of this period remain, however, as the moist coastal atmosphere causes the cedar poles to rot and fall in about 60 to 70 years.

a limited amount of simple geometric design on such things as whalebone clubs and whaling harpoon barbs. Their Coast Salish neighbours used some, but less, representative art, which was similar if looser in style. On Puget Sound there was little representative art; the abstract painted designs on the canoe boards were unlike anything else in the region. Most traditional Chinook art is represented by just a few angular figures incised on mountain sheephorn bowls. In the southernmost part of the culture area, in northwestern California, art generally focused on geometric patterns incised on elkhorn objects and shells.

Weaving was also highly developed. The inner bark of red cedar was stripped, and the long ribbonlike strands were woven into mats and baskets, using a checkerwork technique. The same material could be shredded into finely divided flexible hanks, which were twined together to make a slip-on rain cape shaped like a truncated cone. The softer inner bark of yellow cedar was made into robes. Persons of high status wore robes made of or edged with strips of sea otter fur and yarn made of the wool of mountain goats. Salish groups near the Georgia Strait wove robes of mountain goat wool and also of wool from a special breed of shaggy dog. The Chilkat, a Tlingit group, wove robes and basketry, applying various twilling techniques to fabric and basketry alike. Their blankets bore representations of crests in blue, yellow, black, and white.

Twined basketry made from long flexible splints split from spruce roots illustrated great technical skill. Baskets so tightly woven as to be waterproof were made for cooking in northern and northwestern California; their contents were boiled by placing hot stones into the soup or potage within the basket. Storage containers, receptacles for valuables large and small, and rain hats were also woven. The Coast Salish specialty was coiled baskets.

Dress patterns of the area were fairly simple, and, although ceremonial garments and some hats could be highly embellished, most clothing was worn for protection from the environment rather than for ostentatious display. Both women and men customarily wore some combination of necklaces, earrings, nose rings, bracelets, and anklets; these were made of various materials, mostly shells, copper, wood, and fur. Some individuals rubbed grease and ochre onto their skin to produce a red colour, often accented with black; tattooing was also practiced. Throughout the region women wore skirts or gowns of buckskin, soft leather, or woven wool or plant fibres. Men's dress varied from tribe to tribe but was in general quite minimal—most men wore nothing but ornaments on warm days. Men of the northernmost Tlingit and the Kitksan of the upper Skeena wore tailored buckskin breechcloths, leggings, and shirts in cold weather; elsewhere they wore robes of yellow cedar bark or pelts in cold weather and rain capes in downpours.

KINSHIP AND FAMILY LIFE

While groups in the northern province tended to be matrilineal—passing status, property, and education through the maternal line—those in the other three provinces were generally patrilineal. Marriages were usually arranged by parents, who openly wished to see their children rise (or at least not fall) in status. As with up-marrying slaves, members of the middle classes of a group could marry up if they had distinguished themselves in some way. The children of these marriages would inherit the status of the higher-ranking spouse. If the spouse of lower rank was not distinguished in some way, the children would accrue the lower status; as this was generally seen as an undesirable outcome, such matches occurred relatively rarely.

An interesting aspect of Northwest Coast culture was the emphasis on teaching children etiquette, moral standards, and other traditions of social import. Every society has processes by which children are taught the behaviour proper to their future roles, but often such teaching is not an overt or deliberate process. On the Northwest Coast, however, particularly northward of the Columbia River, children were instructed formally. This instruction began at an age when children were still in their cradles or toddling, and all elder relatives, particularly grandparents, participated in it. Lessons were often delivered gently and humorously through the telling and retelling of folktales. Trickster tales recounting Raven's exploits were especially entertaining, as his troubles were so obviously the result of his dissolute, lazy, gluttonous, and lecherous personality. Children born to high status were given formal instruction throughout childhood and adolescence. They had to learn not only routine etiquette but also the lengthy traditions by which the rank and privileges of their particular group were validated, including rituals, songs, and formulaic prayers.

Changes in status were generally marked by public ceremonies. Formal rituals were considered necessary at each of two or three critical stages in a person's lifetime—birth, a girl's attainment of puberty (there were no boys' puberty rites in the area), and death—because at those times the participants in these events might be especially vulnerable or so filled with power that they could inadvertently harm others. A newborn infant was believed to be in danger of harm by supernatural beings; the infant's parents were simultaneously in danger and potentially dangerous. Mystic forms of vulnerability and volatility also accrued to girls at puberty, to the close kin of a deceased person, and to those who prepared and disposed of the dead. Such perils were avoided by isolating the persons involved—either within a boarded-off cubicle in the house or in a simple structure out in the woods—and by limiting their diet to old dried fish and water. At the conclusion of the isolation period, a formal purification ritual was performed. The intensity of the restrictions varied considerably, not only in different parts of the coast but even within individual houses. Often the pubescent daughter of a chief, for example, was secluded for many months, whereas her low-ranking house sister might have to observe only a few days of confinement.

Over most of the coast there was a very great fear of the dead. A body was usually removed from the house through some makeshift aperture other than the door and disposed of as rapidly as possible. An exception occurred in the northern province, where bodies of chiefs were placed in state for several days while clan dirges were sung. Disposal of the dead varied. In the northern province, cremation was practiced. In the Wakashan and part of the Coast Salish areas, large wooden coffins were suspended from the branches of tall trees or placed in rock shelters. Other Coast Salish deposited their dead in canoes set up on stakes. In southwestern Oregon and northwest California, interment in the ground was preferred.

RELIGION AND THE PERFORMING ARTS

The religions of the Northwest Coast shared several concepts that provided

RAVEN CYCLE

A collection of trickster-transformer tales originated among the Native Americans of the Northwest Pacific Coast from Alaska to British Columbia. These traditional stories feature Raven as a culture hero, an alternately clever and stupid bird-human whose voracious hunger, greed, and erotic appetite give rise to violent and amorous adventures that explain how the world of humans came to be.

As with the trickster-transformer tales of other cultures, stories about Raven often begin with him instigating a crisis that precipitates social or physical chaos. The tales then recount the ultimate resolution of these crises (often at Raven's expense) and the re-creation of order out of chaos. The Raven cycle begins with a boy's birth and relates early adventures that include his seduction of his aunt (sometimes replaced by the daughter of the Sky Chief) and subsequent flight to the sky to escape the flood that ensues from his transgression of incest (or status) rules. Raven, the result of this scandalous union, falls to earth during the flight. There Raven is adopted by a chief.

As an adult, Raven transforms the earth from a dark and arid land inhabited by a variety of ferocious monsters into a land of rivers, lakes, and mountains inhabited by animals and human beings. He travels about changing aspects of the physical environment into their present forms, often through deception. The dozens of tales that recount his activities include Raven's impersonation of a woman to embarrass a man; his killing of a monster by putting hot stones down its throat; and his role as the "bungling host," a common motif of a guest who is fed by an animal wizard, then tries to imitate it in producing food but, lacking his host's magic, fails ignominiously. In other areas of North America, Mink, Blue Jay, Fox, or Coyote replace Raven as the hero of similar tales.

the widespread bases for various kinds of religious activity.

One concept was that salmon were supernatural beings who voluntarily assumed piscine form each year in order to sacrifice themselves for the benefit of humankind. On being caught, these spirit-beings returned to their home beneath the sea, where they were reincarnated if their bones or offal were returned to the water. If offended, however, they would refuse to return to the river. Hence,

there were numerous specific prohibitions on acts believed to offend them and a number of observances designed to propitiate them, chief of which was the first-salmon ceremony. This rite varied in detail but invariably involved honouring the first salmon of the main fishing season by sprinkling them with eagle down, red ochre, or some other sacred substance, welcoming them in a formal speech, cooking them, and distributing their flesh, or morsels of it, communion-fashion, to all the members of the local group and any guests. The maximal elaboration of this rite occurred in northwestern California in what have been called world-renewal ceremonies; these combined first-salmon rituals, first-fruits observances, and dances in which lineage wealth was displayed. Elsewhere the first-salmon rituals were less elaborate but still important, except among the Tlingit, who did not perform them.

Another religious concept was the acquisition of personal power by seeking individual contact with a spirit-being, usually through prayer and a vision. Among Coast Salish all success in life—whether in hunting, woodworking, accumulating wealth, military ventures, or magic—was bestowed by spirit-beings encountered in the vision quest. From these entities each person acquired songs, special regalia, and dances. Collectively, the dances constituted the major ceremonials of the Northwest Coast peoples. Known as the spirit dances, they were performed during the winter months.

In the Wakashan and northern provinces, it was believed that remote ancestors who had undertaken vision quests had been rewarded with totemic symbols or crests. Displaying these hereditary crests and recounting the traditions of their acquisition formed an important part of potlatches. In the Wakashan area certain ceremonial cycles called for the dramatization of the whole tale of the supernatural encounter, which in some cases included the spirit-being's possession of and its eventual exorcism

from the seeker. Such dramas were performed by dancing societies.

Shamanism differed from other acquisitions of supernatural power only in the nature of the power obtained—that is, power to heal the sick through extraction of disease objects or recovery of a strayed soul. It was commonly believed that some shamans, or medicine men and women, had the power to cause infirmities as well as to cure them. Witchcraft was used to kill others or to make them ill and was believed to be carried out by malicious persons who knew secret rituals for that purpose.

CULTURAL CONTINUITY AND CHANGE

The impact of European and Euro-American colonialism on the peoples of the Northwest Coast varied at different periods and in different regions. The Tlingit were the first group to encounter such outsiders, when Russian traders made landfall in Tlingit territory in 1741. These colonizers did not establish a garrison in the region until 1799, and then only after heated resistance. Spain sent parties to the Haida in 1774, Britain to the Nuu-chah-nulth in 1778, and the United States to various groups about 1800.

The colonial expeditions sought sea otter pelts, which were particularly dense and highly prized in the lucrative Chinese market. Although the Russians pressed Aleut men into corvée labour as sea otter hunters, they traded with Northwest Coast peoples for furs and food. In exchange they brought foreign manufactured goods to the tribes. These materials affected indigenous cultures only slightly, as the tribes selected the articles that complemented existing culture patterns. They acquired steel blades, for example, that could be fitted to traditional adzes to cut more efficiently than stone or shell blades, yet initially spurned axe and hatchet blades because these required a drastic change in motor habits and coordination patterns.

By the middle of the 19th century, a number of trading posts had been established in the region. The peoples of the region recognized that fur traders were more interested in commerce than in self-sufficiency; having long been involved in commerce among themselves, indigenous groups found novel ways to profit from this. Tlingit house groups provisioned the trading posts with fish, game, and potatoes; the latter were a South American crop that had by this time circled the globe, having arrived in the Northwest Coast via Russian trade. They sold literally tons of food. Records indicate that in 1847, for instance, the Russians purchased more than 83,000 pounds (37,650 kg) of game and fish plus more than 35,000 pounds (nearly 16,000 kg) of potatoes from the Tlingit.

Other avenues of entrepreneurship were open as well. The Tsimshian and others gained control of major portage routes and shipping lanes, demanding fees for passage and vessel rental. Some of their monopolies were in place for decades. Still other groups hired out their slaves as prostitutes or labourers.

Although the Northwest Coast tribes had quickly found ways to benefit from maritime trade, they found it more difficult to cope with the flood of settlers from the eastern United States and Canada that began in the 1840s. These emigrant farmers were encouraged by their governments to move to what are now western Washington, Oregon, Vancouver Island, and the lower Fraser River valley. In the United States this occupation was accompanied by the removal of the tribes to small reservations in present-day Washington and Oregon, under the provisions of formal treaties. In the area that is now British Columbia, there were no treaties extinguishing native title to the land; undeveloped land was presumed to belong to the crown, and transfers of developed land were private affairs.

Effective missionary activity began in various parts of the coast in conjunction with the settlement movement. Missionaries on the Northwest Coast were very successful at directing culture change, teaching not only Christian precepts but also the precepts of etiquette, sobriety, household hygiene, and punctuality and a host of other requirements for competency in the dominant culture. In addition, the formal schooling of indigenous children was in the hands of missionaries on much of the coast for many decades.

From the late 18th through the entire 19th century, the most disruptive events for Northwest Coast peoples were epidemics of contagious diseases such as smallpox, venereal infections, and measles. These had a profound effect on native society because, never having been exposed to these illnesses before, the people suffered extremely high death rates. It is estimated that between 1780 and 1900, the indigenous population in the region declined by as much as 80 percent. Depopulation forced societies into unusual distributions of roles and status positions. These frequently involved adoptions, the allocation of multiple titles to a single individual, and other compromises that helped to maintain the social system despite rapid population decline. A great deal of ritual and practical knowledge was lost when those who would have passed the information on grew ill and died.

By the second half of the 19th century, trading profits had combined with high mortality and social uncertainty to create increasingly extravagant potlatches. As houses consolidated in response to losses from epidemics, some used this traditional means of display to climb the status hierarchy, while other houses engaged in lavish potlatches to reaffirm or defend their high status. In addition, spirit dancing seems to have become more extravagant and evocative. Unfortunately, both activities were misunderstood by missionaries and government officials—potlatches were seen as foolish "giveaways" that impoverished their host families, while the reenactment of a legend of cannibalism within the spirit dance was misunderstood as the actual consumption of human flesh. As a result, both practices were outlawed in Canada from 1884 to 1951, though they persisted in discreet settings.

In the closing decades of the 19th century, the fur trade collapsed, and the peoples of the Northwest Coast found themselves in dire economic straits. Divested of most of their lands and increasingly dependent upon manufactured goods, they needed to develop new economic resources. Indigenous reasons for the accumulation of wealth differed from those of Euro-Americans, but, as before, the tribes found ways to enter the dominant economic system. Some individuals began by working for wages in a dull day-after-day routine, something that most other Native American peoples refused to do. At first there was less hired work available than potential employees. Jobs were mostly limited to guiding prospectors, backpacking cargo over mountain passes, cutting cordwood for coastal steamers, and working as farm and domestic labour. Yet when the canned salmon industry developed, principally from the Fraser River northward, wage labour boomed.

Native peoples knew more about the habits of the region's salmon population than anyone else, which presented them with a clear advantage, especially given that the commercial salmon fishery began with a very simple technology. The Northwest Coast Indians had long used canoes, spears, nets, and weirs, and over the decades most changes in the fishing industry involved increased mechanization rather than changes in its fundamental premises: motive power changed from paddles and oars to two-cycle gasoline engines, high-speed gasoline engines, and eventually diesel engines; harvesting tools changed from gill nets and crude beach seines to huge purse seines handled with power gear; and navigation changed from dead reckoning to a reliance on tide tables, compasses, and charts. Native American fishers (both men and women) learned the new skills alongside their coworkers, and a number eventually became independent operators. Often these individuals were of hereditary high status and fulfilled traditional expectations for behaviour by employing, feeding, or otherwise aiding the lower-status members of their house group. At the same time, many native people, especially women, were employed in processing the catch—again activities to which they had long been accustomed.

Fishing continues to be a mainstay of the economy in this region, and in the long run the indigenous peoples who are dependent upon the industry face problems common to all commercial fishers: commitment to a short-season industry that ties up capital in expensive boats and nets, seasonal income fluctuation, the potential for accidents, the prospect of overfishing, and the fickle nature of the market.

Having retained a high level of economic independence relative to other North American groups, the peoples of this region were able to organize relatively effectively against government interference. Beginning in 1912, the Tlingit, Haida, and other tribes in southeastern Alaska created political groups called Native Brotherhoods, and in 1923 Native Sisterhoods, to act on behalf of the people in legal and other proceedings; similar groups were subsequently formed in coastal British Columbia. These organizations provided valuable training in modern political processes and negotiations. Their successes are remarkable, given the rampant discrimination faced by indigenous peoples of the region, where some businesses posted signs with statements such as "No natives or dogs allowed" as recently as the 1940s.

The Native Brotherhoods (and the nascent, but not yet chartered, Sisterhoods) pursued a variety of legal strategies to ensure equal treatment under the law, beginning with the 1915 passage of an act granting territorial citizenship to Native Alaskans who met certain criteria. In 1922 they won the acquittal of a traditional leader who had been arrested for voting in the Alaska primary elections, an important precursor to legislation granting U.S. citizenship to all native peoples in 1924 (Canadian federal elections were opened to native peoples in 1960). Also in 1924 a prominent Native Brotherhood leader and lawyer, William L. Paul, Sr. (Tlingit), became the first indigenous person elected to Alaska's territorial legislature.

These victories were followed by a variety of successful antidiscrimination suits and land claims. In the United States the latter were ultimately resolved through the Alaska Native Claims Settlement Act of 1971. This act resolved indigenous claims of illegal takings in Alaska and created a series of for-profit corporations charged with managing a final settlement of some 44 million acres (17.8 million hectares) of land and $962 million; native peoples participate in these corporations as shareholders, directors, and employees. The Canadian organizations effected the repeal, in 1951, of laws prohibiting potlatches and the filing of land claims. After many years of discussion, the provincial government of British Columbia agreed in 1990 to negotiate tribal land claims through a body known as the British Columbia Treaty Commission; the prescribed negotiation process was necessarily painstaking, and the first Agreement-in-Principal between a tribe and the government was signed in 1999. At the turn of the 21st century, progress remained slow and many tribal claims remained in negotiation with the Treaty Commission.

CALIFORNIA INDIAN PEOPLES

Because its mosaic of microenvironments—including seacoasts, tidewaters, rivers, lakes, redwood forests, valleys, deserts, and mountains—provided ample sustenance for its many residents, California was one of the most densely populated culture areas of Northern America. The indigenous peoples of this region were considerably more politically stable, sedentary, and conservative and less in conflict with one another than was generally the case in other parts of North America. Within the culture area, neighbouring groups often developed elaborate systems for the exchange of goods and services. In general, the California tribes reached levels of cultural and material complexity rarely seen among hunting and gathering cultures.

REGIONAL AND TERRITORIAL ORGANIZATION

Each of the many tribes in the California culture area had distinct linguistic, social, and cultural traditions. Except for the Colorado River peoples (Mojave and Quechan) and perhaps some Chumash groups, California peoples avoided centralized governmental structures at the tribal level. Instead, each tribe consisted of several independent geopolitical units, or tribelets. These were tightly organized polities that nonetheless recognized cultural connections to the other polities within the tribe; they were perhaps most analogous to the many independent bands of Sioux. Tribelets generally ranged in size from about a hundred to a few thousand people, depending on the richness of locally available resources; tribelet territories ranged in size from about 50 to 1,000 square miles (130 to 2,600 square km).

Within some tribelets all the people lived in one principal village, from which some of them ranged for short periods of time to collect food, hunt, or visit other tribelets for ritual or economic purposes. In other tribelets there was a principal village to which people living in smaller settlements traveled for ritual, social, economic, and political occasions. A third variation involved two or more large villages, each with various satellite settlements. In such systems, a designated "capital" village would be the residence of the principal chief as well as the setting for major rituals and political and economic negotiations.

SETTLEMENT PATTERNS

In most of California the tribelets established permanent villages that they occupied all year, although small groups routinely left for periods of a few days or weeks to hunt or collect food. In areas with sparse economic resources, people often lived in seminomadic bands of 20 to 30 individuals, gathering together in larger groups only temporarily for such activities as antelope drives and piñon-nut harvests. As a rule, riverine and coastal peoples enjoyed a more settled life than those living in the desert and foothills.

Traditional house types varied from permanent, carefully constructed homes occupied for generations to the most temporary types of structures. Dwellings could

be wood-framed (northern California), earth-covered (various areas), semisubterranean (Sacramento area), or made of brush (desert areas) or thatched palm (southern California). Communal and ceremonial buildings were found throughout the region and were often large enough to hold the several hundred people who could be expected to attend rituals or festivals. Houses ranged in size from 5 or 6 feet (almost 2 metres) in diameter to apartment-style buildings in which several families lived together in adjoining units. Sweat lodges were also common. These earth-covered permanent structures were used by most California tribes (the Colorado River groups and the northern Paiute, on the margins of California, were exceptions), with sweating a daily activity for most men.

PRODUCTION AND TECHNOLOGY

Traditional subsistence in native California centred on hunting, fishing, and collecting wild plant foods. Typically, men hunted and fished while women and children collected plant foods and small game. Hunting and fishing equipment such as bows and arrows, throwing sticks, fishing gear, snares, and traps were made by men; women made nets, baskets, and other gathering implements as well as clothing, pots, and cooking utensils.

Food resources varied across the landscape. Shellfish, deep-sea fish, surf fish, acorns, and game were the main subsistence staples for coastal peoples. Groups living in the foothills and valleys

Southern Miwok woman with a sifting basket, photograph by Edward S. Curtis, c. 1924. Edward S. Curtis Collection/Library of Congress, Washington, D.C. (neg. no. LC-USZ62-114583)

relied on acorns, the shoots and seeds of weedy plants and tule (a type of reed), game, fish, and waterfowl. Desert-dwellers sought piñon nuts, mesquite fruit, and game (especially antelope and rabbit) and engaged in some agriculture.

Native Californians developed a variety of specialized technological devices to help them maximize the productivity of the region's diverse environments. The Chumash of southern coastal California made seaworthy plank canoes from which they hunted large sea mammals. Peoples living on bays and lakes used tule rafts, while riverine groups had flat-bottom dugouts made by hollowing out

large logs. Traditional food-preservation techniques included drying, hermetic sealing, and the leaching of those foods, notably acorns, that were high in acid content. Milling and grinding equipment was also common.

PROPERTY AND EXCHANGE SYSTEMS

Traditional concepts of property tended to vary in degree rather than kind in native California. In general, larger groups such as clans and villages owned the land and protected it against infringement from other groups. Individuals, lineages, and extended families usually did not own land but instead exercised exclusive use rights (usufruct) to certain food-collecting, fishing, and hunting areas within the communal territory. Areas where resources such as medicinal plants or obsidian, a form of volcanic glass used to make very sharp tools, were unevenly distributed over the landscape might be owned by either groups or individuals. Particular articles could be acquired by manufacture, inheritance, purchase, or gift.

Goods and foodstuffs were distributed through reciprocal exchange between kin and through large trading fairs, which were often ritualized. Both operated similarly in that they served as a redistribution and banking system for easily spoiled food; a group with surplus edibles would exchange them for durable goods (such as shells) that could be used in the future to acquire fresh food in return.

Most California groups included professional traders who traveled long distances among the many tribes. Goods from as far away as Arizona and New Mexico could be found among California's coastal peoples. Generally, shells from the coastal areas were valued and exchanged for products of the inland areas, such as obsidian. Medicines, manufactured goods such as baskets, and other objects were also common items of exchange.

LEADERSHIP AND SOCIAL STATUS

For those groups that engaged in centralized forms of organization, the role of chief, or tribelet leader, was generally an inherited position. In some groups, such as the Pomo, women were eligible for chiefly office. Typically the chief was an economic administrator whose work ranged from general admonitions to specific directions for particular tasks, such as indicating where food was available and how many people it would require to collect it. Such leaders redistributed the economic resources of the community and, through donations from its members, maintained resources from which emergency needs could be met. Within their communities, chiefs were the major decision makers and the final authority, although they typically worked with the aid of a council of elders, heads of extended families, ritualists, assistant chiefs, and shamans. In some areas the chief functioned as a priest, maintaining the ceremonial house and ritual objects. The chief was generally a conspicuous person, being wealthier than the average individual, more elaborately dressed, and often displaying symbols of office. Chiefs' families formed a superstratum of the community elites, especially among those tribelets that organized themselves through lineages.

As chiefs led in the political sphere of traditional native California life, shamans led in the sphere in which spiritual and physical health intertwined. The vocation of shaman was open to women and men. Shamans enjoyed a status somewhat similar to that of chief. They served as physical and mental healers, diviners, advisers, artists, and poets. Among other

Hupa Female Shaman, *photograph by Edward S. Curtis, c. 1923.* Edward S. Curtis Collection/ Library of Congress, Washington, D.C. (neg. no. LC-USZ62-101261)

duties, they defined and described the world of the sacred and regulated the fortune of souls before and after death, mediating between the mundane and sacred worlds. Most tribelets in California had one or more shamans, who were active in political life, working with other leaders and placing their powers at the disposal of the community.

Alongside chiefs and shamans were ritualists—dancers, singers, fire tenders, and others—who were carefully trained in their crafts and who functioned intimately within the political, economic, and religious spheres of their communities. These men and women acquired considerable respect and often wealth because of their skills. In effect, they were members of the power elite. When performing, ritualists were usually costumed in headdresses, dance skirts, wands, jewelry, and other regalia.

RELIGION

Native California's traditional religious institutions were intensely and intimately associated with its political, economic, social, and legal systems. Frequently the priests, shamans, and ritualists in a community organized themselves around one of two religious systems: the Kuksu in the north and the Toloache in the south. Both involved the formal indoctrination of initiates and—potentially, depending upon the individual—a series of subsequent status promotions within the religious society; these processes could literally

occupy initiates, members, and mentors throughout their lifetimes. Members of these religious societies exercised considerable economic, political, and social influence in the community.

In the Kuksu religion (common among the Pomo, Yuki, Maidu, and Wintun), colourful and dramatic costumes and equipment were used during ritual impersonations of specific spirit-beings. Within the Toloache religion (as among the Luiseño and Diegueño), initiates performed while drinking a hallucinogenic decoction made of the jimsonweed plant (*Datura meteloides*); the drug put them in a trance and provided them with supernatural knowledge about their future lives and roles as members of the sacred societies.

Religions on the Colorado River differed slightly because they were not concerned with developing formal organizations and recruitment procedures. Individuals received religious information through dreams, and members recited long narrative texts, explaining the creation of the world, the travel of culture heroes, and the adventures of historic figures.

In the northwestern part of the culture area, there was another type of informally structured religious system. Its rituals concerned world renewal (as in the white-deerskin dance) and involved the recitation of myths that were privately owned—that is, for which the prerogative of recitation belonged to only a few individuals. One communal need served by these ceremonies was the reification (or, sometimes, restructuring) of relationships. The display of costumes and valuable possessions (such as white deerskins or delicately chipped obsidian blades) reaffirmed social ranking, and the success of the ritual reaffirmed the orderly relationship of humanity to the supernatural.

The use of supernatural power to control events or transform reality was basic to every California group. Generally magic was used in attempts to control the weather, increase the harvest of crops, and foretell the future. Magic or sorcery was deemed not only the cause of sickness and death, but also the principal means of curing many diseases. Its practices were also considered to be ways to protect oneself, to punish wrongdoers, and to satisfy personal ends.

MARRIAGE AND CHILD REARING

Because of its implications for long-term economic and social bonds and obligations, marriage was almost always a matter arranged by the families of the prospective bride and groom. Generally, the families exchanged goods at the time of the marriage, with the bulk of goods coming from the husband's family. In most cases the wife took up residence with the husband's family and was taught the ways of the group by her mother-in-law.

Adults of childbearing age were generally responsible for providing food for the group; the generation senior to them—their parents, aunts, and uncles— were typically responsible for raising the children of the community. Learning

was a continuous process in which older persons instructed children through elaborate tales containing lessons concerning behaviour and values. Constant supervision, provided by adults, older siblings, and other relatives, reminded younger children about how things should be done.

The educational process became more intense and dramatic during rites of passage, when individuals attained new status and responsibility. The female puberty ritual, for example, generally included a time of isolation, because girls were considered especially empowered (and therefore potentially dangerous on a spiritual level) at menarche. Depending on the tribe, this ritual varied in length from several days to several weeks. During this time, an older woman would care for the girl and instruct her in her role as an adult. Initiation ceremonies for boys were less common and, when carried out, were usually less formal, involving instruction in male occupations and behaviour, and predictions regarding the boy's future religious, economic, or political career.

Adult education could be heavily institutionalized. Young Chumash men, for instance, purchased apprenticeships from guildlike associations of professional artisans. Young Pomo men were also charged a fee to be trained as apprentices by recognized professional craftsmen, albeit without the intervention of a craft association.

Leaders and specialists continued their training on a less-formal level throughout their lifetimes. A person destined to become chief received instruction from others (such as elders, ritualists, and shamans) and continued to receive such counsel after assumption of office.

ARTS

Oral literature—and especially a variety of elaborate creation tales and epic poems—was the art form for which native Californians were most renowned. There were also songs that recounted tales of victory, recent events, daily activities, and romantic love. Songs were usually short but could, in narrative form, last for days. Singing was accompanied by rattles, whistles, or drums.

Visual art forms ranged from decoration on items of daily use, such as baskets and tools, to elaborate rock paintings and rock engravings. Rock paintings were widespread, and, in various parts of the region, designs were incised or pecked into rock surfaces as well. Rock art served a range of functions, from recording individual and group rituals to marking trails.

California peoples were renowned for their exquisite basketwork, though pottery in the eastern desert was also handsomely shaped and decorated. Costuming, particularly in relation to the Kuksu religion, involved the creation of elaborate headdresses, skirts, feathered garments, and other regalia, which were often symbolic of supernatural beings. Body painting was also popular.

Pomo feathered gift basket decorated with shell pendants, c. 1890; in the National Museum of the American Indian, Heye Foundation, New York City. Courtesy of the Museum of the American Indian, Heye Foundation, New York

CULTURAL CONTINUITY AND CHANGE

California was colonized by the Spanish beginning in 1769, when Junípero Serra and his successors began to build a series of missions along the region's southern Pacific coast. Accompanied by soldiers and soon followed by ranchers and other colonial developers, these missionaries upon their arrival initiated a long period of cultural rupture for most of California's indigenous peoples. Native communities were often forcibly dislocated to missions, where they were made to work for the colonizers and to convert to Christianity.

In less than a century, the rest of California had been colonized. In 1812 Russian fur traders founded an outpost at Fort Ross (about 90 miles [140 km] north of present-day San Francisco), and the gold rush that began in 1848 drew some 250,000 Euro-Americans to the California interior over the next five years. Together, these and other events caused the native population to collapse to such an extent—from a precontact high of perhaps 275,000 to perhaps 15,000 in the closing decades of the 19th century—that some have described the period as genocidal.

After a period of intense oversight during the late 19th and early 20th centuries, the U.S. government terminated most of its federal obligations to native Californians in 1955. Indigenous *rancherías*, or reservations, have become relatively autonomous in the period since. Each *ranchería* has an elected body of officials, usually known as a business committee or tribal council, which acts as a liaison between the tribal community and such outside interests as the U.S. Bureau of Indian Affairs, business corporations desiring the purchase or lease of reservation lands, public utilities seeking rights-of-way across lands, and other entities having some form of business with the group. Typically, the council also hears intratribal grievances and participates in planning economic and social development programs.

By the early 21st century, many California Indians were not readily distinguishable from other people residing in California in terms of external factors such as clothing, housing, transportation, or education. However, indigenous attitudes, rituals, and other aspects of traditional culture remained vibrant throughout the state. Many native Californians choose to live in rural areas and reside on reservations; others choose to live in urban or suburban areas; and still others live part of the year on a reservation and spend the rest of the year in a city or suburb.

Throughout California one finds indigenous ceremonial structures, the continued use and manufacture of ritual materials, and the use of traditional foods. Many art forms, especially basket weaving, continue to be passed from one generation to another, and many native languages, though spoken less and less as first languages, are maintained as part of an overall interest in indigenous heritage. Some *rancherías* have cultural centres and museums that help to preserve their cultures and languages, and in some school districts classes in native languages and cultures are being offered to both children and adults.

Traditional culture is less obvious in the major population centres of the state, which now range along the coast and the Central Valley from San Francisco and Oakland south to San Diego. Native culture has not ceased in urban areas but rather has become an important part of a larger tapestry of urban cultural diversity. Growing at a faster rate than the general population, California's indigenous population is the highest in the United States; early 21st-century estimates indicated some 630,000 individuals of indigenous descent residing there. Two California cities are among the 10 U.S. cities with the largest resident populations of Native North Americans—Los Angeles (2nd) and San Diego (9th).

Not all Native Americans living in California are California Indians, and the growth of this population is a relatively recent phenomenon. People from throughout North America, including indigenous individuals, gravitated to the state in large numbers during World War II in order to work in the burgeoning defense industries of that era. A second wave of native migration to California occurred in the 1950s, during

Native Americans occupy Alcatraz Island in San Francisco Bay, March 1964. © Bettmann/Corbis

an aggressive indigenous relocation program carried out by the U.S. Bureau of Indian Affairs.

However well-intended, the Bureau of Indian Affairs' coordination of the relocation plan—which had been designed to move native individuals and families from job-poor reservations to employment-rich urban areas—was often ineptly carried out and frequently abandoned families once they had relocated. As predominantly rural people finding themselves in unfamiliar urban areas with little of the interfamilial social and economic support to which they were accustomed, many newly urban Native Americans sought each other out and developed independent service and support organizations in the cities.

As a result of these migrations, the unique cultural patterns of the many tribes now represented in California are apparent throughout the state, and there is also a strong pantribal ethos that has fostered citywide and statewide recreational, educational, and political groups. For instance, in 1964 a group of Native Americans occupied Alcatraz Island, citing an 1868 treaty allowing them to claim any "unoccupied government land." Although the protestors occupied Alcatraz only for a period of hours, their concerns were later pursued by others. In 1969 a group of approximately 100 individuals calling themselves "Indians of all Tribes" occupied Alcatraz again, this time staying until 1971. The purposes of the occupations were to publicize Indian demands for self-determination, to force negotiations for a Native American cultural centre, museum, and university, and to gain (or, in the occupiers' view, to regain) legal title to the island.

In the early 21st century, California's Native American coalitions were continuing to merge political and educational activism. With organizations such as the American Indian Historical Society and the California Indian Education Association, they are assertively examining, criticizing, and providing new teaching materials for schoolteachers who work with indigenous children and for the state curriculum as it regards Native American life and culture.

CHAPTER 4

PLATEAU AND GREAT BASIN CULTURE AREAS

The Plateau culture area comprises a complex physiographic region that is bounded on the north by low extensions of the Rocky Mountains, such as the Cariboo Mountains; on the east by the Rocky Mountains and the Lewis Range; on the south by the Blue Mountains and the Salmon River (excepting a narrow corridor to present-day California); and on the west by the Canadian Coast Mountains and the Cascade Range. It includes the watersheds of the Columbia and Fraser rivers.

The Great Basin culture area comprises almost all of the present-day states of Utah and Nevada as well as substantial portions of Oregon, Idaho, Wyoming, and Colorado and smaller portions of Arizona, Montana, and California. Great Basin topography includes many small basin and range systems—that is, nearly flat desert plains alternating with many small, roughly parallel mountain ranges—and parts of the mountains, high desert, and low desert that define its external boundaries. The region's northern basin and range systems transition rather gradually to the intermontane plateaus of Idaho and Oregon. Likewise, the differences between the Great Basin Indians and the Plateau Indians are culturally continuous. Anthropologists sometimes refer to the Plateau and Great Basin jointly as the Intermontane culture area.

PLATEAU NATIVE PEOPLES

The climate in which the Plateau peoples live is of the continental type. Temperatures range from -30 °F (-34 °C) in winter to 100 °F (38 °C) in summer. Precipitation is generally low and forms a snow cover during the winter, particularly at higher altitudes. There are three different provinces of vegetation in the region. The Middle Columbia area is a steppe of sagebrush and bunchgrass fringed by yellow pine on higher levels. The Upper Columbia consists mainly of wooded areas, although grassland is found in river valleys. The Fraser area is a semi-open coniferous forest interspersed with dry grassland and a partly maritime flora.

Tribes that live in this environment include the Salish, Flathead, Nez Percé, Yakima, Kutenai, Modoc and Klamath, Spokan, Kalispel, Pend d'Oreille, Coeur d'Alene, Walla Walla, and Umatilla.

LANGUAGE

The peoples of the Plateau belong mainly to four linguistic families: Salishan, Sahaptin, Kutenai, and Modoc and Klamath. The majority of Plateau groups speak Salishan and Sahaptin languages.

The tribes that speak Salishan languages may be conveniently divided into Northern Plateau and Interior Salish; there are also Coast Salish among the Northwest Coast Indians. The Northern Plateau Salish include the Shuswap, Lillooet, and Ntlakapamux (Thompson) tribes. The Interior Salish live mostly in the Upper Columbia area and include the Okanagan, Sinkaietk, Lake Wenatchee, Sanpoil, Nespelem, Spokan, Kalispel, Pend d'Oreille, Coeur d'Alene, and Flathead peoples. Some early works incorrectly denote all Salishan groups as "Flathead."

Speakers of Sahaptin languages may be subdivided into three main groups: the Nez Percé, the Cayuse and Molala, and the Central Sahaptin, comprising the Yakima, Walla Walla, Tenino, Umatilla, and others.

The Kutenai and the Modoc and Klamath language families include the Kutenai and the Modoc and Klamath peoples.

TRADE AND INTERACTION

Its geographic location in the midst of four other culture areas—the Northwest Coast, the Plains, the Great Basin, and California—made the Plateau a crossroads of cultures. An expansive trade network enabled the exchange of goods, ideas, and even people, as slavery was common in the region. The Northwest Coast cultures contributed innovations such as mat-covered houses and pit houses, the carving of animal motifs in wood and bone, and cremation and scaffold burials. Part of this diffusion undoubtedly occurred through trade-based interactions, while other ideas arrived with the Wishram, a Chinook group that migrated from the coast into the Cascade Mountains.

During the 18th century, influences from the south and east grew in importance. The Great Basin's Shoshone had acquired horses by this time and furnished their closest neighbours on the Plains and the Plateau with the new animals. The Plateau tribes placed such a high value on horses that European and Euro-American traders testified that the Nez Percé, Cayuse, Walla Walla, and Flathead had more horses than the tribes of the northern Plains from the early 19th century onward.

During the late 18th and early 19th centuries, the peoples of the Middle Columbia area adopted several kinds of material culture from the Plains. Sahaptin women, for example, made and wore Plains-inspired beaded dresses, men began to wear feathered headdresses and other war regalia, and tepees became popular. Similar innovations occurred on the eastern periphery of the Plateau, especially among the Flathead and the Kutenai. The northwestern Salishan peoples, however, rejected these changes

Kutenai people modeling traditional dress, photograph by J.R. White, c. 1907. Library of Congress, Washington, D.C. (neg. no. LC-USZ61-119219)

in favour of maintaining Plateau traditions. The military ethos common among the Plains peoples was not found uniformly among residents of the Plateau. The Ntlakapamux, Shuswap, Sahaptin, and Klamath did make occasional war raids, dressed in elk hide or wooden slat armour and armed with bows and clubs. Other groups chose to avoid conflict, however. The Flathead in particular were well regarded by visitors for their courtesy, hospitality, honesty, and courage.

SETTLEMENT PATTERNS AND HOUSING

Traditionally, the Plateau peoples resided in permanent villages during the winter, with the remainder of the year divided between those villages and a variety of semipermanent camps conveniently situated for hunting and gathering. As soon as horses were adopted, some groups became more nomadic, using mobile camps as they traversed the Rocky Mountains in order to hunt buffalo on the Plains.

A village was home to between a few hundred and a thousand people, although the community could house more than that during major events. Villages were generally located on waterways, often at rapids or narrows where fish were abundant during the winter season. Communities owned the fishing sites and surrounding area in common. Each village also had an upland for hunting; in contradistinction to the fishing localities,

upland territories were mostly open for people from other villages as well.

Village houses were of two main types, the semisubterranean pit house and the mat-covered surface house. Pit houses were usually circular and typically had a pit 3 to 6 feet (1 to 2 m) deep and a diameter of 25 to 40 feet (7.5 to 12 m), with an interior space of approximately 500 to 1,260 square feet (45 to 115 square m). The roof was usually conical and was supported by a framework of wooden posts, beams, and stringers—long saplings that had been stripped of bark and were used to bridge the area between the beams or from the beams to the ground. The smoke hole in the top was also the entrance to the house; the interior was reached by climbing onto the roof, through the smoke hole, and down a ladder or notched log.

Pit houses were common throughout the Plateau region at one time, but they were eventually supplanted in the southern Plateau by the mat-covered surface house. These homes used a conical or A-frame design that was formed by leaning together stringers or timbers and covering them with mats made of tule, a type of reed. As the availability of Euro-American goods increased, Plateau peoples often covered surface houses with canvas instead of reed mats, which were time-consuming to produce.

Conical houses had one hearth in the centre of the floor and generally sheltered one nuclear or three-generation family. These tepeelike, lightly built

Yakima tepee with reed mat cover, photograph by Edward S. Curtis, c. 1910. Edward S. Curtis
Collection/Library of Congress, Washington, D.C. (neg. no. LC-USZ62-99798)

structures were used in summer when families were engaged in nomadic foraging activities. They averaged perhaps 15 to 30 feet (4.5 to 9 m) in diameter, with an interior space of approximately 175 to 700 square feet (16 to 65 sq m). In contrast, A-frame houses were used as communal winter residences, so they were very large, heavily built, and thoroughly insulated. Early visitors to the Plateau report houses as much as 150 feet (45 m) long. More typical were houses between 25 and 60 feet (7.5 and 18 m) long and perhaps 12 to 15 feet (3.5 to 4.5 m) wide, for an interior of approximately 300 to 900 square feet (28 to 85 sq m). Hearths were placed at intervals down the central aisle and were usually shared by two nuclear families, one on each side of the aisle.

Housing at foraging camps could take a variety of forms, ranging from small conical mat lodges to simple windbreaks. Groups that traveled to the Plains to hunt bison typically used the tepee during those expeditions. As they became increasingly nomadic, many of these groups adopted the tepee as a full-time dwelling.

SUBSISTENCE AND MATERIAL CULTURE

As members of hunting and gathering cultures, the peoples of the Plateau relied upon wild foods for subsistence. Salmon, trout, eels, suckers, and other fish were abundant in the rivers, and fishing was the most important source of food. Fishing was accomplished with one- or three-pronged fish spears, traps, and nets. Communities also built and held in common large fish weirs—stone or wooden enclosures used to "corral" the catch. Substantial quantities of fish were dried on elevated wooden racks and preserved for winter consumption. Hunters used a bow and arrows and sometimes a short spear in their pursuit of such prey. In the winter they wore long and narrow snowshoes to facilitate the tracking of animals.

Wild plant foods were another important source of nutrition. Roots and bulbs were especially important. The major source of starch was the bulb of the camas flower (Camassia esculenta). Bitterroot, onions, wild carrots, and parsnips were also gathered and were generally cooked in earth ovens heated by hot stones. Berries—serviceberries, huckleberries, blueberries, and others—were harvested as well.

The earliest European explorers in the region reported that Plateau clothing comprised a bark breechcloth or apron and a twined bark poncho that fell a little below the waist. During the cold season men wrapped their legs with fur, women had leggings of hemp, and robes or blankets of rabbit or other fur were used. By the 19th century, however, clothing had become similar to that seen on the Plains. Men wore breechcloths, leggings, and shirts, and women wore leggings and dresses. Hair was generally braided, and hats, headbands, feathered battle

Klamath woman preparing food on a stone slab, photograph by Edward S. Curtis, c. 1923. Edward S. Curtis Collection/Library of Congress, Washington, D.C. (neg. no. LC-USZ62-115814)

and ceremonial regalia, and other headgear had also become common.

The Chinook, who traded in slaves, molded the heads of freeborn infants with a device attached to the cradleboard. Despite their name, the Flathead did not engage in this form of modification; some early ethnographers speculated that the apparent misnomer derived from the group's squareness of profile relative to the triangular form seen in skulls that had been altered. Many historic paintings that purport to depict Flathead individuals are actually portraits of members of neighbouring tribes.

Dugout or bark canoes were useful forms of transportation, although long-distance water travel was limited by the many river rapids in the region. Items that were small or could be manufactured by one or two people were typically the property of individuals. Groups whose territory neighboured that of the Northwest Coast Indians engaged in a variety of redistributive events similar to potlatches. Decorative art consisted of pictographic designs with a symbolic content, referring to supernatural beings and cosmic things.

The general ethos emphasized material equality and the sharing of necessities. Food resources, for instance, were generally shared. The Klamath, however, held wealthy persons in greater esteem than others, an ethos that may have derived from the tribe's proximity to the hierarchical societies of the Northwest Coast and California.

POLITICAL ORGANIZATION

In traditional Plateau societies the village formed the key sociopolitical unit, although the political hierarchy used in governing each village varied from tribe to tribe. The Ntlakapamux, for example, used a fairly informal consensus system. The Sanpoil, on the other hand, had a more formal political structure. The village had a chief, a subchief, and a general assembly in which every adult had a vote—except for young men who were not married. The Flathead were perhaps the most hierarchical group, with a head chief of great power and band chiefs under him; the head chief decided on matters of peace and war and was not bound by the recommendations of his council.

In many Plateau societies, chiefs and their families played a prominent role in promoting traditional values. Among the Sinkaietk, for instance, chiefly office was hereditary. While conferring a level of decision-making power, the office also obligated the chief and his family to act in ways that exemplified virtuous behaviour. For this group such behaviour included the placement of a female relative among the chief's advisers. Similar positions for highly respected women also existed in other groups, such as the Coeur d'Alene, and bear witness to the independence of women in many Plateau tribes.

Social control was, as a rule, achieved through social pressure and public

Head Flattening

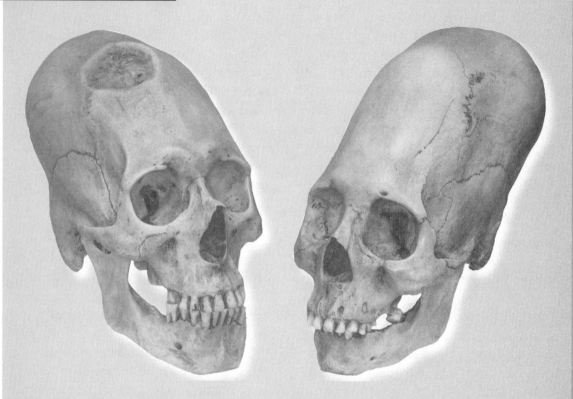

Peruvian elongated skulls, trephined male (left) *and intact female* (right), c. 1000 BC. Courtesy, Skulls Unlimited International, Inc.

The practice of intentionally changing the shape of the human skull was once common in some cultures. Head flattening was practiced by a number of North, Central, and South American Indian tribes, particularly before European colonization. It was most commonly accomplished by securing an infant in a cradleboard that had a moveable cover over the forehead. The pressure of the cover, gently and consistently applied over time, caused the child's forehead to elongate, creating a nearly smooth silhouette from the tip of the nose to the crown of the head. Flattening could also be achieved by binding an infant's head with cloth.

Head flattening appears to have had no effect on an individual's mental capabilities. Deformation of the skull is the best-documented type of modification of the head, largely because archaeological skeletal remains clearly reveal its presence. Cases of cranial modification are known from all continents except Australia and Oceania, although it was rather rare in Africa south of the Sahara and apparently absent from South India.

opinion rather than force. People were not coerced into following the advice of a chief or the decisions of a council meeting. Those who did not agree with a given course of action could simply move to another village or another band, and did so fairly frequently. However, a number of groups allowed chiefs, village councils, or a combination thereof to arbitrate or punish transgressions against the community such as murder or stealing. Arbitrations generally involved a settlement of horses to the injured party, while corporal punishment was usually administered by a delegated village "whipper." Slaves were compelled to follow their owners' wishes.

In some cases, as with the Nez Percé's transition from settled village life to a more nomadic existence, political organization was adjusted. The Nez Percé were originally a village-centred people. Each village had a male chief whose office was hereditary, although poorly qualified sons were generally passed over for the privilege. The chief was advised by a council and was primarily occupied with mediating disputes, displaying exemplary behaviour, and seeing to the general good of his people. By the early 19th century, however, families from different villages had begun to coalesce into mobile bands in order to undertake autumn hunts on the Plains. While the hereditary authority of the village chiefs continued, leadership in the new tasks associated with this change in lifestyle—notably travel, defense, and

raiding—came under the authority of skilled hunters and fighters.

KINSHIP

Bilateral descent systems prevailed in most Plateau groups. In these systems descent is traced equally through the lines of the mother and the father. The average Plateau kin group consisted of a nuclear family and its closest lineal relatives. This was the case among, for instance, the Tenino. Their kinship terminology revealed the close connection between family relatives of the same generation, so that all one's female cousins were called by and treated in the same terms as those used for one's sisters; one's male cousins, likewise, were all one's "brothers."

As notional siblings, first cousins did not marry. Other than this constraint, marriage and divorce were informal affairs. Newlyweds generally resided near the groom's family, and, in case of divorce, the wife simply returned to her parents' home. No particular grounds for separation were necessary, and at a later date both parties usually undertook new marriages. Polygyny, a form of marriage in which several wives share a husband, was an approved but not especially common practice throughout the culture area.

Some Plateau kinship systems included "joking relationships." These could be informal mechanisms for expressing social disapproval or deflating puffed egos, as with the ribbing and practical joking encouraged by the Tenino between a father's sister's husband and his wife's brother's child. The butt of a joke was expected to respond gracefully. Joking relationships could also be ribald, permitting sexual innuendo between a man and his sister-in-law; notably, these individuals were potential marriage partners under the polygyny system.

CHILDHOOD AND SOCIALIZATION

The life cycle of the individual was marked by fixed ritual acts that opened the gateway to the different social roles he had to enact. These rituals began before birth. Among the Sinkaietk, for example, a pregnant woman was supposed to give birth in a lodge that had been constructed for this purpose. A newborn spent its day strapped in a cradleboard. Naming practices varied among the tribes. The training of the child was left to the mother and grandmother, but even as a small boy a Sinkaietk could accompany his father on fishing and small-game hunting trips, while small girls helped their mothers about the house and in gathering wild foods. Children learned to be hardy through activities such as swimming in cold streams; such exertions were generally supervised by grandparents. Disobedience was rare. When it did occur, it was sometimes met with corporal punishment; some groups allowed parents to call upon the village whipper when children misbehaved.

At puberty a boy undertook a vision quest. This rite of passage usually involved spending some days fasting on a mountaintop in hopes of communicating with a guardian spirit. A girl who had her first menstruation was taken to a location some distance from the village and provided with living quarters. During this time she was seen as extremely powerful in the spiritual and supernatural senses and so observed a number of ritual taboos that were meant to protect her and the community. Among other actions, her hair was bound up in rolls that she touched only with a small comb, her face was painted red or yellow, she wore undecorated clothing, and she used a drinking tube rather than taking water directly from a well. After the flow, she ritually purified herself in a sweat lodge. Her seclusion might continue for one or several months, during which time she might undertake a vision quest. She finished her seclusion with evening prayers on a hill. When she returned to the village, she was treated as an adult.

Certain rituals were carried out after an individual's death. To prevent the dead from lingering among the living, some groups demolished homes where death had occurred. Grave sites were often located at riversides, though the specific form of burial—whether the body was intact or cremated, placed on the surface or in the ground, covered with soil or a rockslide, and marked with stones or wood—varied from one tribe to another. For about one year after the death, the decedent's spouse (or spouses, in polygynous marriages) was expected to demonstrate grief by wearing old or ragged clothing and was also expected to delay remarriage during this period.

BELIEF SYSTEMS

Religion was, like the rest of the culture, closely intertwined with the region's ecology. Plateau religions shared several features with indigenous North American religions in general, most notably in their emphases on animism, shamanism, and individual communion with the spirit world.

The main rituals were the vision quest; the firstling, or first foods, rites; and the winter dance. The vision quest was compulsory for boys and recommended for girls. The spirit-beings who engaged with humans were thought to guide individuals to particular vocations, such as hunting, warfare, or healing. Both boys and girls could become shamans, though it was seen as a more suitable occupation for the former. They cured diseases by extracting a bad spirit or an object that had entered the patient's body. On the northern Plateau they also brought back souls that had been stolen by the dead and were known to publicize their feats through dramatic pantomimes. Because their work included healing the living and contacting the dead, shamans tended to be both wealthy and respected—and even feared.

Firstling rites celebrated and honoured the first foods that were caught or gathered in the spring. The first salmon ceremony celebrated the arrival of the salmon run. The first fish caught was ritually sliced, small pieces of it were distributed among the people and eaten, and the carcass was returned to the water accompanied by prayers and thanks. This ritual ensured that the salmon would return and have a good run the next year. Some Salish had a "salmon chief" who organized the ritual. The Okanagan, Ntlakapamux, and Lillooet celebrated similar rites for the first berries rather than the first salmon.

The winter or spirit dance was a ceremonial meeting at which participants personified their respective guardian spirits. Among the Nez Percé the dramatic performances and the songs were thought to bring warm weather, plentiful game, and successful hunts.

As in much of Northern America, folklore in the Plateau generally emphasized the creator, trickster, and culture hero Coyote. The subject of innumerable trickster tales, Coyote (or alternative trickster figures such as Blue Jay) undertook exploits that reflected common foibles and reinforced the social mores of the people.

CULTURAL CONTINUITY AND CHANGE

The cultures of the Plateau changed with time and place. The most dynamic period of cultural change occurred after the arrival of the horse in the early 18th century. Horse technology inspired innovations in subsistence, political organization, housing, and other aspects of traditional life. It could also displace people: Pressure from the nomadic Blackfoot in approximately 1800 forced the Flathead and Kutenai to withdraw from their home quarters on the plains of western Montana. They resettled in the intermontane valleys of the Rockies and from there made occasional buffalo hunts on the Plains in the company of other Plateau tribes such as the Coeur d'Alene and Nez Percé.

The 19th Century: Syncretism and Disenfranchisement

Other innovations arose from different causes. Direct contact between indigenous groups and Euro-Americans were relatively brief at first and included the provision of boats and food to the Lewis and Clark expedition, which traversed the region in 1805 and again in 1806. Early in the 19th century the fur trade brought Native American and Euro-American trappers from the east into the country, particularly to the northern Plateau. These groups included a relatively large number of Iroquois men who had adopted Roman Catholicism; they propagated Christianity among the Flathead, who thereafter visited St. Louis to call on missionaries. Proselytizing missionaries were a strong force in the area from the 1820s to the '50s.

By the 1830s Plateau peoples were engaging in syncretic religious practices through millenarian movements that came to be known collectively as the Prophet Dance. The major impetus for the movement appears to have been despair over the devastating loss of life caused by the epidemic diseases that had accompanied European colonization. The eponymous prophets were charismatic leaders who were said to have received supernatural instructions for hastening the renewal of the world and the return of the dead. The Prophet Dance movement appeared before that of the Ghost Dance. As with the Ghost Dance, variations on the Prophet Dance persisted into the 21st century.

By the 1840s the United States was subject to a burgeoning homestead movement that inspired thousands of emigrants to move to the Willamette valley and other parts of what would become the Oregon Territory. Many of these settlers traveled through the Plateau, often trespassing on tribal lands. Native peoples also noted with consternation that disease seemed to follow the Euro-American missionaries and settlers. Conflict ensued, and by the 1850s the United States had begun to negotiate treaties with the resident tribes. For the most part these involved setting terms for regional development and delineating specific tracts of land as belonging to either the tribes or the government. The treaty process was disrupted in 1857, before completion, when the discovery of gold on the Thompson River spurred a great influx of settlers and miners. Gold strikes were soon found on several other rivers in the region. Tensions rose; crowded mining camps bred infectious diseases, and the men drawn to such enterprises were often corrupt and predatory.

The remainder of the 19th century was a turbulent period during which many Plateau tribes struggled economically. The United States and Canada invoked a series of public policies to assimilate indigenous peoples: Tribes were confined to reservations, subsistence practices were forcibly shifted from hunting and gathering to agriculture, and children were sent to boarding schools where they were often physically abused. The region was also affected by placer mining, a technique in which water from high-pressure hoses is used to strip soil from hillsides into rivers; this greatly increased the sediment load of waterways and depleted crucial salmon stocks. Fisheries were further decimated by industrial harvesting at the mouths of the great rivers. Used to supply a burgeoning cannery industry, the new techniques not only caught enormous quantities of fish but did so before the salmon could reach their spawning grounds and reproduce.

As subsistence became increasingly difficult, some indigenous groups became more resistant to government policies. In the early 1870s a band of Modoc, dissatisfied with farming life and the suppression of their religious practices, left their assigned reservation and returned to their original land near Tule Lake. The Modoc War (1872–73) comprised the federal government's attempt to return this band to the reservation; unable to apprehend the group, the military finally used siege tactics to force its surrender.

The Nez Percé War of 1877 resulted from two otherwise unrelated events: a shady treaty negotiation that ceded some tribal lands and a raid in the Wallowa valley in which several settlers were killed. Following the raid, the United States ordered all bands of Nez Percé off of the ceded lands, including the Wallowa valley. The band that had remained resident there was led by Chief Joseph and comprised more than 500 individuals, many of them women, children, or elders. Fearing disproportionate reprisals from the military, the band fled. The group was eventually captured, but only after a chase of more than three months during which the people traveled some 1,600 to 1,700 miles (2,575 to 2,700 km).

In the 1880s, in a process known as "allotment," the common title to land that had been conferred to each tribe was replaced with individual titles to farm-sized acreages; the remainder was then sold, severely reducing indigenous landholdings in the Plateau. Although legal safeguards were put into place to protect indigenous landowners from exploitation and corruption, such laws were poorly enforced. As a result, allotment initiated a period of increasing poverty for many Plateau tribes.

THE 20TH AND 21ST CENTURIES: REGAINING SOVEREIGNTY

In the 1930s, after decades of paternalism, the U.S. Bureau of Indian Affairs engaged in a series of policy revisions that authorized tribes to create governments and corporations, and take charge of other aspects of community life, such as the administration of schools. Many tribes chartered constitutions or similar documents, elected councils, and engaged in other forms of self-governance during this period.

In 1954 the federal government terminated its relationship with the inhabitants of the Modoc and Klamath reservation, stripping the tribe of federal recognition and the benefits and protections associated with that status. Termination was a national policy. The hope was that the elimination of the special relationship between the federal government and indigenous peoples would encourage economic development on reservations. The reservation land that had survived allotment was condemned and sold, with the proceeds distributed among the former residents. The loss of federal support for health care and schools devastated the community. The Modoc and Klamath people sued to regain federal recognition, which they achieved in 1986, but they did not regain their former lands.

As the 20th century progressed, many tribes sued the governments of Canada and the United States in order to reclaim territory, generally claiming illegal takings due to treaty violations or unconscionably low compensation. A number of these suits were successful and resulted in awards in the tens of millions of dollars. Most of the monetary awards were distributed among all members of a tribe rather than held as common assets, however, and so were not available for reservationwide improvements. Treaty-ensured fishing rights were also the substance of legal action, especially after major dam construction on the Columbia and other rivers abrogated those rights by destroying traditional fishing sites. Again, the tribes were generally successful in gaining compensation for their losses.

In the late 20th and early 21st centuries, many Plateau tribes had regrouped from the economic devastation of the previous 100 years or more. Several had added tourist resorts and casinos to their extant timber, ranching, and fishing operations. Funds from these enterprises were used for a variety of community purposes, including education, health care, rural development, and cultural preservation.

PEOPLES OF THE GREAT BASIN

The Great Basin is arid to semiarid, with annual average precipitation ranging from as little as 2.1 inches (5.3 cm) in Death Valley to 20 to 25 inches (50.8 to 63.5 cm) in mountainous areas. Precipitation falls primarily in the form of snow, especially in the high country. Because of the surrounding topography, water does not leave the basin except by evaporation or industrial means; brackish and even salty water are common on basin floors, as at the Great Salt Lake. The area is characterized by a vertical succession of ecological zones, each with a dominant xerophytic (desert-type) flora and related fauna. Before industrialization, the region's population density was sparse, ranging from 0.8 to 11.7 persons per 100 square miles (259 square kilometres).

The Great Basin is home to Washoe, Mono, Paiute, Bannock, Shoshone, Ute, and Gosiute tribes.

LANGUAGE

This region was originally home to peoples representing two widely divergent language families. The Washoe, whose territory centred on Lake Tahoe, spoke a Hokan language related to those spoken in parts of what are now California, Arizona, and Baja California, Mexico. The remainder of the Great Basin was occupied by speakers of Numic languages. Numic, formerly called Plateau Shoshonean, is a division of the Uto-Aztecan language family, a group of related languages widely distributed in the western United States and Mexico. Linguists distinguish Western, Central, and Southern branches of Numic.

Western Numic languages are spoken by the Owens Valley Paiute (Eastern Mono), several Northern Paiute groups, and the Bannock. Central Numic languages are spoken by the Panamint (Koso) and several Shoshone groups, including the Gosiute, Timbisha, Western Shoshone, and Comanche. Although they originated in the Great Basin, the Comanche acquired horses during the early colonial period, moved to present-day Texas, and became nomadic buffalo hunters; they are thus typically regarded as Plains Indians.

Southern Numic languages are spoken by the Kawaiisu and a number of Ute and Southern Paiute groups including the Chemehuevi. The distinction between Southern Paiute and Ute is cultural rather than linguistic; Ute speakers who had horses in the early historic period are regarded as Ute, and those who did not readily adopt horses are regarded as Southern Paiute.

The Numic peoples called themselves "Numa," "Nungwu," or "Numu," meaning "people" or "human beings"; the various tribal names such as Paiute and Shoshone were designations given them by other tribes. The Washoe called themselves "Washoe," a true self-name. Linguistic and archaeological evidence indicates that the Washoe separated from other California Hokan-speaking groups as long as several millennia ago. Similar evidence indicates that the Numic peoples may have been spreading across the Great Basin from southeastern California for the last 2,000 years, reaching their northernmost areas less than 1,000 years ago.

TECHNOLOGY AND ECONOMY

The traditional cultures of the Great Basin are often characterized according to their use or rejection of horses, although people inhabited the region for thousands of years before horses became available. Groups that used the horse generally occupied the northern and eastern sections of the culture area. The Southern Ute and Eastern Shoshone were among the first peoples north of the Spanish settlements of New Mexico to obtain horses, perhaps by the mid-1600s. These bands subsequently acted as middlemen in the transmission of horses and horse culture from New Mexico to the northern Plains. As the Northern Shoshone of Idaho obtained horses in the 18th century, they were joined by Northern Paiute speakers from eastern Oregon and northern Nevada to form the Shoshone-Bannock bands of historic times. By 1800 the Southern and Northern Ute, the Ute of central Utah, the Eastern Shoshone, the Lemhi Shoshone, and the Shoshone-Bannock had large herds of horses, used tepees or grass-covered domed wickiups, and were increasingly oriented toward the tribes and practices found on the Plain. Bison became their major prey animal, and they began to engage more heavily in the kinds of inter-tribal trade and warfare characteristic of the Plains Indians.

The tribes to the south and west in the Great Basin proper and on the western Colorado Plateau did not take up the general use of horses until 1850–60. The Washoe did not use horses prior to colonial settlement in the region and rarely used them thereafter. The Numu and the Washoe built two types of shelters: semicircular brush windbreaks in the summer and domed brush, bark-slab, grass, or reed-mat wickiups in the winter. Whether equestrian or pedestrian, Great Basin peoples generally sited their winter villages along the edge of valley floors near water and firewood; their summer encampments were moved frequently so as not to exhaust the food resources in any given locale.

Aside from horse-related technology, such as halters and saddles, the tools of equestrians and pedestrians were quite similar and very typical of hunting and gathering cultures: the bow and arrow, stone knife, rabbit stick, digging stick, basket, net, and flat seed-grinding slab and hand stone. Some Western Shoshone, Southern Paiute, and Southern Ute groups made a coarse brownware pottery; some Northern Shoshone made steatite jars and cups. Lines and hooks, harpoons, nets, and willow fish weirs were used on rivers and lakes. Rodents were taken with snares and traps or pulled from burrows with long hooked sticks. Rabbits were driven into nets and clubbed or were shot with bows and arrows; rabbit drives provided an occasion for people to congregate and socialize, gamble, dance, and court. Antelope were driven into corrals and traps. Waterfowl were netted, trapped, or shot with arrows that had rounded heads and were intended to stun the bird; some groups made decoys of tule reeds covered with duck skins. Deer, elk, and mountain sheep were taken by individual hunters with bows and arrows or in traps or deadfalls.

Great Basin peoples followed an annual round that encompassed several ecological zones, exploiting plant and animal resources as they became available. Typically, more than 70 percent of the food supply was vegetal. More than 200 species of plants were named and used, principally seed and root plants. Pedestrian groups gathered nuts from piñon pine groves in the upland areas of Nevada and central Utah each autumn, storing large quantities for winter use; early spring was a difficult time, as such resources were often exhausted, plants immature, and prey animals lean and wary. Some Southern Paiute bands practiced limited horticulture along the Colorado and Virgin rivers, and some bands of Owens Valley Paiute, Northern Paiute, and Western Shoshone irrigated patches of wild seed plants to increase their yield. Groups with large lakes in their territories did considerable fishing, especially during spawning runs.

Like the pedestrian peoples of the Great Basin, the horse-using groups followed an annual round. However, the latter were able to range over a much larger area than those on foot. They hunted bison, deer, elk, and mountain sheep and collected seed and root foods as these became available. After autumn bison hunts on the northern Plains, groups returned to the Bridger Basin, the Snake River area, or the Colorado mountains for the winter. Shoshone and Shoshone-Bannock peoples caught salmon during the annual spawning run each spring; fresh salmon was an important food source after the long winter, and some salmon was also dried or smoked for later use. Certain kinds of roots, and especially camas, were also an important

Petroglyphs located in the Paria Canyon–Vermilion Cliffs Wilderness Area, near the Arizona-Utah border. © Carol Jean Smetana

food source, although the latter's onion-like bulbs required detoxifying by pit roasting or steaming.

Clothing for those groups that did not use horses consisted of sage bark aprons and breechcloths, augmented by rabbit-skin robes in the winter; their artistic efforts were often expressed through fine basketry and rock art (petroglyphs and pictographs). The horse-using peoples wore Plains-style tailored skin garments. Like their Plains trade partners, these groups painted their tepees, rawhide shields, and bags and containers, as well as decorating clothing and other soft goods with dyed porcupine quills and, later, glass beads.

Traditionally, western Great Basin groups engaged in trade involving shells (including marine shells), tanned hides, baskets, and foodstuffs. Horse-using groups actively traded among themselves and with others, including fur traders; Shoshone clothing was particularly prized in trade for its beauty and durability. Between about 1800 and 1850, mounted Ute and Navajo bands preyed on Southern Paiute, Western Shoshone, and Gosiute bands for slaves, capturing and sometimes trading women and children to be sold in the Spanish settlements of New Mexico and southern California.

SOCIAL ORGANIZATION

The social organization of the Great Basin's pedestrian bands reflected the rather difficult arid environment of the culture area. Groups were typically small,

moved frequently, and had very fluid membership. These mobile bands moved through a given territory on an annual round, exploiting the available food resources within a particular valley and its adjacent mountains. Food supplies were seldom adequate to permit groups of any size to remain together for more than a few days. People usually came together in larger groups only for certain brief periods—during rabbit drives in the spring or during the piñon nut season in the autumn. Where conditions allowed, as for the Washoe at Lake Tahoe and the Northern Paiute and Ute groups at lakes in their districts, people would also aggregate when fish were spawning. These periodic gatherings are perhaps best understood as aggregations of several extended families; they involved no sustained sense of political cohesion.

The same fluidity of social organization was characteristic of the equestrian bands. Possession of horses permitted larger numbers of people to remain together for much of the year, but this did not lead to the development of formal political hierarchies within the tribes. Among both equestrian and pedestrian groups, a particular leader was followed as long as he was successful in leading people to food or in war. If he failed, people would simply join other bands or form new ones.

KINSHIP AND MARRIAGE

The basic social unit usually consisted of a two- or three-generation family or the nuclear families of two brothers, augmented occasionally by other individuals with ties to the core group. Kin ties were reckoned bilaterally, through both the mother and the father, and were widely extended to distant relatives. Such extension permitted people to invoke kin ties and the customs of hospitality that rested upon them in order to move from one group to another if circumstances warranted.

Marriage practices varied across the culture area, with a tendency among some groups to marry true cross-cousins (mother's brother's or father's sister's child) or pseudo cross-cousins (mother's brother's or father's sister's stepchild). Both the sororate (marriage between a widower and his dead wife's sister) and the levirate (marriage between a widow and her dead husband's brother) were practiced, as were their logical extensions, sororal polygyny and fraternal polyandry. Although polygynous marriages were formally recognized by communities, polyandry was usually informal, consisting only of a couple extending sexual privileges to the husband's brother for a limited period of time.

There was no set pattern of postmarital residence. A newly married couple might live with the bride's family for the first few years until children were born, but the availability of food supplies was the key factor in determining residence. Marriages could be brittle, especially between young adults; divorce was easy and socially acceptable. Nonetheless, the difficult environment favoured a division of labour that led most individuals to be married (whether to one person or in a series of partnerships) during most of their adult lives.

Children began to learn about and participate in the food quest while very young. Grandparents were responsible for most caregiving and for teaching children appropriate behaviour and survival skills; adults of childbearing age were engaged in providing most of the food for the group. There was little emphasis on puberty rites except among the Washoe, who held a special dance and put a girl through various tests at the time of menarche.

RELIGION AND RITUAL

Religious concepts derived from a mythical cosmogony, beliefs in powerful spirit-beings, and a belief in a dualistic soul. Mythology provided a cosmogony and cosmography of the world in which anthropomorphic animal progenitors, notably Wolf, Coyote, Rabbit, Bear, and Mountain Lion, were supposed to have lived before the human age. During that period they were able to speak and act as humans do; they created the world and were responsible for present-day topography, ecology, food resources, seasons of the year, and distribution of tribes. They set the nature of social relations—that is, they defined how various classes of kin should behave toward each other—and set the customs surrounding birth, marriage, puberty, and death. Their actions in the mythic realm set moral and ethical precepts and determined the physical and behavioral characteristics of the modern animals. Most of the motifs and tale plots of Great Basin mythology are found widely throughout North America.

Spirit-beings were animals, birds, or natural or supernatural phenomena, each thought to have a specific power according to an observed characteristic. Some such beings were thought to be benevolent, or at least neutral, toward humans. Others, such as water babies—small long-haired creatures who lured people to their death in springs or lakes and who ate children—were malevolent and feared. Great Basin peoples also had conceptions of a variety of other beings, such as the Southern Paiute *unupits*, mischievous spirits who caused illness.

Shamanism was prominent in all Great Basin groups. Both men and women might become shamans. One was called to shamanism by a spirit-being who came unsought; it was considered dangerous to resist this call, for those who did sometimes died. The being became a tutelary guide, instructing an individual in curing and sources of power. Some shamans had several tutelary spirit-beings, each providing instruction for specific practices, such as the power to cure disease, to foretell the future, or to practice sorcery. Among Northern Paiute and Washoe and probably elsewhere, a person who had received power became an apprentice to an older, practicing shaman and from that mentor learned a variety of rituals, cures, and feats of legerdemain associated with curing performances.

Curing ceremonies were performed with family members and others present and might last several days. The widespread Native American practice of sucking an object said to cause the disease from the patient's body was often employed. Shamans who lost too many patients were sometimes killed.

In the western Great Basin, some men were thought to have powers to charm antelope and so led communal antelope drives. Beliefs that some men were arrow-proof (and, after the introduction of guns, bulletproof) are reported for the Northern Paiute and Gosiute but were probably general throughout the area. Among the Eastern Shoshone, young men sought contact with spirit-beings by undertaking the vision quest. The Eastern Shoshone probably learned this practice from their Plains neighbours, although the characteristics of the beings sought were those common to Great Basin beliefs.

There was a concept of soul dualism among most, if not all, Numic peoples. One soul, or soul aspect, represented vitality or life; the other represented the individual as he was in a dream or vision state. During dreams or visions, the latter soul left the body and moved in the spirit realm; at those times, the person could be subject to soul loss. At death, both souls left the body. Death rites were usually minimal; an individual was buried with his possessions, or they were destroyed. The Washoe traditionally abandoned or burned a dwelling in which a death had occurred.

MODERN DEVELOPMENTS

Contact with Spanish and Euro-American colonizers drastically altered Great Basin societies and cultures. The Southern Ute were in sustained contact with the Spanish in New Mexico as early as the 1600s, but other Great Basin groups had little or no direct or continued contact with Europeans or Euro-Americans until after 1800. Between 1810 and 1840, the fur trade brought new tools and implements to those residing in the eastern part of the region. In the 1840s, Euro-American settlement of the Great Basin began, and a surge of emigrants traveled through the area on their way to Oregon and California.

As elsewhere in the United States, government policy in the Great Basin was overtly designed to assimilate the tribes into Euro-American society. Assimilation was accomplished by undercutting the indigenous subsistence economy, removing Native American children to distant boarding schools, and suppressing native religions in favour of Christianity. Beginning in the 1840s, for instance, private-property laws favouring Euro-American mining, ranching, and farming interests either destroyed or privatized most indigenous food-gathering areas. Piñon groves were cut for firewood, fence posts, and mining timbers, and the delicate regional ecosystem was disrupted by an influx of humans and livestock.

The indigenous peoples of the Great Basin attempted to resist colonial encroachment. Mounted bands of Ute, Shoshone, Shoshone-Bannock, and Northern Paiute fought with ranchers and attacked wagon trains in attempts to drive the intruders away. The struggle culminated in several local wars and massacres in the 1850s and '60s. After 1870 the tribes were forced onto reservations or into small groups on the edges of Euro-American settlements; their land base was reduced to a small fraction of its former size. This forced the abandonment of most aboriginal subsistence patterns in favour of agriculture and ranching, in those areas where land remained in native hands, or in wage work, usually as farmhands and ranch hands.

The Great Basin peoples were perhaps most successful in resisting religious assimilation. In 1870 and again in 1890, so-called Ghost Dance movements started among the Northern Paiute of western Nevada. The dances were millenarian, nostalgic, and peaceful in character. The 1870 movement, led by the Paiute prophet Wodziwob, centred in Nevada and California. It was an elaboration of the round dance, a traditional ceremony for the renewal and abundance of life. Wodziwob's vision indicated that the dance would resurrect the victims of an epidemic that had decimated the region a year earlier.

The 1890 movement, led by the Northern Paiute prophet Wovoka, was adopted by many tribes in the western United States. Wovoka's movement stressed peace, accommodation of Euro-American development projects,

GHOST DANCE

In the complex of late 19th-century religious movements are two distinct Ghost Dance cults. These represented an attempt of Indians in the western United States to rehabilitate their traditional cultures. Both cults arose from Northern Paiute prophet-dreamers in western Nevada who announced the imminent return of the dead (hence "ghost"), the ousting of the whites, and the restoration of Indian lands, food supplies, and way of life. These ends, it was believed, would be hastened by the dances and songs revealed to the prophets in their vision visits to the spirit world and also by strict observance of a moral code that resembled Christian teaching and forbade war against Indians or whites. Many dancers fell into trances and received new songs from the dead they met in visions or were healed by Ghost Dance rituals.

The first Ghost Dance developed in 1869 around the dreamer Wodziwob (d. c. 1872) and in 1871–73 spread to California and Oregon tribes; it soon died out or was transformed into other cults. The second derived from Wovoka (c. 1856–1932), whose father, Tavibo, had assisted Wodziwob. Wovoka had been influenced by Presbyterians on whose ranch he worked, by Mormons, and by the Indian Shaker Church. During a solar eclipse in January 1889, he had a vision of dying, speaking with God in heaven, and being commissioned to teach the new dance and millennial message. Indians from many tribes traveled to learn from Wovoka, whose self-inflicted stigmata on hands and feet encouraged belief in him as a new messiah, or Jesus Christ, come to the Indians.

Thus, the Ghost Dance spread as far as the Missouri River, the Canadian border, the Sierra Nevada, and northern Texas. Early in 1890 it reached the Sioux and coincided with the rise of the Sioux outbreak of late 1890, for which the cult was wrongly blamed. This outbreak culminated in the massacre at Wounded Knee, S.D., where the "ghost shirts" failed to protect the wearers, as promised by Wovoka.

As conditions changed, the second Ghost Dance became obsolete, though it continued in the 20th century in attenuated form among a few tribes. Both cults helped to reshape traditional shamanism (a belief system based on the healing and psychic transformation powers of the shaman, or medicine man) and prepared for further Christianization and accommodation to white culture.

truthfulness, self-discipline, and other tenets of "right living," including performance of the round dance; his message was so apt for the time that he was soon mentoring novitiates from throughout the trans-Mississippi West. Despite Wovoka's best efforts at promoting the core aspects of the new religion, the Ghost Dance message evolved from one of renewal to one of destruction as it was taken home by novitiates from the Plains. Particularly among the many bands of Sioux, ghost dancing was thought to have the power to effect an apocalypse; if properly performed, it was believed, the tribes would have the opportunity to annihilate the colonizers (or at least drive them back to the sea), the dead would be resurrected, the bison herds would be repopulated, and traditional ways of life would be restored. Ultimately, Euro-American fears related to the movement contributed to the 1890 massacre of Lakota at Wounded Knee Creek (in present-day South Dakota). In the Great Basin, however, the movement's original message endured, and Ghost Dance congregations became important reservoirs of traditional culture that persist into the 21st century.

The 20th century fostered other religious movements in the Great Basin as well. The practice of ingesting peyote in a religious context was introduced to the Ute and Eastern Shoshone in the early 1900s by Oklahoma Indians. It later spread to other peoples in the region. Most peyote groups became part of the Native American Church, a nationally recognized religious organization. Great Basin peyote rituals are generally a mixture of aboriginal and Christian elements. Ceremonies are led by experienced individuals known as "road chiefs," because they lead believers down the peyote "road" or way. A peyote ceremony, which typically lasts all night, includes singing, praying, and ingesting those parts of the peyote cactus that produce a mild hallucinogenic experience. The tenets of the Native American Church stress moral and ethical precepts and behaviour. The Eastern Shoshone and Ute also adopted the Sun Dance from the Plains tribes. The four-day dance continues to be performed, usually annually, to ensure health for the community and valour for the participants. The Sun Dance spread to some other Great Basin groups in the second half of the 20th century. For the Ute, the bear dance, a spring ceremony, also remains important.

The U.S. Indian Reorganization Act (1934) led to the establishment of local elected tribal councils for the various reservations and colonies in the region. These councils have since developed a number of tribally based economic enterprises, including ranching, light industry, and tourism. They have also been plaintiffs in lawsuits seeking to reclaim ancestral lands. In 1950, for instance, the U.S. judicial system found that the Ute tribe had been illegally defrauded of land in the 19th century; while the courts did not revert title to the land, they did mandate substantial monetary compensation.

In the 1950s many tribes in the United States—including several bands of Utes and Southern Paiutes—were subject to termination, a process whereby they lost federal recognition of their Indian status and thus their eligibility for federal support of health care and other services. Although most bands fought this process, some did not regain federal status until the 1980s. Others continued to fight for recognition and land well into the early 21st century; the Western Shoshone, for instance, turned to the international court system in their efforts to regain their traditional landholdings.

CHAPTER 5

SOUTHWEST AND PLAINS CULTURE AREAS

The Southwest culture area is located between the Rocky Mountains and the Mexican Sierra Madre. The Continental Divide separates the landscape into the watersheds of two great river systems: the Colorado–Gila–San Juan, in the west, and the Rio Grande–Pecos, in the east. The environment is arid, with some areas averaging less than 4 inches (10 cm) of precipitation each year; droughts are common. Despite its low moisture content, coarse texture, and occasional salty patches, the soil of most of the Southwest is relatively fertile.

The Plains culture area embraces the Great Plains of the United States and Canada. It comprises a vast grassland between the Mississippi River and the Rocky Mountains and from the present-day provinces of Alberta and Saskatchewan in Canada through the present-day state of Texas in the United States. The area is drained principally by the Missouri and Mississippi rivers; the valleys of this watershed are the most reliable sites from which to obtain fresh water, wood, and most plant foods. The climate is continental, with annual temperatures ranging from below 0 °F (−18 °C) to as high as 110 °F (43 °C).

SOUTHWEST INDIAN PEOPLES

The people of the Cochise culture were among the earliest residents of the Southwest. A desert-adapted hunting and

The Cliff Palace, which has 150 rooms, 23 kivas, and several towers, at Mesa Verde National Park in Colorado. © C. McIntyre—PhotoLink/Getty Images

gathering culture whose diet emphasized plant foods and small game, this group lived in the region as early as *c.* 7000 BC.

Farming became important for subsequent residents including the Ancestral Pueblo (Anasazi; *c.* AD 100–1600), the Mogollon (*c.* AD 200–1450), and the Hohokam (*c.* AD 200–1400). These groups lived in permanent and semipermanent settlements that they sometimes built near (or even on) sheltering cliffs; developed various forms of irrigation; grew crops of corn (maize), beans, and squash; and had complex social and ritual habits. It is believed that the Ancestral Pueblo were the ancestors of the modern Pueblo Indians, that the Hohokam were the ancestors of the Pima and Tohono O'odham (Papago), and that the Mogollon dispersed or joined other communities.

LANGUAGE

The Southwest was home to representatives from several North American Indian language families, including Hokan, Uto-Aztecan, Tanoan, Keresan, Kiowa-Tanoan, Penutian, and Athabaskan.

The Hokan-speaking Yuman peoples were the westernmost residents of the region; they lived in the river valleys and the higher elevations of the basin and range system there. The so-called River Yumans, including the Quechan (Yuma), Mojave, Cocopa, and Maricopa, resided on the Lower Colorado and the Gila River. Their cultures combined some traditions of the Southwest culture area with others of the California Indians. The Upland Yumans, including the Havasupai, Hualapai, and Yavapai, lived on secondary and ephemeral streams in the western basins and ranges.

Two groups that spoke Uto-Aztecan languages resided in the southwestern portion of the culture area, near the border between the present-day states of Arizona (U.S.) and Sonora (Mexico). The Tohono O'odham were located west of the Santa Cruz River. The closely related Pima lived along the middle Gila River.

The Pueblo Indians were linguistically diverse. Those living along the Rio Grande and its tributaries are generally referred to as the eastern Pueblos, while those on the Colorado Plateau are assigned to the western division. The eastern group included the Keresan-speaking Zia, Santa Ana, San Felipe, Santo Domingo, and Cochiti, and representatives of three members of the Kiowa-Tanoan language family: the Tewa-speaking San Ildefonso, San Juan, Santa Clara, Tesuque, and Nambe; the Tiwa-speaking Isleta, Sandia, Taos, and Picuris; and the Towa-speaking Jemez. The western Pueblo tribes included the Hopi (Uto-Aztecan), Hano (Tanoan), Zuni (Penutian), and Acoma and Laguna (Keresan).

The Navajo and the closely related Apache spoke Athabaskan languages. The Navajo lived on the Colorado Plateau near the Hopi villages. The Apache traditionally resided in the range and basin systems south of the plateau. The major Apache tribes included the Western Apache, Chiricahua, Mescalero, Jicarilla, Lipan, and Kiowa Apache. The Athabaskan-speaking groups migrated from northwestern North America to the Southwest and probably did not reach the area until sometime between AD 1100 and 1500.

SUBSISTENCE, SETTLEMENT PATTERNS, AND SOCIAL ORGANIZATION

Most peoples of the Southwest engaged in both farming and hunting and gathering. The degree to which a given culture relied upon domesticated or wild foods was primarily a matter of the group's proximity to water. A number of domesticated resources were more or less ubiquitous throughout the culture area, including corn (maize), beans, squash, cotton, turkeys, and dogs. During the period of Spanish colonization, horses, burros, and sheep were added to the agricultural repertoire, as were new varieties of beans, plus wheat, melons, apricots, peaches, and other cultigens.

Most groups coped with the desert environment by occupying sites on waterways. These ranged in quality and reliability from large permanent rivers such as the Colorado, through secondary streams, to washes or gullies that channeled seasonal rainfall but were dry most of the year. Precipitation was unpredictable and fell in just a few major rains each year, compelling many groups to engage in irrigation. While settlements along major waterways could rely almost entirely on agriculture for food, groups whose access was limited to ephemeral waterways typically used farming to supplement hunting and gathering, relying on wild foods during much of the year.

THE YUMANS, PIMA, AND TOHONO O'ODHAM

The western and southern reaches of the culture area were home to the Hokan-speaking Yuman groups and the Uto-Aztecan-speaking Pima and Tohono O'odham. These peoples shared a number of cultural features, principally in terms of kinship and social organization, although their specific subsistence strategies represented a continuum from full-time agriculture to full-time foraging.

Kinship was usually reckoned bilaterally, through both the male and female lines. For those groups that raised crops, the male line was somewhat privileged as fields were commonly passed from father to son. Most couples chose to reside near the husband's family (patrilocality), and clan membership was patrilineal. In general women were responsible for most domestic tasks, such as food preparation and child-rearing, while male

tasks included the clearing of fields and hunting.

The most important social unit was the extended family, a group of related individuals who lived and worked together; groups of families living in a given locale formed bands. Typically the male head of each family participated in an informal band council that settled disputes (often over land ownership, among the farming groups) and made decisions regarding community problems. Band leadership accrued to those with proven skills in activities such as farming, hunting, and consensus-building. A number of bands constituted the tribe. Tribes were usually organized quite loosely—the Pima were the only group with a formally elected tribal chief—but were politically important as the unit that determined whether relations with neighbouring groups were harmonious or agitated. Among the Yumans, the tribe provided the people with a strong ethnic identity, although in other cases most individuals identified more strongly with the family or band.

The most desirable bottomlands along the Colorado and Gila rivers were densely settled by the so-called River Yumans, including the Mojave, Quechan, Cocopa, and Maricopa. They lived in riverside hamlets and their dwellings included houses made of log frameworks covered with sand, brush, or wattle-and-daub. The rivers provided plentiful water despite a minimum of rainfall and the hot desert climate. Overflowing their banks

Mojave men, photograph by Timothy O'Sullivan, c. 1871. Library of Congress, Washington, D.C.

each spring, they provided fresh silt and moisture to small, irregular fields where people cultivated several varieties of corn as well as beans, pumpkins, melons, and grasses. Abundant harvests were supplemented with wild fruits and seeds, fish, and small game.

The Upland Yumans (including the Hualapai, Havasupai, and Yavapai), the Pima, and the Tohono O'odham lived on the Gila and Salt rivers, along smaller streams, and along seasonal waterways. The degree to which they relied upon agriculture depended upon their distance from permanently flowing water. Those who lived near such waterways built stone canals with which they irrigated fields of corn, beans, and squash. Those with no permanently flowing water planted crops in the alluvial fans at the mouths of washes and built low walls or check dams to slow the torrents caused by brief but intense summer rains. These latter groups relied more extensively on wild foods than on agriculture; some engaged in no agriculture whatsoever, instead living in a fashion similar to the Great Basin Indians.

Upland settlement patterns also reflected differential access to water. Hamlets near permanent streams were occupied all year and included dome-shaped houses with walls and roofs of wattle-and-daub or thatch. The groups that relied on ephemeral streams divided their time between summer settlements near their crops and dry-season camps at higher elevations where fresh water and game were more readily available. Summer residences were usually dome-shaped and built of thatch, while lean-tos and windbreaks served as shelter during the rest of the year.

THE PUEBLOS

Traditional social and religious practices are fairly well understood for the western Pueblo peoples because distance and the rugged landscape of the Colorado Plateau afforded them some protection from the depredations of Spanish, and later American, colonizers. Less is known of the pre-conquest practices of the eastern Pueblos. Their location on the banks of the Rio Grande made them easily accessible to colonizers, whose approaches to assimilation were often brutal. Many Pueblos, both eastern and western, took their traditional practices underground during the colonial period in order to avoid persecution; to a great extent they continue to protect their traditional cultures with silence. Their secret societies, each of which had a specific theme such as religion, war, policing, hunting, or healing, have proved quite difficult to investigate. Undoubtedly, however, they were and are important venues for social interaction and cultural transmission.

The Pueblo peoples lived in compact, permanent villages and resided in multifamily buildings. The women of a household cared for young children; cultivated spring-irrigated gardens; produced fine baskets and pottery; had charge of

Taos Pueblo, N.M., with domed oven in the foreground. Ray Manley—Shostal/EB Inc.

the preservation, storage, and cooking of food; and cared for certain clan fetishes (sacred objects carved of stone). The men of a household wove cloth, herded sheep, and raised field and dune crops of corn (maize), squash, beans, and cotton. A wide trade network brought materials such as turquoise, shell, copper, and macaw feathers to the Pueblo tribes; many of these exotic materials appear to have come from Mexico.

The family was a key social grouping; extended family households of three generations were typical. The western Pueblos and the eastern Keresan-speaking groups reckoned kinship through the female line (matrilineally),

while the remaining eastern Pueblos reckoned kinship patrilineally or bilaterally, through both parents. Residence usually coincided with kinship; among the matrilineal Zuni, for instance, a husband joined his wife's natal residence (matrilocality). A Zuni household would typically include a senior woman, her husband, and their unmarried children, plus the couple's married daughters, sons-in-law, and their children.

Related families formed a lineage, a kin group that could trace its ancestry directly to a known figure in the historical or legendary past. Lineages were often conceived of as timeless, extending backwards into the remote past and

Pueblo Indian pottery: (left) *Acoma water jar, c. 1890;* (centre) *Santa Clara vase, c. 1880;* (right) *San Ildefonso water jar, c. 1906; in the Denver Art Museum.* Courtesy of the Denver Art Museum, Denver, Colorado

forward through generations yet unborn. Among the western Pueblo and the eastern Keresan-speakers, several related lineages were combined to form a clan; many villages had dozens of clans, which were often named for animals, plants, or other natural phenomena.

Instead of using clans, some Pueblos grouped lineages directly into two units called moieties. This was particularly prevalent among the eastern Pueblos, many of whom organized themselves into paired groups such as the "Squash People" and "Turquoise People" or the "Summer People" and "Winter People."

Clans and moieties acted as corporate groups; they were responsible for sponsoring certain rituals and for organizing many aspects of community life. Among the matrilineal Hopi, for instance, each clan owned specific fields and ritual paraphernalia and the oldest active woman functioned as the clan's administrative leader. Her brother assumed the responsibilities of ceremonial leader, supervising annual reenactments of events that were part of clan history or tradition. At San Juan pueblo in the east, the kinship system was bilateral, and the fluidity inherent in a bilateral system was reflected in the moiety system as well: One was born into membership in one's father's moiety, but upon marriage a young woman became a member of her husband's division. At San Juan the leaders of the Summer and the Winter moieties were each responsible for village administration during their respective season (spring and summer were grouped together, as were autumn and winter). Many activities were limited to just one of the seasons; trading and hunting, for instance, could only take place under the authority of the Winter moiety, while the gathering of wild plants was limited to the period of the Summer People's administration.

Clan and moiety systems were important tools for managing the delegation of ritual and mundane tasks, but were also important in achieving harmony in other ways. Membership in these groups was symbolically extended to specific animals, plants, and other classes of natural and supernatural phenomena, metaphysically linking all aspects of the social, natural, and spiritual worlds together for a given tribe. In a concrete political sense, as well, the common (though not universal) custom of clan or moiety exogamy, or out-marriage, smoothed social relations by ensuring that households included members of different corporate groups.

The Navajo and Apache

While the peoples mentioned thus far all have very ancient roots in the Southwest, the Navajo and Apache are relative newcomers. Linguistic, archaeological, and historical evidence indicate that the ancestors of these groups were members of hunting and gathering cultures that migrated to the region from present-day Canada, arriving by approximately AD 1500, although no earlier than AD 1100. The Navajo occupied a portion of the Colorado Plateau adjacent to Hopi lands. The Apache claimed the basin and range country east and south of the Plateau and surrounding the Rio Grande pueblos.

Together, the Navajo and Apache are referred to as Apacheans.

By the early 17th century the Navajo and the Jicarilla, Lipan, and Western Apache had begun to engage in a relatively settled way of life, farming indigenous crops; after the advent of Spanish colonization, they incorporated new products such as sheep and cattle into their economies. The Chiricahua and Mescalero Apache continued to rely on hunting and gathering as the mainstay of their economies. All the groups raided the Pueblo tribes and later the Spanish and American colonizers. Raids were often (although not always) undertaken in stealth; the goal was generally to seize livestock and food stores rather than to engage in battle.

In general, Apachean women were responsible for raising their children; gathering and processing edible seeds and other wild plants, such as mescal, a cactus that provided food, juice, and fibres; collecting firewood and water; producing buckskin clothing, baskets, and pottery; and building the home. The Navajo were an exception to the last rule, as they viewed home construction as men's work. Apachean men hunted, fought, and raided. Among the more sedentary groups, women tended gardens, men tended fields, and both engaged in shepherding and weaving.

As their territories were generally unfavourable to the support of concentrated populations, the Apacheans tended to reside in dispersed groups. Although the Navajo and Western Apache had exogamous matrilineal clans, kinship was generally reckoned bilaterally and clans played little role among the other Apachean groups. The basic socioeconomic unit was the matrilocal extended family, a group of one or more related women, their husbands and unmarried sons, and their daughters, sons-in-law, and grandchildren. Within this group each nuclear family—or each wife and her children, if two or more women shared a husband—occupied a separate dwelling. Among the Navajo the preferred house form was the hogan, a circular lodge made of logs or stone and covered with a roof of earth; some hogans also had earth-berm walls. Among the Apache, the wickiup and tepee were used. The ramada, a free-standing rectangular arbour, was used by both groups for shade.

Among the Apache, a kin-based group of perhaps 20 to 30 individuals who lived and worked together constituted a band, the most important social group in daily life. Among the Navajo, similarly sized "outfits," or neighbouring extended families, cooperated in resolving issues such as range management and water use. Bands and outfits were organized under the direction of a leader chosen for his wisdom and previous success. They functioned on the basis of consensus, and individuals could, and often did, move to another group if they were uncomfortable with their current situation. A tribe comprised a group of bands that shared bonds of tradition, language, and culture; they were usually not formal political entities. The small bands that functioned as basic social units should not be confused with larger groups, such as the Mescalero, that are sometimes referred to as bands but are in fact tribes.

SOCIALIZATION AND EDUCATION

All of the Southwestern tribes viewed the raising of children as a serious adult responsibility. Most felt that each child had to be "made into" a member of the tribe and that adults had to engage in frequent self-reflection and redirection to remain a tribal member; in other words, ethnic identity was something that had to be achieved rather than taken for granted.

Children were generally treated with warmth and permissiveness until they were weaned, a period that might last from one to three or four years. Care was taken not to agitate a child unduly: young children nursed on demand, and weaning and toilet training were gradual. Children were protected from harm through careful tending and by means of magical prophylactics. Cradles and cradleboards were used, especially during the first year of life; the Hopi viewed swaddling as the first of many periods of conditioning that helped the individual to gain self-control. From birth, children were treated as an integral part of the family; among the Navajo, for instance, the cradleboard was hung on a wall or pillar so that the child would be at eye level with others seated in the family circle.

From the beginning of childhood there was training in customary gender roles; little girls began to learn food

Mizheh and Babe, *portrait of an Apache woman holding a child in a cradleboard, photograph by Edward S. Curtis, c. 1906.* Library of Congress, Washington, D.C. (neg. no. LC-USZ62-46949)

processing and childcare, and little boys were given chores such as collecting firewood or tending animals. However, the most important work of childhood was the internalization of the abiding precept that individuals were expected to pull their own weight, at every age grade, according to their gender, strength, and talent.

When they were between five and seven years old, boys began to associate almost exclusively with the men of their households, who from then on directed their education into masculine tasks and lore. At about the same age, girls began to take on increasing responsibility for the exacting tasks of the household. Among the more nomadic groups, particularly the Apacheans, the physical strength, stoicism, and skill needed for battle were stressed, and training in the arts of war intensified as a youth grew to young manhood. Even among the more pacifist Pueblos, however, boys learned agility, endurance, and speed in running. Racing was important to the Pueblos because it was considered to possess magical efficacy in helping plants, animals, and human beings to grow.

Despite these similarities, tribes did show some marked differences in their child-rearing practices. The children of the Tohono O'odham and Pima were probably allowed the greatest freedom of action. This does not imply that Tohono O'odham and Pima children went untrained: They were expected to recognize seniority and show respect for age, regardless of sex; to promote group solidarity; and to respect the role, function, and opinion of every member of the band. Children were considered accomplished provided they made age-appropriate progress in these areas and in contributing to the group's subsistence.

In contrast, Pueblo children were subjected to extremes of control. These tribes stressed life-crisis ceremonies that offered symbolic resolution to the major problems faced by the community. Children who failed to reach certain (usually behavioural) benchmarks in a timely manner were pushed in prescribed ways to meet the standard. For example, all Hopi children participated in the kachina ceremony at about seven years of age; its purpose was to initiate them into the tribe and to facilitate their introduction to the supernatural. During the ceremony, it is reported that all the children were ritually whipped to exorcise evil influences, but those children who frequently misbehaved or showed a lack of self-control were whipped more severely than the others.

BELIEF AND AESTHETIC SYSTEMS

Like most Native American religions, those of the Southwest Indians were generally characterized by animism and shamanism. Animists perceive the world as filled with living entities: spirit-beings that animate the sun, moon, rain, thunder, animals, plants, topographic features, and many other natural phenomena. Shamans are men and women who have achieved a level of knowledge or power regarding physiological and spiritual health, especially its maintenance, recovery, or destruction. Always in a somewhat liminal state, shamans had to be acutely aware of the community's goings-on or risk the consequences: A number of 19th-century accounts report the execution of Pima shamans who were believed to have caused people to sicken and die.

The spectacular, communally centred Pueblo ceremonies for rain and growth reflected a conception of the universe in which every person, animal, plant, and supernatural being was considered significant. Without the active participation of every individual in the group, it was believed that the life-giving sun would not return from his "winter house" after the solstice, the rain would not fall, and the crops would not grow. In fact, Pueblo groups generally believed that the cosmic order was in perpetual danger of breaking down and that an annual cycle of ceremonies was a crucial factor in the continued existence of the world.

In the Pueblo view, humans affected the world through their actions, emotions, and attitudes, among other things, and communities that fostered metaphysical harmony were visited by spirit-beings called kachinas (*katsinas*) each year. The number and form of the spirit-beings varied from one community to the next and reflected the concerns and consequences of life in a desert environment. Many of the more than 500 kachinas known to scholars were spirits of corn, squash, and rain; there were also kachinas of trickster clowns, ogres, hunters, and many animals. Each individual kachina had a distinctive appearance, and during annual rituals they were thought to possess or share the bodies of dancers whose regalia matched that appearance. Small representations of kachinas were made for children; they were beautiful objects as well as useful items for teaching cultural traditions. The kachina religion was most active among the western Pueblos and was less important as one traveled east.

The Apache conceived of the universe as inhabited by a great variety of powerful entities, including animals, plants, witches (evil shamans), superhuman beings, rocks, and mountains. Each could exert force in the world for good or ill and required individual propitiation. Each was personalized, talked to, sung to, scolded, or praised. Apache ceremonies were concerned mainly with the magical coercion of these powerful entities for the curing of disease and the acquisition of personal success in hunting and warfare.

Navajo ceremonies were based on an elaboration of a similarly animistic view of the universe, with the power sources both diffuse and specific. Power was localized in a great many autonomous beings who were dangerous and unpredictable. These were of two classes: Earth Surface People (human beings, ghosts, and witches) and Holy People (supernaturals who could aid or harm Earth Surface People by sending sickness). As they turned away from hunting and raiding in favour of agriculture and herding, the Navajo focused their attention on elaborate rituals or "sings" that aimed to cure sickness and bring an individual into harmony with his family group, nature, and the supernatural.

In contrast to the animistic religions of other Southwest tribes, the River Yumans believed that a single animating principle or deity was the source of all supernatural power. There was only one medium, dreaming, for acquiring the supernatural protection, guidance, and power that were considered necessary for success in life. Sequences of traditional myths acquired through dreaming were converted into songs and acted out in ceremonies. The pursuit of such power sometimes caused an individual religious or war leader to abandon all other activities—farming, food collecting, and even hunting. It seems to have been no coincidence that this form of spiritual quest occurred only where one could count on regular and plentiful crops.

The religion of the Tohono O'odham seems to reflect their position between the River Yumans and the Pueblos. Not only did they "sing for power" and go on individual vision quests like the former, but they also held regular communal ceremonies to keep the world in order.

BLESSINGWAY

The Blessingway is a central ceremony of a complex system of Navajo healing ceremonies known as sings, or chants, that are designed to restore equilibrium to the cosmos. Anthropologists have grouped these ceremonies into six major divisions: Blessingways, Holyways, Lifeways, Evilways, War Ceremonials, and Gameways.

Parts of the general Blessingway, especially the songs, are included in most Navajo ceremonies. Unlike the other healing ceremonies, the Blessingways are not intended to cure illness but are used to invoke positive blessings and to avert misfortune. The Blessingway is comparatively short, lasting only two nights, and is often part of longer rites. Among other things, it is performed to bless and protect the home, to prevent complications of pregnancy, and to enhance the good fortune that attendees and participants hope to foster through the kinaalda (girl's puberty rites). As a part of Navajo religious practices, the Blessingway is considered to be a highly spiritual, sacred, and private event.

This ceremony and others are celebrated by crime-fiction writer Tony Hillerman, two of whose main characters—Joe Leaphorn and Jim Chee—are Navajo tribal policemen.

CULTURAL CONTINUITY AND CHANGE

Traditionally, each community in the Southwest culture area tried to maintain a delicate balance between population and natural resources. If the population outgrew the capacities of the resource base, a segment might split off and form a colony in a favourable habitat resembling that of its parent group. Under normal conditions the new colony was so constituted to reproduce as far as possible the parent culture even in its most esoteric aspects. If prolonged drought occurred, an entire community might migrate. Alternatively human pressures from without, such as raids by marauding bands or aggressive missionization, could cause a tribe to consolidate and move to more easily defended sites. In the 1700s, for instance, Tohono O'odham settlements consolidated into large compact villages for defense against the Apache.

COLONIZATION AND RESISTANCE

Spain hoped to gain gold, slaves, and converts to Roman Catholicism from its New World colonies; soldiers and missionaries who undertook the work of conquest were promised a portion of those riches. Not surprisingly, rumours of golden cities soon abounded, though of course none was actually discovered. In 1536 the Spanish explorer Álvar Núñez Cabeza de Vaca recounted stories of golden cities rumoured to be somewhere in the North American interior. His report spurred the government to sponsor an exploratory trip by the friar Marcos de Niza (1539), who reported seeing from afar cities of vast riches. These were probably the Zuni pueblos and the friar's mistake is understandable given that the Zuni towns were larger than many of the Spanish outposts in Mexico.

Francisco Vázquez de Coronado subsequently led an expedition (1540–42) that included some 300 soldiers, several missionaries, approximately 1,000 indigenous labourers, and some 1,000 pack animals. Overwintering on the Rio Grande, Coronado demanded provisions from nearby pueblos; his men also molested several Pueblo women. Indigenous resistance was met with force: the Spanish executed some 200 Pueblo individuals, many through burning at the stake; Spain was in the throes of the Inquisition during this period, the methods of which had been quickly transferred to the Americas. The surviving Pueblos in the area were horrified and they fled.

Permanent colonial occupation of the Southwest was initiated in 1598 under the leadership of Juan de Oñate, who had been commissioned to found a series of Spanish towns in the region. When Oñate's troops met with resistance at Acoma pueblo in 1599, they killed perhaps 800 of the town's 6,000 residents. The 80 surviving men of Acoma were punished by the amputation of a foot, the women and adolescents were sentenced to 20 years of slavery, and children under age 12 were given to the missions.

The next eight decades saw the spread of Catholicism and the establishment of the *encomienda*, a system of tribute paid through indigenous labour and foodstuffs. Although these changes were burdensome, the penalties the Pueblos felt for engaging in traditional religious activities such as kachina dances were far worse. These rituals were seen by the Catholic priests as abominations, and, in order to stamp out traditional religion, the missionaries destroyed regalia and punished religious leaders severely; reports of tortures such as flaying and dismemberment are common during this period.

By about 1670 it had become increasingly clear to the Pueblos that the world was sliding into chaos. In addition to deaths from torture and execution, many Pueblos died during recurrent epidemics of smallpox and other Old World diseases to which they had little resistance. Further, the Apachean tribes had begun to raid freely; raids combined with a series of devastating droughts and the *encomienda* to cause mass starvation in the pueblos. Given their worldview, the Pueblo peoples thought it imperative to reestablish their religious observances. In 1680 they effected an organized revolt against the Spanish, killing nearly all the Catholic priests and driving the conquerors out of the region.

ACCOMMODATION AND CULTURAL PRESERVATION

Between 1680 and 1692 the Pueblos were free from foreign rule. When soldiers and missionaries returned they employed a divide and conquer process, overcoming each pueblo individually; by 1696 Spanish rule again prevailed in the Southwest. Having had a period in which to reorganize and reevaluate their position vis-à-vis the colonizers, the Pueblos appeared to accede to missionization. They did not, however, abandon their traditional religious and cultural practices; instead, they took such practices underground and thus preserved many aspects of their pre-Columbian cultural traditions.

With differing levels of exposure to colonial conquest, it is to be expected that the traditions of the eastern and western Pueblos were differentially preserved. Unless totally destroyed, the western Pueblos did not surrender structurally to foreign control. Social organization among these groups was characterized by robust and cross-cutting levels of clan and secret society memberships. These were rather easily disguised, and the people were thus able to resist (or only superficially absorb) externally imposed social change.

In contrast, the eastern Pueblos had more centralized forms of social organization based on moieties, which, in turn, were the foundation of both civil and spiritual life. When combined with the greater levels of subjugation to which these groups were exposed, the moiety systems proved vulnerable to attack at both the sociopolitical and the ceremonial levels. Most of the eastern Pueblos incorporated at least some aspects of the Spanish system into their own structures,

creating a syncretic blend of the two. The Tohono O'odham produced their own Christian sect, a blend of native and mission practices known as Sonoran Catholicism.

During the 16th, 17th, and 18th centuries, the Apachean tribes fought the foreign control of the Spanish and attempted to gain and hold territory surrounding the Pueblo communities. They also took note of the material conditions of these groups—indigenous and Spanish—and selectively incorporated such things as horses, sheep, cattle, woven goods, and dry land agricultural techniques. While fiercely preserving their unique tribal identities, the Apacheans also engaged in a long period of cultural acquisition and remodeling.

In the 19th century, a period of relative peace for the Pueblo groups, the Apachean peoples encountered considerable difficulty. During this period the Southwest was ceded by Spain to Mexico (1821) and later became part of the United States (1848). Although the American Civil War slowed U.S. colonization of the region, Apachean actions against settlers were reported in newspapers and caused great public outcry. In 1863, Kit Carson was ordered to pacify the Navajo and led U.S. Army forces in the systematic destruction of the tribe's fields and livestock. Carson's forces captured some 8,000 Navajo who subsequently endured the "Long Walk" from their homeland near Canyon de Chelly in northeastern Arizona to Fort Sumner, N.M., some 300 miles (482 km) away; they were interred at the nearby Bosque Redondo camp from 1864 to 1868. After their release, the Navajo returned to their communities and began the rebuilding process.

The Apache were more difficult to conquer, particularly as several incidents of treachery, rape, and murder by members of the U.S. military instigated extreme wariness on the part of these tribes. Military pressure did cause some of the more sedentary Apache bands to move to reservations following the Civil War, but many did not trust promises of peace and chose to flee to the canyon country of the Colorado Plateau or southward, to Mexico. Although most were captured and removed to reservations by 1875, others, led by luminaries including Geronimo, continued to engage in spirited resistance until their final capture in 1886. Those who had continued armed resistance were transported to Florida, and later to Alabama, only returning to the Southwest in 1894. Geronimo, however, was seen as a figurehead of resistance and so was not allowed to return; he died in custody in 1909.

THE 20TH AND 21ST CENTURIES

The processes of change accelerated at the end of the 19th century and the beginning of the 20th century. The isolation of the region had combined with its arid climate and the fierce resistance of the Apacheans to slow Euro-American settlement and urbanization. At the same time military defeat, the loss of traditional lands, and missionary efforts to change their religious beliefs and practices had fostered among many tribes a sense of rejection and bitterness against colonizers.

U.S. policies towards indigenous peoples in most of the 20th century were disparate and often unevenly applied, but shared the common goal of assimilation. In the first half of the century tribal governments were developed and empowered with legal authority. A variety of rural development projects also took place, including rural electrification and the building of schools, hospitals, irrigation systems, highways, and telephone lines. The 1950s, '60s, and '70s saw the advancement of a policy called termination, in which many tribes lost their status as sovereign entities. By the late 20th century some "terminated" Southwestern groups had filed petitions to regain federal status.

Despite rural development and other projects, reservation life remained generally difficult when compared to that of the rest of the American population, especially among the Tohono O'odham, Hopi, Fort Apache, and some of the highland Yuman tribes. Farming and sheep operations remained economic mainstays in much of the region. The reassignment of a substantial portion of Hopi common lands to the Navajo, an action that the Hopi claim abrogated federal treaties, contributed to Hopi impoverishment; although the federal judiciary ruled the taking was legal and the United States Congress in 1996 passed legislation it hoped would resolve the dispute, the reassignment remained a point of contention into the 21st century.

By the early 21st century the tribes of the Southwest had formed a variety of business development units, tribally owned enterprises, and other economic ventures. Many had developed tourism programs; these, in turn, provided jobs and a venue for the sale of indigenous arts such as jewelry, pottery, and textiles. Some tribes chose to allow the development of their rich mineral resources, principally coal and uranium, under closely monitored conditions. However, the ecological and spiritual costs of large mining operations made many skeptical of this form of development.

PLAINS INDIAN PEOPLES

Perhaps because they were among the last indigenous peoples to be conquered in North America—some bands continued armed resistance to colonial demands into the 1880s—the tribes of the Great Plains are often regarded in popular culture as the archetypal American Indians. This view was heavily promoted by traveling exhibits such as George Catlin's *Indian Gallery*, "Wild West shows" such as the one directed by William F. ("Buffalo Bill") Cody, and a multitude of toys, collectibles, pulp novels, films, television shows, and other items marketed to consumers.

LINGUISTIC ORGANIZATION

Six distinct American Indian language families or stocks were represented in the Plains. Those speaking the same language are generally referred to as a tribe or nation, but this naming convention frequently masks the existence of a number of completely autonomous political divisions, or bands, within a given tribe. For instance, the Blackfoot tribe included three independent bands, the Piegan, Blood, and Northern Blackfoot.

Each language family included groups that lived in other culture areas, and the speakers of the several languages within a stock were not always geographically contiguous. Thus, the speakers of Algonquian languages included the Blackfoot, Arapaho, Atsina, Plains Cree, and Saulteaux (Plains Ojibwa), all in the northern Plains, while Cheyenne, also an Algonquian language, was spoken in the central Plains.

The speakers of Siouan languages included the Mandan, Hidatsa, Crow, Assiniboin, Omaha, Ponca, Osage, Kansa, Iowa, Oto, and Missouri. Dakota, Lakota, and Nakota were spoken by the bands of the Santee, Teton, and Yankton Sioux tribes, respectively.

The Pawnee, Arikara, and Wichita were Caddoan-speakers, whereas the Wind River Shoshone and the Comanche were of the Uto-Aztecan language family. The Athabaskan (Na-Dené) stock was represented by the Sarcee in the northern Plains, while the Kiowa-Tanoan stock was represented by the Kiowa.

Two other communication systems bear mention. The Métis of the Canadian Plains spoke Michif, a trade dialect that combined Plains Cree, an Algonquian language, and French. Michif was spoken over a wide area; in other areas many tribes used Plains sign language as a means of communication. This was a system of fixed hand and finger positions symbolizing ideas, the meanings of which were known to the majority of the tribes of the area.

The Role of the Horse in Plains Life

The introduction of the horse had a profound effect on the material life of the Plains peoples. Horses greatly increased human mobility and productivity in the region—so much so that many scholars divide Plains history into two periods, one before and one after the arrival of the horse. Horses became available gradually over the course of at least a century; before AD 1650 horses were fairly rare, and by 1750 they had become relatively common.

Plains Life Before the Horse

From at least 10,000 years ago to approximately AD 1100, the Plains were very sparsely populated by humans. Typical of hunting and gathering cultures worldwide, Plains residents lived in small family-based groups, usually of no more than a few dozen individuals, and foraged widely over the landscape. The peoples of deep prehistory in this region are referred to as Paleo-Indians, Archaic cultures, and Plains Woodland cultures.

By approximately AD 850, some residents of the central Plains had shifted from foraging to farming for a significant portion of their subsistence and were living in settlements comprising a number of large earth-berm homes. As early as 1100, and no later than about 1250, most Plains residents had made this shift and were living in substantial villages and hamlets along the Missouri River and its tributaries; from north to south these groups eventually included the Hidatsa, Mandan, Arikara, Ponca, Omaha, Pawnee, Kansa, Osage, and Wichita. Some villages reached populations of up to a few thousand people. These groups, known as Plains Village cultures, grew corn (maize), beans, squash, and sunflowers in the easily tilled land along the river bottoms. Women were responsible for agricultural production and cultivated their crops using antler rakes, wooden digging sticks, and hoes made from the shoulder blades of elk or buffalo. Women also collected medicinal plants and wild produce such as prairie turnips and chokecherries. Men grew tobacco and hunted bison, elk, deer, and other game; whole communities would also participate in driving herds of big game over cliffs. Fish, fowl, and small game were also eaten.

Until the horse the only domesticated animals were dogs, which were sometimes eaten but were mostly used as draft animals. Dogs drew the travois, a vehicle consisting of two poles in the shape of a V, with the open end of the V dragging on the ground; burdens were placed on a platform that bridged the two poles. Because of the limitations inherent in

Bird's-Eye View of the Mandan Village, 1800 Miles Above St. Louis, *detail of painting by George Catlin, 1837–39; in the National Museum of American Art, Washington, D.C.* National Museum of American Art, Washington, D.C., gift of Mrs. Sarah Harrison

using only dogs and people to carry loads, Plains peoples did not generally engage in extensive travel before the horse. However, Francisco Vázquez de Coronado's expedition in 1541 reported encounters with fully nomadic buffalo-hunting tribes on the southern Plains who had only dogs for transport.

Before horses became available, intertribal warfare was relatively rare and few battles were deadly. However, a period of exceptional conflict occurred in the 14th century, probably due to the same kinds of drought-induced crop failure that caused the dispersal of the Ancestral Pueblo and Hohokam cultures

of the Southwest at approximately the same time.

PLAINS LIFE AFTER THE HORSE

As the European colonization of North America's Atlantic coast began, epidemic diseases and colonizers swept across the landscape. Indigenous communities in the path of destruction fled, displacing their neighbours and creating a kind of domino effect in which nearly every Northeast Indian tribe shifted location; eventually groups as far inland as present-day Minnesota and Ontario were displaced westward to the Plains. Those who eventually resettled on the Plains included the Santee, Yankton, and Teton Sioux and the Saulteaux, Cheyenne, Iowa, Oto, and Missouri.

By the mid-18th century horses had also arrived, coming from the Southwest via trade with the Spanish and the expansion of herds of escaped animals. Guns were also entering the Plains, via the fur trade. Plains peoples, whether established residents or newcomers, quickly combined horses and guns to their advantage. Unlike pedestrian hunters, mounted groups could keep pace with the region's large buffalo herds and thereby support themselves on the grasslands. Most hunters initially chose to use bows and arrows in the mounted hunt, as these provided greater accuracy than early guns. However, as firearms became more accurate, they were readily adopted.

As tribes became more reliant on equestrian hunting, they adjusted their annual round to match that of their primary food source, the buffalo. As a rule, the largest bands or tribes came together en masse only in late spring and summer. During this period the buffalo congregated for calving, allowing hunters to supply enough food to support extensive gatherings of people. During the remainder of the year, the buffalo dispersed into smaller herds, and the nomadic tribes and bands followed suit.

The seasonal round of the village groups may be illustrated by the Arikara, who planted their crops in the spring, spent the summer as nomadic hunters, and returned to their villages in the autumn for the harvest. After a brief period of hunting in the late autumn, they moved to winter hamlets of a few homes each in the wooded bottomlands, which provided shelter from winter storms. They returned to their villages in the spring to begin the cycle anew.

Dogs continued to be used as draft animals, particularly for mundane and short-distance tasks such as hauling water and firewood from a valley to a nearby village or camp. Horses were generally considered too valuable for these activities.

Settlement Patterns and Housing

All Plains peoples used tepees, although villagers resided for most of the year in earth lodges. The tepee is a conical tent, its foundation being either three or four poles; other poles placed around these formed a roughly circular base. Before the horse, tepees averaged about 10 feet (3 m) in diameter, encompassing approximately 80 square feet (7.5 sq m). Later, they averaged about 15 feet in diameter (4.5 m), for an interior of some 175 square feet (16.25 sq m). A teepee would usually house a two- or three-generation family. The cover was made from dressed buffalo skins carefully fitted and sewn together and often painted with representations of the visions or war exploits of the eldest male resident.

When a large group assembled, a camp circle was usually formed, leaving the space in the centre for ceremonial structures. Among some peoples, such as the Cheyenne and Atsina, each subgroup had a defined place in the circle. Among many tribes, too, the orientation of the lodges and the opening of the circle were toward the rising sun.

The earth lodge, the dwelling used by most village tribes, was much larger than a tepee. Earth lodges averaged 40 to 60 feet (12 to 18 m) in diameter, encompassing approximately 1,250 to 2,825 square feet (116 to 263 sq m), and generally housed three-generation families. Like tepees, they had a roughly circular floor plan; unlike tepees, they were dome-shaped, roofed and walled with earth, and entered by means of a covered passage. A rattle made of deer hooves often served as a door knocker in these residences.

The placement of an earth lodge within a village varied from one tribe to the next and often was determined by

Wichita grass lodge, photograph by Edward S. Curtis, c. 1927. Edward S. Curtis Collection/ Library of Congress, Washington, D.C. (neg. no. LC-USZ62-118773)

TEPEE

The conical tent common to the North American Plains Indians is the tepee (tipi). Although a number of Native American groups used similar structures during the hunting season, only the Plains Indians adopted tepees as year-round dwellings, and then only from the 17th century onward. At that time the Spanish introduction of horses, guns, and metal implements enabled Plains peoples to become mounted nomads. The tepee was an ideal dwelling for these groups, as it could be easily disassembled and transported.

The tepee was generally made by stretching a cover sewn of dressed buffalo skins over a framework of wooden poles; in some cases reed mats, canvas, sheets of bark, or other materials were used for the covering. Women were responsible for tepee construction and maintenance. In raising a tepee, a woman would begin with three or four poles, depending upon her tribe's preferences. These first few poles acted as the keystones of a conical framework that was augmented by some 20 to 30 lighter poles, all leaning toward a central point and tied together a short distance from the top.

When very large shelters were needed, two pole frameworks could be set adjacent to one another in a figure-eight shape, with poles and covers left out of the adjoining walls. Many examples are known of small tepees sized for children's playhouses and very small tepees sized for dollhouses.

An adjustable flap was left open at the top to allow smoke to escape, and a flap at the bottom served as a doorway. Early travelers reported that one scratched or rubbed on the tent wall in lieu of knocking. A hearth in the centre provided heat and light; a smoke hole at the top could be closed in bad weather, and in warm weather the sides could be rolled up for additional ventilation.

It was common for Native Americans to devote much of the winter season to decorating their tepees with colourful paintings of animals and the hunt. The beauty and gracefulness of the tepee made it the popular image of the home of all indigenous Americans, although the wickiup (wigwam), hogan, igloo, longhouse, pueblo, and earth lodge were equally important examples of Native American dwellings.

the eldest male resident; however, the homes themselves typically belonged to the women of the household. Earth lodge villages were generally protected by a defensive ditch and palisade.

The construction of Osage and Wichita houses was similar to that of the wickiup of the Northeast. The dwellings of the Osage were oval in ground plan, composed of upright poles arched over on top, interlaced with horizontal withes, and covered with mats or skins. Wichita houses were more conical in shape and thatched with grass. They were otherwise similar in size and occupancy to earth lodges.

MATERIAL CULTURE AND TRADE

On the northern Plains men wore a shirt, leggings reaching to the hips, moccasins, and, in cold weather, a buffalo robe painted to depict the war deeds of the owner. Among the villagers and some southern nomads, men traditionally left the upper part of the body bare and frequently tattooed the chest, shoulders, and arms. Women's clothing typically consisted of a long dress, leggings to the knee, and moccasins. Clothes were decorated with porcupine-quill embroidery, fringe, and in later times, beadwork. Often, the eyeteeth of elk were pierced and used to decorate dresses; as each elk had at most two suitable teeth, a highly decorated dress conspicuously displayed the skill and dedication of the hunters in a woman's or girl's family. Billed caps and fur hats were used for protection from the bright sun and the cold. Elaborate headgear and other regalia were reserved for ceremonial occasions.

Bullboats, a round watercraft created by stretching a bison skin over a framework of willow withes, were often used to

Plains bullboats, in Mih-tutta-Hangkusch, a Mandan village, one of a series of aquatint engravings by Karl Bodmer, 1843–44. Library of Congress, Washington, D.C.

transport large quantities of meat or trade goods downstream. Pipe bowls were usually of stone but could also be ceramic, and pipe stems were generally made of wood. Receptacles of various kinds were made from rawhide, leather, and fascia such as the pericardium, which was used as a tough, collapsible bucket. Basketry and pottery were characteristic products of the villagers, although nomadic groups such as the Cheyenne, Comanche, and Arapaho made basketry gambling trays. A few nomadic tribes, such as the Atsina, Blackfoot, and Cree, claimed to have made earthenware in the past but to have given up the practice because the resulting vessels were too fragile for travois transport. Tools were made of fibre, bone, horn, antler, stone; many traditional tools, including hide scrapers, cooking vessels, knives, and arrowheads, were made from metal once it became available through the fur trade.

Differences in wealth arose from the increased productivity enabled by the horse. There was a flowering of what one authority has termed luxury developments—"showy clothing, embroidered footgear, medicine-bundle purchases, elaborate rituals [culminating in the Sun Dance], [and especially] gratuitous and time-consuming warfare." Horses became so valuable that horse stealing became a major reason for raiding; in the villages the best horses were even brought inside the earth lodge at night. The man who had many horses could use this wealth for a variety of purposes, such as giving

them to those in need, offering them as bridewealth, or trading them for other materials.

Because most material goods other than horses were readily available to all members of a given community, there was very little intratribal trade in them. There was, however, much exchange of ritual knowledge and other intangibles. Knowledge of war medicine and of curing rites was a valuable asset, and in almost all of the tribes the acquisition of this information was costly. For example, in the 1830s an individual who wished to gain the spiritual benefit believed to accrue from viewing the contents of a Mandan sacred bundle (a group of sacred and ceremonial objects) was expected to pay the bundle's guardian cash, horses, or goods equivalent to about a year's wages for the typical manual labourer.

Apprenticeships in craft production were also purchased. Hidatsa customs, for instance, required men who wished to learn to chip flint arrowheads to purchase instruction from the guardians of the bundles associated with arrow-making songs; similarly, women who wished to learn to make pottery or earth lodges had to purchase apprenticeships from recognized craft and ritual specialists.

Trade between members of different tribes was common and often involved an exchange of products between nomads and villagers, as in the trade of buffalo robes for corn. Intertribal trading relationships were often smoothed by the practice of ritual adoption, as when two men or two women would adopt one another as "brothers" or "sisters." As most social expectations were framed by kinship, adoption defined a clear role for each member of the partnership. The Cheyenne were middlemen in the trade of horses between the tribes of the southern Plains and those of the north-central Plains, while the Assiniboin, Hidatsa, Mandan, Arikara, and later some eastern Sioux groups brokered the guns and other materials such as blankets, beads, cloth, and kettles that flowed from the British and French for pelts and buffalo robes from groups to the west. Conflicts often stemmed from competition among tribes that wished the sole control of a specific trade route.

POLITICAL ORGANIZATION

The political structures of most Plains tribes functioned at the level of the band. Bands were fluid groups that could range in size from a few dozen to a few hundred people who lived, worked, and traveled together. Nomadic tribes generally comprised several large independent bands that coalesced and dispersed over the course of the year. Village groups functioned similarly. A group of related villages might coalesce for a band-level hunt, while smaller groups were the more usual parties for work and socializing.

Band organization relied upon a combination of individual leaders and military societies. Leaders had to prove themselves. Although some social status derived from one's family, those who were to be entrusted with the community good had to demonstrate individual productivity, wisdom, bravery, and success. Talent and skill played strong roles in leadership as many traditional activities were quite complex—managing a large summer hunt, a communal ritual, a seasonal dispersal, a period of raiding or defense, the building of new earth lodges, or the timing of the planting or the harvesting of a crop—and were often crucial to the group's continued survival. Military societies, in turn, kept the general order and enforced the decisions of leaders.

Each band centred its activities in a loosely defined area within a broader tribal territory. The bands within a tribe did not fight one another, but the degree to which they acted in concert varied. Among the nomadic Comanche, for instance, bands changed membership with ease and the people chose not to have a formal tribal council. Similarly, residency in each of the three Hidatsa villages was quite fluid, but each village nonetheless identified itself as a band and remained politically independent from the others. In contrast, the Skidi band of the Pawnee lived in 19 separate villages that were united in maintaining their political independence from the other three bands within the Pawnee nation. The Cheyenne were the most politically hierarchical Plains group; their 10 bands sent representatives to a council of 44 peace chiefs, whose decrees were binding on the entire tribe.

Kinship and Family

Some Plains cultures reckoned descent bilaterally, or equally in both the male and female lines. Others reckoned descent exclusively in either the male or female line; in those cultures a child automatically became a member of either the father's or mother's lineage (a group that could trace its ancestry to a known individual) and clan (a group of lineages). This did not mean that there was no recognition of the other parent and his or her relatives; to the contrary, both parents and their kin usually had specific roles to fill. Frequently a child was treated indulgently by lineal or clan relatives, who taught him ordinary life skills such as hunting (for boys) or agriculture (for girls), while non-lineal relatives were more authoritarian and acted as spiritual mentors.

For instance, although they had a matrilineal clan system, tracing descent through the mother's line and back to a common female ancestor, a Hidatsa child had important relationships with the father and his clan. These kin were always treated with respect, often presented with gifts, had the privilege of naming children, and had important mentoring roles in warfare and ritual performances such as the Sun Dance. The Mandan and Crow also had matrilineal clan systems. The patrilineal clan system was characteristic of the Iowa, Kansa, Omaha, Osage, and Ponca, and probably the Blackfoot and Atsina.

In some tribes certain clans regarded themselves as more closely related to each other than to other clans. Among the Kansa the 16 clans were grouped into seven larger units (phratries) that regulated marriage and certain other activities. Occasionally phratries were further grouped into two complementary units, or moieties. The Ponca moieties, for instance, were each composed of two phratries, each consisting of two clans. A key feature of the clan system was its ability to transcend band differences within the tribes. One was generally expected to provide hospitality to clan relatives regardless of their band loyalties, thus integrating the tribe as a whole.

Every group had regulations governing marriage. Some, such as the Atsina and Blackfoot, did not tolerate marriage between consanguineous (genetic) relatives, no matter how distant the tie, and others proscribed marriage within varying degrees of relationship. However, unions between affines—those who were already connected through marriage—were often preferred. The levirate and sorarate were common customs in which, respectively, a man married the widow of his deceased brother or a woman married the widower of her deceased sister. Most marriages were monogamous, although polygyny was also common; polygynous marriages usually involved sisters sharing a husband, as this built on established bonds and ensured that friendly parties would share in raising the household's children and caring for its elders.

Ideally marriages were arranged between the families of the bride and groom, the latter usually paying bridewealth. Sometimes, as among the Mandan, this was a purely symbolic exchange as each side provided exactly equivalent gifts. Virginity was highly prized among most of the tribes, particularly the Cheyenne. Among the Blackfoot, women known to be chaste were selected for roles in important ceremonies. A double standard prevailed, however, and men in all of the tribes were expected to pursue sexual conquests. Elopement was not unknown, but attitudes varied; the Teton tolerated the couple on their return, while the Cheyenne considered the girl disgraced forever.

Most Plains tribes had definite rules governing conduct between marriage partners and their opposite-sex parents-in-law. Their interactions were typically characterized by avoidance behaviour; this so-called mother-in-law taboo in which a man and his wife's mother showed their mutual respect by not speaking to, or in some cases not even looking at, each other was usually paralleled by a father-in-law taboo, in which a woman and her husband's father would avoid one another for the same reasons. The Atsina and a few other tribes required brothers-in-law to be very circumspect in their speech, avoiding any reference to sex no matter how indirect.

Most Plains tribes also had joking relationships between particular categories of kin. Perhaps the most universally recognized joking relatives were grandparents and grandchildren. Although parents, especially mothers, were often visibly fond of their children, the latter were expected to treat their parents with respect. In contrast, grandchildren and grandparents often engaged in mild ribbing. When praise for good behaviour proved insufficient, this was the preferred way to remind a child of appropriate comportment. Most kinship systems delineated a wide network of additional joking relatives. Teasing, roughhousing, and practical joking was expected within these cohorts and one was to respond to them in a good-natured manner or risk losing prestige. As everyone from the highest chief to the poorest orphan had joking relatives, this custom provided a mechanism for registering social approval or disapproval and for deflating puffed egos.

Some joking relationships were quite ribald; many of the tribes adhering strictly to the avoidance taboo permitted great freedom between a man and his sisters-in-law. Among the Crow they were expected to romp with each other and to talk to each other in vile or sexually explicit language. The Atsina encouraged mutual practical joking and teasing, and the Blackfoot allowed the same freedom as between man and wife. It is notable that, according to marriage rules on the Plains, the parties to these joking relationships were potential mates.

SOCIALIZATION AND EDUCATION

Training began early for Plains children, as part of their play. As children were usually raised in extended families, grandparents were often heavily engaged in their socialization. Older children were also charged with watching after their younger counterparts.

Plains tribes typically had a distinct division of labour in which women were responsible for producing children, raising and gathering plant foods, constructing and maintaining the home, cooking, and providing clothing and other domestic accoutrements, while men hunted for the household and provided defense for the community. In preparation for her adult role, a young girl would be given a doll to play with and care for. As she grew older her family might make her child-sized hide-scraping tools, which her female relatives would teach her to use. She would learn to sew by making clothes for her doll and to keep house in a child-sized tepee.

Likewise, a young boy would be given a bow and arrows with knobbed tips; as he grew stronger he would receive larger, heavier bows and be shown how to stalk small game and to hit moving targets. Groups of boys engaged in shooting matches and play battles, the winners receiving acclaim from their elders; the losers were praised if they had fought bravely. Girls played a game in which a ball was kept in the air without using the hands. Children also engaged in horse races, foot races, swimming, and games of chance.

The young were encouraged to behave in desired ways by praise and reward, with many of the tribes giving special praise for the first successful completion of a task or skill. Thus, an Oto father publicly gave away property to honour his son when the boy first walked, when he brought in his first small game, when he killed his first deer, and when he returned from his first war party. When a Crow boy killed his first big game animal, he was given public recognition; a song celebrating the achievement was sung at a ceremony similar to that which would mark his return from a first war party. Progress toward maturity was generally rewarded by removing restrictions and granting special privileges. Blackfoot boys who won shooting matches were allowed to wear feathers in their hair. As soon as he went on his first war party, a Cheyenne boy was relieved from the duty of herding horses and also from the necessity of listening to long lectures on proper behaviour.

Girls were similarly recognized for their accomplishments in food production, cooking, quilling, beading, hide processing, and the like. A few tribes, including the Plains Cree, ritually marked the occurrence of the girl's first menses.

In a number of tribes the mother's brother and the father's sister played important roles as mentors and disciplinarians. Among the matrilineal Hidatsa, the maternal uncle was responsible for the direction and supervision of his nephews; he guided them and punished them, but also praised them. Arapaho parents relied on the father's sister to instruct a girl in proper behaviour and to reprimand her if necessary. Physical punishment was seldom employed. Praise and reward for achievement seem to have been generally emphasized more than ridicule and admonishment for failure, although a child's joking relatives were a constant presence and their potential for teasing provided a strong incentive for socially acceptable interaction.

SOCIAL RANK AND WARFARE

Traditional Plains peoples shared a cultural ethos that interwove expectations of individual competency with those of obligation to the community. For instance, the status of an individual or family was enhanced when they were generous to the poor, shared goods with relatives, engaged in lavish hospitality, and cooperated with others.

There were no hereditary social classes, but there was ranking of individuals. The son of a wealthy family would have an early advantage over a poor child in that he could rely on his family for the material support necessary to pay for craft and ritual apprenticeships, initiation fees for military societies, bridewealth, and feasts. As time passed, however, such a man would have to prove himself independently. A poor man, in contrast, might spend his youth in straightened circumstances but could win wealth and standing through prowess at war or ritual. In some tribes orphans were the preferred marriage partners, as they had proved themselves to be responsible individuals and capable providers at a young age.

Most tribes ranked war exploits, but they did not all evaluate particular deeds alike. Intertribal fighting seldom involved major tribal forces; it was carried out mainly by raiding parties of a few warriors to avenge a death, to steal horses, and especially to gain glory. Counting coup—touching an enemy's body in battle—was generally considered of greater moment than killing him. Stealing a valuable horse that had been picketed at its owner's lodge was also considered a feat of renown; in many tribes, groups of young boys developed stealth by the socially approved practice of attempting to steal food from their neighbours' lodges. In the event of a group's success, the lodge residents often held a feast in the boys' honour; such a celebration of the thieves' skill exempted the household from further plunder.

Most tribes had a number of religious and secular associations. Among the latter were military groups, such as the Hidatsa Dog Society, which generally functioned as police and sometimes as rivals for battle honours. Among the Crow, for example, there were two outstanding societies, the Lumpwoods and the Foxes, that were of equal rank and competed fiercely in feats of war. The Arapaho, Atsina, Blackfoot, Mandan, and Hidatsa ranked their military societies in a series of age sets, groups of individuals of a similar age who functioned as a cohort. Distinctive regalia and membership privileges in each society were purchased collectively by each age set from the next older group, the exchange continuing until the oldest group sold all their materials and retired from the system. The

Dancer of the Hidatsa Dog Society, aquatint by Karl Bodmer, 1834. Courtesy of the Rare Book Division, the New York Public Library, Astor, Lenox and Tilden Foundations

number of societies varied. The Hidatsa at one time had as many as 10 military societies.

Women had their own ritual and secular associations. Where men's groups were generally oriented toward raiding, women's societies generally focused on the fertility of humans, animals, and crops, and on the turning of the seasons. Among the Mandan and Hidatsa, women's societies were also age-graded; it has been reported that such women's societies also existed among the Blackfoot, Arapaho, and Atsina.

Belief Systems

The Plains tribes did not distinguish sharply between the sacred and the secular, although they certainly acknowledged that some things, such as the contents of sacred bundles, had more supernatural power than others. They attached much importance to visions and their cultures generally included aspects of animism, a belief system in which natural phenomena such as animals, plants, the sun, moon, stars, thunder, and lighting are physical manifestations of spirit-beings.

Success in life was believed to depend in large measure on the intervention of these spirit-beings. The usual procedure for obtaining spirit help was to undertake a vision quest, in which a person would go to some lonely spot to fast and beg for aid; men might also mortify the flesh, though women usually did not. If the suppliant was successful, the spirit-being would provide detailed instructions for winning immunity in battle, curing illness, or obtaining other skills or powers. Those who were very respectful might gain the protection of a guardian spirit. The quest for supernatural power through a vision or dream was important among all of the tribes and among both girls and boys; vision quests were often begun when a child was as young as six or seven years of age. Not everyone was successful in the vision quest, and among the Crow and some other tribes those with power were permitted to transfer it to others less fortunate.

All of the tribes had people who communed with the spirit world in order to perform acts of healing and shamanism. In most of the groups ordinary illnesses such as dysentery or headaches would be treated with common herbal remedies, while a shaman would be called in to diagnose and treat more serious illnesses. It was widely believed that illness was caused by intrusion of a foreign object in the body and that the shaman could cure the patient by extracting the item. If the extraction failed, there had presumably been some unwitting infraction of the rules as laid down by the shaman's supernatural sponsor. Shamans were not required to take every case, as their reputation depended upon their ability to cure; among the Teton, they could refuse after examining a patient. Other services they might render included locating enemies and game animals and even finding lost objects. Arapaho, Atsina, and Cheyenne shamans were reported to walk on fire as a proof of their powers.

In some tribes it is difficult to distinguish the role of the shaman, who had direct contact with the supernatural, from that of the priest, who obtained his knowledge from other practitioners. In some cases the two roles were more or less combined. Among the Cheyenne, the main road to supernatural power was through acquisition of ritual knowledge from one who was already a priest, although power was also sought through visions. Thus, the same individual may have acted in some situations as a shaman and in others as a priest.

Among the tribes having a clear belief in a spirit superior to all other spirits were the Cheyenne, the Atsina, and the Pawnee. The Cheyenne, for instance, held that "the Wise One above" knew better than all other creatures. Further, he had long ago left the Earth and retired to the sky. In smoking ceremonies the first offering of the pipe was always made to him. Some of the other tribes, such as the Crow, believed instead in multiplicity of deities, each of whom possessed more or less equal power.

Ceremonial and ritual were well developed on the Plains. They ranged from very simple rites to complicated proceedings involving weeks of preparation and performances that lasted for several days. A number of common ritual elements were used alone or combined in various ways. Sacred bundles, also called medicine bundles, figured prominently in rituals throughout the area. In some cases the bundle was a personal one, the contents of which had been suggested by a guardian spirit, while in others it was a tribal property with a long, or even mythological, history. Bundles were handled reverently and opened according to definite rules. The opening of the Cheyenne sacred arrow bundle, for instance, was the focus of an elaborate tribal rite extending over four days.

The sacred number for most tribes was four, often said to represent the cardinal directions. A less common number was seven, representing the cardinal direction plus "up" or the sky, "down" or the world below, and "centre" or the location of the ritual. Often dances, songs, or other parts of a ritual were performed in or by groups of four or seven. Many rituals used an altar or other specially prepared space in a ceremonial structure for arranging sacred objects or smoking them with incense. The dimensions of the altar and the symbols that were used varied with the tribe and the ceremony. Ritual purification in a sweat lodge was required in connection with many ceremonies.

One important ritual found among about 20 tribes is known inaccurately in English as the Sun Dance. The indigenous terms for this ritual varied: the Cheyenne phrase may be translated as "New Life Lodge"; the Atsina term means "Sacrifice Lodge." While the central features were the same among all the tribes, there were many differences in detail. The sacrament was always held in summer, when the whole tribe could gather; those pledging to undertake the most arduous form of the ritual usually did so in thanks for having been relieved of some grave difficulty.

The ceremony was an annual event among the Teton but occurred at quite irregular intervals among the Crow. The pledger was instructed by a priest or ritual specialist; weeks or even months were needed for spiritual preparation and to gather the food, gifts, and other materials the pledger and his family were expected to provide. A ceremonial structure was built in the centre of the camp circle (or among the Mandan, in a very large earth lodge dedicated to this and other rituals); before it was erected, offerings were placed in the fork of the central log. Within the structure was an altar upon which buffalo skulls were laid. The pledger and other participants fasted and danced for several days, praying for power. A widespread, though not universal, feature of the ceremony was self-mortification by some of the participants. A ritual expert pinched a centimetre or two of skin on the pledger's breast or back, pierced through it with a sharp instrument, and inserted a wooden skewer through the piercing. One end of a rope or thong was tied to the skewer, the other end being attached to the centre pole or a buffalo skull. The dancer leaned back until the line was taut and strained until the line tore through his piercings. Among the Teton the practice also involved piercing the dancers' legs.

CULTURAL CONTINUITY AND CHANGE

Although little direct contact occurred between Plains peoples and Europeans before the 18th century, the fur trade had brought manufactured articles such as guns, metal utensils, axes, knives, blankets, and cloth to the region much earlier. In some cases the new materials were seen by indigenous peoples as superior to the traditional ones. The durability of brass kettles caused them to be preferred over traditional clay pottery, for instance, as the latter were easily broken and time-consuming to produce. Similarly, glass beads were substituted for porcupine quills and metal tools for stone tools, and some traditional arts and crafts declined.

Paradoxically, however, some aspects of social life were intensified as a result of the fur trade. For example, the new purchasing power ascribed to an old product, buffalo robes, indirectly increased polygyny: Women were responsible for dressing hides, so the wives of successful hunters sought to bring new partners into the marriage (often their sisters) to share this arduous work. Religion was affected in a similarly indirect manner, insofar as wealth brought by the fur trade encouraged the more frequent transfer of medicine bundles and drove up the cost of gaining ritual knowledge.

Direct contact with Europeans and Euro-Americans began in earnest in the late 18th century. In addition to fur traders and explorers, a number of artists and scientists traveled to the region and created unusually complete records of the indigenous cultures and their responses to colonialism. The 1830s were particularly well documented through the journals and paintings created by the pioneering ethnologist Prince

Maximilian of Wied-Neuwied and his companion, the Swiss artist Karl Bodmer, as well as the aforementioned American artist George Catlin.

By the 1840s the opening of the Oregon Trail and other routes across the Plains spurred the burgeoning Homestead Movement in the United States. Discussions of tribal unification began as increasing numbers of Euro-American settlers crossed sovereign territory on the way to California and the Pacific Northwest. Some tribes objected to trespass so strongly that they attacked the travelers.

A major conference between tribal leaders and the U.S. government was convened at Fort Laramie in 1851. The United States desired to delineate which lands were to belong to tribes and which to the United States, to establish an inter-tribal peace, to allow the development of transportation systems and supporting fortresses in the region, and to guarantee the safety of settlers en route to the West Coast; the tribes desired to establish legal title to their land and guarantees that such title would be held inviolate. Negotiations were successfully completed and brought a period of relative tranquility to the Plains.

THE PLAINS WARS

Renewed development, particularly an influx of settlers who staked claims under the Homestead Act of 1862, reignited tensions in the region. In the Sioux Uprising of the same year, Santee bands that had remained in Minnesota sought to drive away settlers whom they felt were encroaching on indigenous lands, although most of the areas in question had been ceded to the United States under previous treaties. By the end of the conflict some 400 settlers, 70 U.S. soldiers, and 30 Santee had been killed and more than 300 Santee men were sentenced to death by hanging; President Abraham Lincoln later commuted most of these sentences.

Relations between the region's nomadic peoples and the United States declined precipitously from that point onward. The retaliatory efforts by each side of the conflict were plentiful and horrific. Examples include the Sand Creek Massacre (1864), in which Colorado militia attacked a Cheyenne village and killed between 150 and 500 people, mostly women and children; the Fetterman Massacre (1866), in which Teton warriors killed an entire unit of 80 U.S. soldiers; and the Washita River Massacre (1868), in which George Armstong Custer and the 7th Cavalry killed a reported 103 Cheyenne. The large number of battles during this period has caused some historians to name the conflict as a whole the "Indian Wars" or "Plains Wars."

Notably, the village tribes generally sided with the United States during this period; many of their young men acted as scouts for the U.S. military. In following this strategy, the village groups were acting in their own best interests and suffered far fewer casualties during this period than the nomads. The nomads had arrived on the Plains only a few generations before and were often seen as interlopers by the villagers; although specific bands of nomads and villagers had long-standing trade relations, the groups generally viewed one another as enemies. Alliance with the United States enabled Arikara, Hidatsa, Mandan, Pawnee, and other men to gain battle honours against traditional foes without breaking the Fort Laramie treaty's prohibitions against intertribal warfare. Further, many village leaders perceived that the United States would become the regional hegemon and that cooperation with that government was the best strategy for retaining possession of tribal land.

The nomadic tribes created an atmosphere in which many settlers eventually abandoned their claims. A second treaty convention at Fort Laramie, held in 1868, was intended to reestablish the peace and did so for a time. However, the United States abrogated the treaty in 1874, opening the Black Hills to development when gold was discovered there. Conflicts were

Commercial buffalo hunters curing buffalo hides and bones, wood engraving by Paul Frenzeny and Jules Tavernier in Harper's Weekly, *1874.* Library of Congress, Washington, D.C. (neg. no. LC-USZ62-100250)

renewed and ultimately several bands of Sioux and Cheyenne united, annihilating Custer and his 7th Cavalry at the Battle of the Little Bighorn (1876).

Acknowledging that military actions against guerillas who were defending their home territories was a difficult and expensive proposition at best, U.S. policy makers turned to the destruction of the indigenous food supply. Buffalo hunting had already been undertaken on a massive scale by private parties and needed little encouragement to become terribly efficient. As the buffalo disappeared, the Plains Indians began to starve, and by the early 1880s most bands had acceded to confinement on reservations.

SYNCRETISM, ASSIMILATION, AND SELF-DETERMINATION

New religious movements were adopted during the early reservation period—first the Ghost Dance and later peyotism. Both were syncretic, combining elements of traditional religions with those of Christianity. The Ghost Dance began as a redemptive movement in the Great Basin culture area but became quite millenarian as it spread to the Plains, where believers danced in the hopes that the settlers would disappear, that the buffalo would return, and that their people would be impervious to attack. Concerns that Ghost Dancing would reignite the Plains Wars led to the massacre at Wounded Knee in 1890, in which more than 200 Miniconjou Sioux were killed by the reconstituted U.S. 7th Cavalry. This was the final major armed engagement of the Plains Wars.

Peyotism centred on a type of cactus—the peyote—the fruit of which caused hallucinations or visions when eaten or imbibed. As both the government and Christian missionaries considered this practice dangerous, they made efforts to suppress it. However, adherents of the peyote religion were incorporated in 1918 as the Native American Church, which continued to be a strong organization in the early 21st century. Sun dancing, which had been subject to similar efforts at suppression, also continued to be practiced in the early 21st century.

Canadian tribes were also affected by development and particularly by the political changes that flowed from the British creation of the Dominion of Canada in 1867. The new Canadian government quickly stated its intent to annex the northern Plains, most of which had until then been part of Rupert's Land, a territory of the Hudson's Bay Company. Annexation proceeded without consultation with the area's resident tribes.

Powerful groups such as the Plains Cree, Blackfoot, Saulteaux, and Métis knew that annexation presaged the potential destruction of their way of life; many of these groups had provided refuge to tribes fleeing the conflicts in the United States and were well informed regarding the processes and consequences of colonial expansion. The Métis soon instigated the Red

River Rebellion (1869–70). As a result, the Canadian government and the rebels agreed that the latter would have a strong presence in provincial government. Canada's Numbered Treaties were subsequently executed; similar to the first Fort Laramie treaty, these agreements delineated tribal and governmental title to lands and the terms of development in the area, among other things. In 1885 a second rebellion was instigated in response to the repression of local rule, but it was quashed and its leaders hanged or imprisoned.

By the end of the 19th century both the United States and Canada had begun to pursue assimilationist programs designed to replace traditional cultures with Euro-American ways of life. Those sent to implement these programs were often corrupt or incompetent, and even the most professional among them encountered many obstacles. The nomadic groups were loath to become sedentary, cattle were universally derided as a poor substitute for buffalo, and reservation land was often unsuitable for agriculture. Cultivation was traditionally women's work and the basis of their economic empowerment, and women and men alike resisted the change in the division of labour brought by the plow.

Confusion resulted when officials insisted on listing families by surnames, which few indigenous peoples used. Additional misunderstandings arose within the matrilineal tribes when Euro-Americans insisted that property should pass from father to son rather than from mother to daughter.

Government-sponsored boarding schools were also given the mission of assimilating indigenous children. Attendance was mandatory and children were forced to leave their homes for months or years at a time. Some staff members used extremely harsh measures to force children to give up their traditional cultures and languages. The extent of abuse that occurred in these institutions, including sexual abuse, is perhaps best represented by the Canadian government's 2006 offer of some $2 billion in reparations to former residential school pupils.

SOVEREIGNTY, ECONOMIC DEVELOPMENT, AND CULTURAL REVITALIZATION

Assimilationist policies such as those mandating confinement to reservations were governmental challenges to tribal sovereignty. Regaining self-determination in these and other areas became the defining goal of the Plains tribes in the 20th and 21st centuries. Many tribes in the United States were economically devastated by the Pick-Sloan plan, a post-World War II federal development program that placed major dams on the Missouri River and numerous smaller dams on its tributaries. This project flooded hundreds of square miles of the tribes' most economically productive land and forced the relocation of some 1,000 extended-family households. The dams also created lakes so large that they were difficult to bridge, thus isolating reservation communities whose residents had once been able to visit with relative ease.

As with other rural communities, many Plains tribes had instituted formal plans for economic growth by the late 20th and early 21st centuries. Many of these plans were designed to resolve common rural development issues, such as underemployment and lack of services, while also instituting programs for cultural revitalization. For instance, when tribal schools were opened to replace the boarding schools, many employed tribal elders to instruct children in indigenous languages. Several tribes implemented buffalo ranching operations with programs that were hoped to aid in the restoration of the Plains ecosystem. A number of groups own casinos and hotels; other tribal enterprises include manufacturing, trucking, and construction.

CHAPTER 6

NORTHEAST AND SOUTHEAST CULTURE AREAS

When discussed jointly, the Southeast and Northeast culture areas are sometimes referred to as the Eastern Woodlands. Because of the potential for confusion of this term with that of the Eastern Woodland cultures, a term that describes a group of prehistoric societies rather than a culture area per se, the groups of these regions are here referred to as Northeast and Southeast cultures. They are not sharply divided. To the south the traditions of the Northeast gradually transition to those of the Southeast Indians.

The term Northeast is used to describe the Native American peoples living at the time of European contact in the area roughly bounded in the north by the transition from predominantly deciduous forest to the taiga, in the east by the Atlantic Ocean, in the west by the Mississippi River valley, and in the south by an arc from the present-day North Carolina coast northwest to the Ohio River and thence southwest to its confluence with the Mississippi River. The Northeast culture area comprises a mosaic of temperate forests, meadows, wetlands, waterways, and coastal zones.

The term Southeast refers to any of the Native American peoples of the southeastern United States. The boundaries of this culture area are somewhat difficult to delineate, because the traditional cultures in the Southeast shared many characteristics with those from neighbouring regions. Thus, most scholars define the region's eastern and southern boundaries as the Atlantic Ocean and the Gulf of Mexico, although some assign the southern portion of aboriginal Florida to the circum-Caribbean culture area. To the west the Southeastern peoples merge with those of the southern Plains Indians and the most easterly of the Southwest Indians.

NORTHEAST INDIAN PEOPLES

The Northeast region was occupied by many different groups, each of which was a member of either the Algonquian, Iroquoian, or Siouan language families. As with linguistically related groups elsewhere (e.g., the French, Italian, and Spanish peoples within the Romance language family), each Native American language family comprised a number of distinct peoples.

TERRITORIAL AND POLITICAL ORGANIZATION

Of the three language families represented in the Northeast, Algonquian groups were the most widely distributed. Their territories comprised the entire region except the areas immediately surrounding Lakes Erie and Ontario, some parts of the present-day states of Wisconsin and Minnesota, and a portion of the interior of present-day Virginia and North Carolina. The major speakers of Algonquian languages include the Passamaquoddy, Malecite, Mi'kmaq (Micmac), Abenaki, Penobscot,

Pennacook, Massachuset, Nauset, Wampanoag, Narragansett, Niantic, Pequot, Mohegan, Nipmuc, Pocomtuc, Mohican (Mahican), Wappinger, Montauk, Delaware, Powhatan, Ojibwa, Menominee, Sauk, Kickapoo, Miami, Shawnee, and Illinois.

The territory around Lakes Ontario and Erie was controlled by peoples speaking Iroquoian languages, including the Mohawk, Oneida, Onondaga, Cayuga, Seneca, Huron, Tionontati, Neutral, Wenrohronon, Erie, Susquehannock, and Laurentian Iroquois. The Tuscarora, who also spoke an Iroquoian language, lived in the coastal hills of present-day North Carolina and Virginia.

Although many Siouan-speaking tribes once lived in the Northeast culture area, only the Ho-Chunk (Winnebago) people continue to reside there in large numbers. Most tribes within the Sioux nation moved west in the 16th and 17th centuries, as the effects of colonialism rippled across the continent. Although the Santee Sioux bands had the highest level of conflict with their Ojibwa neighbours, the Teton and Yankton Sioux bands moved the farthest west from their original territory. These bands, as well as most other Siouan-speaking groups, are usually considered to be part of the Plains Indian culture area despite their extended period of residence in the forests.

The most elaborate and powerful political organization in the Northeast was that of the Iroquois Confederacy. A loose coalition of tribes, it originally comprised the Mohawk, Oneida, Onondaga,

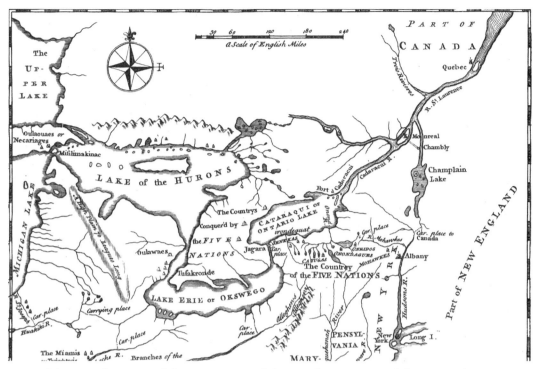

Map of the initial nations of the Iroquois Confederacy, from History of the Five Indian Nations Depending on the Province of New-York, *by Cadwallader Colden, 1755.* Library of Congress, Rare Book Division, Washington, D.C.

Cayuga, and Seneca. Later the Tuscarora joined as well. Indigenous traditions hold that the league was formed as a result of the efforts of the leaders Dekanawida and Hiawatha, probably during the 15th or the 16th century.

The original intent of the coalition was to establish peace among the member tribes. One of the most important things it established was a standardized rate for blood money, the compensation paid to the family of a murder victim. Providing compensation for the loss of a family member was a long-standing practice, but, before the confederacy was established, entire tribes could go to war

if an offer was deemed inadequate. The fixing of blood money rates prevented such conflicts from occurring within the league, although not between members of the league and other tribes.

Notably, the value of both the victim's life and that of the murderer were part of the compensation, as the murderer had notionally forfeited the right to live by committing such violence. The agreed-upon rate was 10 strings of symbolically important shell beads, or wampum, for the life of a man and 20 strings of wampum for the life of a woman; thus, the total compensation for murder of a man by a man was

20 strings, of a woman by a woman 40 strings, and so on.

The Iroquois Confederacy was a league of peace to its members, yet peace within the league also freed the tribes of the Confederacy to focus their military power on the conquest of other indigenous groups. Military activities were a primary occupation among men throughout the Northeast, and military honours were the primary gauge of a man's status within many tribes. Raids provided room for expansion as well as captive women and children; such captives were often adopted into the tribe in order to replace family members lost to death or capture. Captive adult men, however, generally fared less well than women and children. Among the Iroquois Confederacy, other Iroquoian speakers, and perhaps a few Algonquian groups, men taken during raids might be either tortured to death or adopted into the tribe. If the captive had been taken to compensate for a murder, his fate was usually determined by the family of the deceased. If their decision was to torture, the captive tried to avoid crying out, a practice that contributed to the stereotype of the stoicism among indigenous Americans. Among the Iroquois it was not uncommon to close the event by cannibalizing the body, a practice that alienated surrounding tribes.

Although conflicts between the Iroquois Confederacy and neighbouring tribes certainly antedated colonization, it is equally certain that the confederacy increased its raiding activity during the ensuing centuries. This occurred for a number of reasons—some, such as demographic collapse, indirectly promoted violence, while others, such as economic pressures, were direct instigators of conflict. Although it is nearly impossible to completely untangle the ways that these processes interacted, it is useful to consider them both.

Europeans who traveled to the Americas brought with them diseases to which indigenous peoples had no immunity. These new diseases proved much more deadly to Amerindians than they had been to Europeans and ultimately precipitated a pancontinental demographic collapse. The introduced diseases proved especially virulent in the concentrated settlements of the Iroquoians, who began to suffer heavier population losses than their neighbours. In attempting to replace those who had died during epidemics, the tribes of the Iroquois Confederacy seemed to have taken kidnapping to unprecedented levels.

Economic disruptions related to the commercialization of animal resources also instigated intertribal conflict. By the early 17th century, trapping had severely depleted the beaver population around the Great Lakes. At that time beaver pelts were the most important commodity in the fur trade economy and could easily be bartered for guns, ammunition, and other goods necessary to ensure a tribe's safety, or even preeminence, in a region. The Iroquois Confederacy occupied some of the more depleted beaver habitat and began a military campaign intended to effect expansion into territory that had not been overhunted.

While raiding for expansionist purposes might have differed from raiding intended to take captives, those tribes that were put on the defensive created several alliances to repel confederacy attacks. A prominent example was an alliance known as the Wendat Confederacy, which comprised several Huron bands and the Tionontati. The Wenrohronon and the Neutral tribes also formed loose defensive coalitions. Ultimately, however, these alliances proved ineffective. The Iroquois Confederacy conquered the Wendat in 1648–50, the Neutrals in 1651, the Erie in 1656, and the Susquehannock in 1676.

SUBSISTENCE, SETTLEMENT PATTERNS, AND HOUSING

The Northeast culture area comprises a mosaic of temperate forests, meadows, wetlands, and waterways. The traditional diet consisted of a wide variety of cultivated, hunted, and gathered foods, including corn (maize), beans, squash, deer, fish, waterbirds, leaves, seeds, tubers, berries, roots, nuts, and maple syrup.

Rivers in the northern and eastern parts of the culture area had annual runs of anadromous fish such as salmon; in the north people tended to rely more upon fish than on crops as the latter were frequently destroyed by frost. Similarly, groups in the upper Great Lakes relied more upon wild rice (*Zizania aquatica*) than on crops, and peoples on

the western fringes of the culture area relied more upon hunting the bison that roamed the local tallgrass prairies than on agriculture. On the Atlantic coast and along major inland rivers, shellfish were plentiful and played an important part in the diet. In contrast, residents of the central and southern parts of the culture area tended to rely quite heavily upon crops, because wild resources such as rice, anadromous fish, shellfish, and bison were unavailable. Notably, the geographic distribution of those areas where domesticated plants were essential mirrors the distribution of Iroquoians, while the Algonquian and Siouan groups generally lived in the areas of enriched wild resources.

This is not to imply that the Algonquians and Siouans did not farm. All the Northeastern tribes were familiar with corn, beans, and squash—often referred to as the "three sisters" for their complementary growing habits, nutritional value, and ease of storage. Fields were created by girdling trees and burning any undergrowth; fruit and nut trees were not girdled but rather became part of the larger garden or field system. Crops were planted in small mounds or hills about 3 feet (1 metre) across. Corn was planted in the centre of the mound, beans in a ring around the corn, and squash around the beans. As the plants grew, bean runners used the corn stalks as a support, and the broad leaves of the squash plants shaded out weeds and conserved soil moisture. The nitrogen depletion caused by intensive corn

Secoton, a Powhatan Village, watercolour drawing by John White, c. 1587; in the British Museum, London. Courtesy of the trustees of the British Museum

production was repaired by the beans' ability to fix nitrogen to the soil, and in combination the plant trio provided a wide complement of proteins and vitamins. Harvested produce was eaten fresh or dried and stored for winter meals, as were wild foods.

The tribes that relied most heavily upon agriculture tended to coalesce into the largest settlements, perhaps because they needed to store and defend the harvest. Large Iroquoian villages, for instance, were protected by as many as three concentric palisades at the time of initial European contact, indicating that these groups were quite concerned about raids from fellow tribes. In contrast, Algonquian and Siouan oral traditions and early European reports indicate that the peoples living in areas with enriched wild food sources such as wild rice or salmon tended to live in relatively smaller and less protected villages and to spend more of their time in dispersed hunting and gathering camps. By the first half of the 17th century, however, nearly every village was ringed by a protective palisade.

Algonquian and Siouan homes were wickiups or wigwams; Iroquoians lived in longhouses. Wickiups were made by driving a number of pointed poles into the ground to make a circular or oval floor plan ranging from 15 to 20 feet (4.5 to 6 metres) in diameter. These poles were tied together with strips of bark and reinforced with other poles tied horizontally to make a dome-shaped framework that was covered with bark, reeds, or woven mats, the type of covering depending on the availability of materials in the area. A single fire in the centre provided heat for cooking and for warmth. Typically, a wickiup would house a single two- or three-generation family, although two close families would occasionally share a home.

Traditional longhouses were also made of a framework of poles covered with bark sheets but were roughly rectangular in floor plan, with a door at either end and an arched roof; in terms of construction, a longhouse was rather like a greatly elongated wickiup. After European contact, longhouse construction techniques changed so that walls were built to remain vertical, rather than to create a roof arch, and were topped with a gable roof. A longhouse was usually some 22 to 23 feet (6 to 7 m) wide and might be anywhere from 40 to 400 feet (12 to 122 m) in length depending on the number of families living in it. Interior walls divided longhouses into compartments, and usually one nuclear family would reside in each. A series of hearths was placed down the middle of the structure, with the families on either side of the central walkway sharing the fire in the middle. The average longhouse probably had 5 fires and 10 families.

PRODUCTION AND TECHNOLOGY

In keeping with the forested environment of the region, most materials produced in

Northeast Indian moccasins decorated with quillwork, glass beads, and strips of wool.
© Lee Boltin

the Northeast were made of wood. Dishes and spoons were made of bark or carved wood and an invitation to a feast was often phrased, "Come, and bring your bowl and spoon." Corn-based potages were a dietary staple and were usually cooked in ceramic pots or birch-bark baskets (hot stones were placed in the latter); brass pots and kettles were prized for cooking once they became available as trade items. Corn was generally converted to hominy by soaking the kernels in ashes, removing the hulls, and pounding the remaining mass with a wooden pestle in a mortar hollowed out of a tree trunk. Occasionally, however, the corn was ground between two flat stones.

Wooden dugouts and bark canoes were used for transport on the region's many lakes and streams; birch bark made the best canoes in terms of the ratio between strength and weight. The forest also provided materials for the frames of snowshoes, which made travel in the winter easier and which were essential in the north. The shafts for bows, arrows, and spears were also made of wood, while points for the arrows and spears were

Hair worn in the traditional roach style common to some Northeast Indian nations. Ma-Ka-Tai-Me-She-Kia-Kiah, or Black Hawk, a Saukie Brave, *lithograph by I.T. Bowen's Lithographic Establishment, c. 1838.* Library of Congress, Washington, D.C.

chipped from stone, as were many knives and other sharp-edged implements. A variety of bone tools were also made, primarily for processing animal hides into soft leather. European metal goods became very popular replacements for bone tools and stone arrowheads and knives, and indigenous peoples often fashioned the metal from damaged kettles into these familiar tools.

Typically, labour was divided on the basis of gender and age. Grandparents, great-aunts and great-uncles, and older siblings and cousins helped parents care for children from toddlerhood on, teaching them the ways of the group. Women cared for infants, cooked, made clothing and basketry containers, gathered wild plants and shellfish, fished, and made the tools necessary for these tasks. They also planted, weeded, and harvested all crops; in total, women typically grew, gathered, or caught the majority of the food consumed by a group. Men held councils, warred, built houses, hunted, fished, and made the implements they needed for these activities.

Although housing and the reliance upon agriculture varied from tribe to tribe, clothing was fairly similar throughout the Northeast culture area. The basic item of men's dress was the breechcloth, a strip of soft leather drawn between the legs and held in place by looping it over a belt at the waist. For protection from the cold or while traveling in the forest, leggings—basically, two tubes of leather or fur also attached to the waist belt—were added. A cape or robe of leather or fur was also worn in cold weather. The basic item of women's dress was a skirt, to which might be added leggings tied at the knee and a cape or robe. Both men and women wore moccasins, the soft-soled and heelless shoe adapted, among other things, for use with the snowshoe.

Clothing might be decorated with painting, porcupine-quill embroidery, shells, or shell beads; glass beads, cloth, and ribbons were highly sought after once the fur trade made them available. For special occasions such as feasts and war expeditions, the body might also be decorated with paint and jewelry. Body modification and ornamentation were common; many individuals had tattoos, especially on the face, long hair was admired and might be greased to add lustre, and a number of men plucked out some hair and cut the remainder to form roaches (a hairstyle now commonly referred to as a "Mohawk") or other distinctive hairstyles.

SOCIAL ORGANIZATION

Northeastern cultures used two approaches to social organization. One was based on linguistic and cultural affiliation and comprised tribes made up of bands (for predominantly mobile groups) or villages (for more sedentary peoples). The other was based on kinship and included nuclear families, clans, and groups of clans called moieties or phratries. These two organizational structures often intersected at the lowest levels; one's nuclear family, for instance, was generally

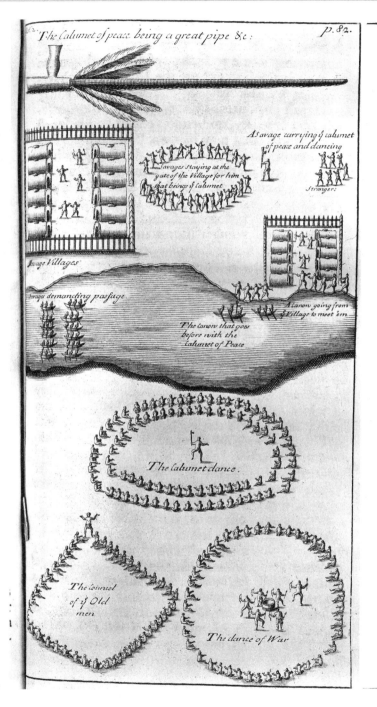

Stages in the calumet (sacred pipe) ceremony, engraving from a watercolour by John White, c. 1585. Library of Congress, Washington, D.C.

part of one's village. However, kin connections often smoothed social interaction at the tribal and intertribal levels.

A band or village was a loosely organized collection of people who occupied a particular locale and who recognized a common identity. Bands tended to be smaller and to live in the resource-enriched parts of the region, while villages tended to be larger and more dependent upon agricultural produce. Each typically had a unique name for itself; a number of what were originally band or village appellations are now thought of as tribal names. In some cases, Europeans conflated the identities of a people, their geographic locale, and their leader, as with the people of the Powhatan confederacy, the village known as Powhatan, and the leader Powhatan. Several bands or villages comprised a tribe, which was also loosely organized and which in many parts of the area was not so much a political or decision-making unit as a group of people who spoke a common language and had similar customs.

Although chieftainships often were inherited, personal ability was the basis for the influence that was exercised by a chief, or sachem. Leaders of various levels gathered frequently for councils, which might include 50 or more individuals. Such gatherings normally opened with prayers and an offering of tobacco to the divine, followed by the smoking of a sacred pipe, or calumet. West and south of the Great Lakes, this practice was elaborated into the calumet ceremony, and it is from this custom that phrases such as "sharing the peace pipe" are derived.

Persuasion was an important skill for leaders because most communities used a consensus model for decision making; issues were discussed until there was broad agreement on a course of action. Any dissidents would either leave the group or continue to express their opposition until a change was made; in either case, the effectiveness of the community would be weakened. As a result, oratory was highly valued and developed into a fine art; even in English translations, the power of Northeast Indian oratory is evident. Speech making served as a means of ascertaining the diversity of opinion within the group and the manner in which consensus could be reached, for commonly each speaker summarized the opinions previously expressed before offering his own.

KINSHIP AND FAMILY LIFE

Clans were perhaps the most important and stable social group in the Northeast. They served to divide the community into smaller cooperating units and to create a means for uniting people from different villages or bands. Members of a clan had certain obligations toward one another, such as providing hospitality to visitors of the same clan, regardless of tribal or community affiliations.

Clan names often referred to an animal. The Seneca clans, for example, were called Turtle, Bear, Beaver, Wolf, Snipe,

Hawk, Deer, and Heron. The animal, or totem, had a special relationship to the members of its clan; indeed, the word *totem* was adopted into English from an Ojibwa word denoting the close and mutually protective relationship one has with a sister or brother. Members of a clan considered themselves to be related whether or not a definitive genetic relationship could be traced. Because they represented groups of kin, clans were exogamous, or out-marrying, throughout the Northeast. Ideal marriage partners were often drawn from a specific clan that was seen as the complement of one's own. Some tribes also grouped clans into moieties (when the clans were evenly distributed) or phratries (when the clans were unevenly distributed). These larger groups had reciprocal obligations. Among many Iroquoians, for example, an important moiety responsibility was to bury the dead of the opposite group.

Among the Iroquoians and the Delaware, clans were matrilineal (sibs); a child was automatically a member of the mother's clan. Patrilineal clans (gentes) were found among the Ho-Chunk and many other upper Great Lakes Algonquian tribes; a child in these tribes was a member of the father's clan. Thus, an Iroquois child whose father belonged to the Wolf clan and whose mother belonged to the Turtle clan was a member of the Turtle clan. Further, the child could not marry (without being accused of committing incest) any other members of the Turtle clan. Membership in a clan was for life; it did not change upon marriage. Because clan affiliation was so important in structuring community life, those who were born outside the system and were later adopted into a tribe were also adopted into a clan of that tribe.

Clan membership was an important stabilizing device within native societies, as divorce and deaths from battle, childbirth, accident, and illness could change one's fortunes quite precipitously. A clan was responsible for the well-being of its members and ensured that those least able to provide for themselves—an orphaned child, an elder whose children had died or been killed, a widow or widower with several young children—were cared for. In longhouse societies, the very large houses, each of which was essentially a subset of a specific clan, would often bear these responsibilities.

Each clan owned a number of names, and a newborn child was given a name that was not currently in use; a name would fall out of use when its owner died or took a new name because of a life-changing event. Certain names carried special responsibilities, such as those belonging to the chiefs of the Iroquois Confederacy. When one of those leaders died, the women of his clan decided on a successor who was a member of the same clan. If the successor was approved by the other chiefs, he was given the name of the deceased chief in a condolence ceremony that "raised up" and resuscitated the decedent by giving his name to the successor.

POWWOW

Native Americans in regalia gathering for a parade at Crow Fair, an annual powwow held in Montana by the Crow (Absaroka) Nation. Travel Montana

Celebrations of American Indian culture in which people from diverse indigenous nations gather for the purpose of dancing, singing, and honouring the traditions of their ancestors are called powwows. The term powwow, which derives from a curing ritual, originated in one of the Algonquian nations of the Northeast Indians. During the early 1800s, traveling medicine shows selling cure-all tonics used "powwow" to describe their wares. These vendors often employed local Indians to dance for the entertainment of potential customers, who soon applied the term to the exhibition dancing as well as to the patent medicines. The name took hold, and Indians themselves added to it their nomenclature to describe dancing for an audience in an exhibition.

Today powwows take place over a period of one to four days and often draw dancers, singers, artists, and traders from hundreds of miles away. Spectators (including non-Indians) are welcome to attend, as participants seek to share the positive aspects of their culture with outsiders. Modern powwows can be grouped into two broad divisions: "competition" (or "contest") events and those referred to as "traditional." Competition events offer substantial prize money in various standardized dance and music categories. In contrast, traditional powwows offer small amounts of "day money" to all or some portion of the participants (such as the first 10, 20, or 30 dancers to register) and do not have competitive dancing or singing. Both divisions share the same order of events and styles of singing and dancing.

The songs and dances performed at 21st-century powwows derive primarily from those practiced by the warrior societies of the Plains Indians, with the greatest influences coming from the Heluska Warrior Society styles common to the Omaha and Ponca peoples. After the reservation period began (c. 1880), Indian dancers and singers started traveling with Wild West shows such as the one directed by William F. ("Buffalo Bill") Cody. They soon added an element of crowd-pleasing showmanship, known as "fancying it up." They also developed an opening parade into the arena, made in precise order. This practice is the direct ancestor of the contemporary powwow's Grand Entry, during which groups of dancers follow a colour guard into the arena in a predetermined sequence. The Grand Entry not only marks the beginning of the event but also motivates dancers to arrive in a timely manner, because competition points are deducted from those who miss it.

RELIGION

Animism pervaded many aspects of life for the Northeastern tribes, although it was expressed in a wide variety of ways. Among many upper Great Lakes tribes, each clan owned a bundle of sacred objects. In aggregate the objects in the bundle were seen as spirit-beings that were in some sense alive; the clan was responsible for performing the rituals that insured those beings' health and beneficence. The Iroquois had no comparable clan ceremonies; rather, a significant part of their ritual life centred on ceremonies in recognition of foods as they matured. These rituals included festivals celebrating the maple, strawberry, bean, and green corn harvests, as well as a midwinter ceremony.

Medicine societies, so termed because one of their important functions was curing and because their membership consisted of individuals who had undergone such cures, were also important. Typically their practices combined the use of medicinal plants with what would now be considered psychiatric care or psychological support. The most famous medicine society among the upper Great Lakes Algonquians was the Midewiwin, or Grand Medicine Society, whose elaborate annual or semiannual meetings included the performance of various magical feats. Of the various Iroquois medicine societies, the False Face Society is perhaps best known. The wooden masks worn by members of this society during their rituals were carved from living trees; the masks were believed to be powerful living entities capable of curing the sick when properly cared for or of causing great harm when treated disrespectfully. False Face masks were once commonly found exhibited in museums and pictured in books on Native American art; by the early 21st century, however, many tribes preferred to remove their masks from the public eye as a mark of respect for the sacred.

Not all curing was performed by members of medicine societies. Certain individuals—often termed medicine men, shamans, or powwows (a term that has changed meaning over time)—had the power to cure, a power that was often indicated in a vision or dream. Dreams were especially important, because they indicated not only the causes of illness and an individual's power to cure but also the means of maintaining good fortune in various aspects of life. So much attention was paid to dreams that among some peoples a mother asked her children each morning if they had dreamed in order to teach them to cultivate and attend to these experiences. Dreams could also influence the decisions of councils. Although boys might undertake a vision quest (particularly around the time of puberty), this was not as important in the Northeast as it was among the Plains Indians.

The reliance on dreams should not be interpreted as an indication that these people lived in a fantasy world. Because their cultures placed great emphasis on self-reliance and individual competence, attention to the content of dreams provided a means of understanding oneself and of bringing to consciousness knowledge stored in the unconscious, including knowledge as to where one's greatest abilities lay; dreams and visions might indicate whether one had special ability in warfare, hunting, and other such activities.

Cultural Continuity and Change

When Europeans arrived on the North American continent, they brought manufactured goods that the Indians welcomed and new diseases that they did not. Certain of these diseases proved particularly devastating to Native Americans because they did not have the immunity that the colonial populations had developed through centuries of exposure. For example, the first epidemic recorded in New England took place in 1616–17; while the very early date of this pestilence makes it difficult to determine exactly what disease was involved, most historical epidemiologists and demographers believe it was probably smallpox. As no census figures for Native Americans are available for this period, the number of individuals who perished is similarly difficult to discern. Historically, however, the mortality rates for populations experiencing smallpox for the first time have ranged from 20 to 90 percent. The mortality rates appear to have been quite high in this case, as the Puritans who landed at Plymouth in 1620 remarked upon the large number of abandoned villages near their settlement. They interpreted this obvious and recent depopulation of the region as a sign of divine favour—believing that God had used the epidemic to rid the area of indigenous nonbelievers who would have hindered Puritan expansion.

The extensive trade that developed between Northeastern peoples and the French, English, and Dutch who colonized the region rested on mutual desire. The Europeans desired furs, especially beaver fur, as the undercoat of a beaver pelt could be processed into a strong felt that was used in making hats. The Northeastern peoples desired objects such as guns, brass pots and kettles, metal needles and fishhooks, glass beads, and cloth.

The colonizers soon discovered the value of wampum and established workshops to mass-produce the material on Long Island and in present-day New Jersey. Wampum was used symbolically as blood money, for jewelry and gifts, and as a mnemonic for significant occasions. Important messages, for instance, were accompanied by strings of wampum that had been fashioned using colours or designs that referred symbolically to the communication's content; the making of treaties likewise involved the exchange of wampum belts to confirm the sincerity of the parties and to symbolically record the agreement. Belts or strings of wampum were also used on other political and religious occasions and kept as reminders of those events. Because it was valuable, wampum became a medium of exchange not only between Indians and traders but also among the colonists. Because the coinage in common use in the colonies was already diverse, including Spanish, Portuguese, French, and Dutch coins as well as English ones,

the adoption of wampum as another medium of exchange was an easy matter. Wampum, however, was not used as money before European contact.

The initial European settlement clung to the Atlantic coast—the sea provided the lifeline to the European homeland that the colonists needed—and thus coastal groups were first affected by the newcomers' desire for land. They were ill equipped to counter the invasion. Not only were their numbers relatively small (and made even smaller by the epidemics), but their political organization was not of the kind that easily led to unified action of numbers of men. Friction with the colonists did occasionally erupt, however, as in the Pequot War (1637) and King Philip's War (1675–76). Such resistance could not be maintained for long, however, and indigenous peoples began to adopt European ways as a means of survival. This often involved the acceptance and practice of Christianity; some missionaries were especially influential. John Eliot, for example, accomplished the monumental task of translating the Bible into Algonquian, publishing the translation in two volumes that appeared in 1661 and 1663.

The Iroquoians fared somewhat better than the coastal Algonquians. In the 17th and 18th centuries, their inland location protected them from European settlement, although part of their eastern territory was colonized. In addition, European traders wished to retain the Iroquoians' services as middlemen who would take the risks associated with transporting manufactured goods and furs over long distances. The Iroquoians understood their positional advantage and engaged in both war and diplomacy to maintain their grip on the region. Their power was finally broken during the American Revolution, when George Washington, aware of the alliance of a number of Iroquoian tribes with the British, sent a punitive expedition into what is now upstate New York. After the Revolution, many of these peoples moved to Canada; others remained in New York state, and some (predominantly Oneida) moved to present-day Wisconsin.

Like native peoples farther east, those of the upper Great Lakes area were greatly affected by the fur trade. The French established a series of trading posts there, and the English challenged them for control of the area. Indians from the east, such as the Delaware, Ottawa, and Shawnee, drifted into the area seeking furs and land. The result was a series of wars and skirmishes involving various combinations of the tribes, the English, and the French. In the 18th and 19th centuries, several prophets attempted to revitalize indigenous culture, and a series of chiefs worked to unite various tribes for the purposes of war. Notable among these were Pontiac (Ottawa), Little Turtle (Miami), Tecumseh and his half-brother The Prophet (Shawnee), Keokuk (Sauk), and Black Hawk (Sauk).

Eventually the tribes entered into treaty relations with the governments of the United States or Canada, although the terms of these agreements were generally quite unfavourable to the tribes. Despite heroic efforts to protect their homelands, all of the Northeastern peoples who survived the early colonial period had been either moved to far-flung reservations or disenfranchised of their land by the end of the 19th century.

Despite having been removed to reservations distant from their original homes—or, conversely, being forced to partition communally owned tribal land into private holdings in order to retain title thereof (thus losing tribal status)—many of the Northeastern tribes persisted in having active tribal governments and councils and in engaging in a variety of traditional cultural activities. These actions were important as the tribes dealt with a variety of governmental policies during the 20th century, including urban relocation programs and termination, a policy that removed federal recognition from tribes. They were also crucial in the creation of a variety of tribal development projects that include timber mills, manufacturing centres, and casinos. By the late 20th and early 21st centuries, many groups that had lost tribal status had successfully petitioned the U.S. government to reinstitute their sovereignty. For instance, the Menominee of Wisconsin represented one of the first tribes to be reinstated (1973) after termination, while the Mashpee Wampanoag of Massachusetts, long declared "extinct," were granted federal acknowledgement of tribal status in 2007.

SOUTHEAST INDIAN PEOPLES

The Southeast environment is composed of a series of physiographic and ecological zones. A coastal lowland belt broadly encompasses the subtropical zone of southern Florida. To the north, this gives way to the scrub forest, sandy soil, and savanna grassland of the coastal plains, as well as the alluvial floodplains of the Mississippi River. Moving inland, one finds the piedmont, a landscape of rolling hills and major river systems that is predominantly covered with forests of oak and hickory. A third zone is characterized by the portion of the Appalachian Mountains that lies in present-day eastern Tennessee, northern Georgia, and the western Carolinas—a land of high peaks, deeply etched valleys, hardwood forests, and, at high elevations, flora and fauna typical of more-northerly regions.

The native peoples originally from this region include the Cherokee, Choctaw, Chickasaw, Creek, Seminole, Natchez, Caddo, Apalachee, Timucua, and Guale.

TRADITIONAL CULTURE PATTERNS

Scholarly knowledge of the Southeastern cultures relies on evidence from diverse sources, including artifacts, historical documents, ethnography, linguistics, folklore, and oral history. Many cultural traditions reported by the earliest European explorers, such as the use of ceremonial mounds, the heavy reliance on corn (maize), and the importance of social stratification in some areas, were clearly developed during the Mississippian culture period (c. AD 700–1600). The Mississippians maintained fine craft traditions and also engaged in long-distance trade throughout the Southeast and the surrounding culture areas. The ceremonial centre, Cahokia, was home to many thousands at its climax about AD 1100 (estimates range from 8,000 to 20,000 people). The Natchez are perhaps the best-known members of the Mississippian culture to survive relatively intact into the colonial period.

LANGUAGE

The indigenous peoples of the Southeast represent members of the Muskogean, Siouan, Iroquoian, and Caddoan language families. The region was also home to several linguistic isolates, or languages that have only tenuous connections to a major language family.

Muskogean-speaking peoples constituted the largest linguistic group in the aboriginal Southeast and minimally included the Choctaw, Chickasaw, Apalachee, Creek, Seminole, Alabama, Koasati, Hitchiti, and Mikasuki branches.

Four tribes of the lower Mississippi valley—the Natchez, Chitimachas, Tunicas, and Atakapas—spoke languages with a distant affinity to Muskogean. However, their languages show sufficient divergence from the main Muskogean languages and from each other to warrant semi-independent status as linguistic isolates.

The Tutelos, Biloxis, Ofos (Mosopeleas), and Catawbas spoke Siouan languages. These tribes were widely scattered and probably represent different prehistoric penetrations of Siouan speakers into the Southeast. The Yuchi language also demonstrates distant affinities to Siouan but is sufficiently distinctive to be classified as an isolate. Many small piedmont groups were probably Siouan-speaking peoples, but surviving data are insufficient to make definite identifications.

The Cherokees represent the sole speakers of an Iroquoian language in the Southeast, although the Iroquoian-speaking Tuscaroras, Nottaways, and Meherrins, residing on the northerly margin of the region, are included in the Southeast in some culture area maps. The Caddoan speakers on the western boundary of the region belong to a distinctive language family that shows remote relationships to the Siouan and Iroquoian families.

The present status of the language spoken by the Timucuas, once the predominant tribe of northern Florida, is problematic; linguists have suggested that it is related to such diverse groups as the Muskogean, Siouan, Algonquian, and Arawakan families. Mobilian was an important trade language containing many Choctaw components and served as a lingua franca in the Mississippi Valley.

SUBSISTENCE AND MATERIAL CULTURE

The Southeast was one of the more densely populated areas of native North America at the time of European contact. Most groups resided in the piedmont, where they took advantage of extensive game resources, wild plant foods, and an abundance of arable land. The peoples of south Florida were an exception, as they adjusted to an essentially subtropical maritime way of life.

The primary division of labour was by gender. Women were responsible for cultivating the fields, gathering wild plant foods, cooking and preserving food, taking care of young children and elders, and manufacturing cordage, baskets, pottery, clothing, and other goods. Men assumed duties associated with war, trade, and the hunt; they were often away from the community for extended periods of time. Men also assisted in the harvest, cleared the fields by girdling trees, and constructed houses and public buildings. Both genders manufactured ceremonial objects.

The economic mainstay of the Southeast was corn. Several varieties were grown, including "little corn" (related to popcorn); flint, or hominy, corn; and flour, or dent, corn. Some varieties were baked or roasted on the cob, while others were boiled into a succotash, a dish of stewed corn and beans. Still others were pounded into hominy or cornmeal in wooden mortars made of large upright, partly hollowed logs. Domesticated varieties of beans and

Timucua Indians preparing land and sowing seeds, engraving by Theodor de Bry from a drawing by Jacques Le Moyne, c. 1564; first published in 1591. Library of Congress, Washington, D.C. (neg. no. LC-USZ62-31869)

squash were also important in the diet, as were wild greens.

Fields were prepared with mattocks and hoes and planted by punching holes in the ground with digging sticks, inserting seed corn, and covering the holes with earth to form a mound about 2 feet (½ metre) in diameter; in some areas the soil was instead hilled into a series of linear mounds or ridges some 3 feet (1 metre) across. Typically, beans and squash were planted adjacent to the corn. The bean vines used corn stalks as trellises, while the broad leaves of squash shaded the soil, minimizing weed growth and conserving moisture. Most fields belonged to individual households, although some tribes also cultivated communal fields. Communally grown produce was given to chiefs for redistribution to the needy and for use in various ceremonies and festivals.

The importance of corn in the Southeast cannot be overemphasized. It provided a high yield of nutritious food with a minimal expenditure of labour; further, corn, beans, and squash were easily dried and stored for later consumption. This reliable food base freed people for lengthy hunting, trading, and war expeditions. It also enabled a complex civil-religious hierarchy in which political, priestly, and sometimes heredi-tary offices and privileges coincided.

Other cultivated plants included the sunflower, which was processed for its oil; *Chenopodium* and orache, which pro-duced starchy seeds and spinachlike greens; and tobacco. Many additional plants, such as wild grapes, plums, and perhaps walnut and pecan trees, were in a condition of incipient domestication; indigenous peoples exerted some effect on the propagation of these plants but did not fully domesticate them. Other important plant foods included berries, nuts, acorns, potatoes, zamia roots (simi-lar to turnips), amaranths and smilax (providing shoots and seeds), and maple and honey locust sap. Two species of holly (*Ilex cassine* and *I. vomitoria*) were ingredients in a special decoction, the "black drink," which was used to induce sweating and vomiting in ceremonial and medical contexts. The economic botany of the region also encompassed a vast array of plants used for cordage, clothing, dyes, fish poisons, medicines, building materials, and various tools and utensils.

Before European colonization, the only domesticated animal in the South-east was the dog. In this region canines were used to a minor extent in hunting and as food but were probably most important as sentinels that warned of approaching strangers. In accounts of the Hernando de Soto expedition (1539–43), there are several references to small, fat, barkless dogs that were served to the Spanish visitors by their indigenous

hosts. Some of the 300 or more trail hogs that were transported by de Soto to feed his troops escaped and became the ances-tors of the modern razorback hog. The Spanish also brought horses to North America, but their use was primarily con-fined to the Southwest and Mexico; as a result, the Southeastern peoples gener-ally obtained horses at a much later date, through trade with Plains tribes.

Most of the region teemed with wild game: deer, black bears, a forest-dwelling subspecies of bison, elks, beavers, squir-rels, rabbits, otters, and raccoons. In Florida, turtles and alligators played an important part in subsistence. Wild tur-keys were the principal fowl taken, but partridges, quail, and seasonal flights of pigeons, ducks, and geese also contrib-uted to the diet. The feathers of eagles, hawks, swans, and cranes were highly val-ued for ornamentation, and in some tribes a special status was reserved for an eagle hunter.

In both salt and fresh waters a wide variety of fish were taken. Fishing equip-ment included weirs (underwater corrals or pens), traps, dip nets, dragnets, hooks and lines, bows and arrows, and spears. Botanical poisons were administered in ponds and sluggish or dammed streams, creating a rich harvest of stunned, but edible, fish. Coastal groups gathered oys-ters, clams, mussels, cockles, and crabs, while those residing in the interior col-lected freshwater mussels and crayfish.

The peoples of the Southeast altered the landscape significantly by girdling trees and by the controlled use of fire. These activities created large areas of secondary growth that favoured certain types of berry bushes and other useful plants. The presence of this secondary-growth flora was essential for supporting the large populations of browsing deer, squirrels, rabbits, and wild turkeys on which people depended for sustenance. These environmental changes, combined with hunting, probably accelerated the decline of the wood bison and in some places other species; in areas with intensive corn cultivation, such as the lower Mississippi, early European explorers reported that game animals were scarce. In the central Southeast, however, native groups maintained an equilibrated balance with nature.

TRADE

The external relations of this culture area were complex. A lack of geographic barriers to the north and west allowed significant cultural interchange with Northeastern and Plains peoples. There is evidence of overseas cultural connections with the Antilles; the dominant direction of this diffusion seems to have been from the mainland to the islands. Pre-Columbian interaction with Mesoamerican Indians, while indirect, nonetheless introduced corn, beans, and squash to the Southeast. Many scholars maintain that the building of mounds and the use of certain symbolic motifs also derive from Mesoamerica, although

some believe these were developed independently by the Mississippians and their predecessors. Culture traits such as the cane blowgun, double-weave basketry, fibre-tempered pottery, and certain musical, ritual, and mythological elements suggest at least limited contact with South American peoples as well.

As each household was fairly self-sufficient, the economic specializations and trade networks that developed tended to centre on subsidiary and luxury items. For instance, as salt deposits were unequally distributed, salt became an important trade item. There was regular trade between the coast and the interior; shells, which were used for beads and pendants and to decorate ritual objects, were exchanged for soapstone, flint, furs, and other inland resources. Pottery made with distinctive types of red clay and artifacts made of native copper suggest important trade connections with the western Great Lakes groups that controlled the locales where these raw materials were found.

SETTLEMENT PATTERNS AND HOUSING

The basic settlement unit throughout the Southeast was the local village or town. These varied in size and configuration depending on local ecological resources and cultural preferences. Some towns attained populations of more than 1,000 individuals, but the more typical village was home to fewer than 500 residents. Settlement patterns conformed to two basic types. Dispersed hamlets, each of which might contain storage buildings and a special cookhouse in addition to one or more dwellings, were arrayed along the valley bottoms or the course of streams. In contrast were tightly nucleated settlements, often surrounded with protective timber palisades. Usually each group of hamlets was associated with a palisaded town where the community as a whole gathered for celebrations and ritual events.

In general, settlements were semipermanent and located near rich alluvial soil or, in the lower Mississippi region, near natural levees. Such land was easily tilled, possessed adequate drainage, and enjoyed renewable productivity. Fertility was enhanced by burning off any stalks or vines that remained from the previous harvest. The length of the growing season in the Southeast allowed many fields to be planted twice each year. The first planting was done in spring, and some produce was available by midsummer, when a second planting was undertaken. The major harvest time, in late summer and early fall, was a time of plenty during

A Timucua village, engraving by Theodore de Bry from a drawing by Jacques Le Moyne, c. 1564; first published in 1591. Library of Congress, Washington, D.C.

which most of the major ceremonies were celebrated. Many villages emptied somewhat during the winter months, when households took to the woods in search of game; individuals with limited mobility, however, would remain at home. Men also undertook a shorter hunt in late spring and early summer, after the first crops had been planted.

The heart of a town was typically a ceremonial centre consisting of a council house or temple, which in the interior region might be semisubterranean or located on an earthen mound; a central plaza or square, which, among the Muskogean speakers, was usually surrounded by three or four benches or arbours oriented in the cardinal directions; a ball pole or scalp post sometimes topped with a carved animal emblem; the residences of the chief and other important local dignitaries; and sometimes granaries or other structures for storing communal produce.

Considerable variation in house types existed. In much of the region, people built circular, conical-roofed winter "hot houses" that were sealed tight except for an entryway and smoke hole. Summer dwellings tended to be rectangular, gabled, thatch-roofed structures made from a framework of upright poles and walled with wattle and daub. To the south, especially from the early 19th century onward, houses often had raised floors, palmetto-thatched roofs, and open sides. To the west, the Caddoans lived in domed grass houses.

POLITICAL ORGANIZATION

The picture of the Southeast that emerges at the time of first European contact is one of intensive cultural change. The final centuries before contact appear to have been a period of cultural leveling marked by considerable population movement, warfare, and the formation of chieftains. Early written reports describe the political organization of the Southeast as including independent villages, autonomous village clusters, and "tribelets," independent polities that recognized cultural connections with the other groups or polities within the same tribe. Perhaps most analogous to the many independent polities of the California Indians, tribelets generally ranged in size from about a hundred to a few thousand people, depending on the richness of locally available resources.

Generally speaking, each community was fairly autonomous. A village might be linked to others in the same area by ties of kinship, language, and shared cultural traditions; nevertheless, each claimed sovereignty over its locale and was governed by its own religio-political chiefs (during peacetime) and a complementary group of war leaders (during periods of conflict). Superordinate control at the tribal level was generally avoided, although the consolidation of tribelets into larger coalescent groups and even the formation of intertribal confederacies occurred as European settlements spread in the region.

Over most of the Southeast, religio-political chieftainship was hereditary within certain lineages. The degree of chiefly power and authority varied, however, from the almost divine kingship of the Great Sun among the theocratic Natchez to the self-effacing status of the peacemaking, consensus-seeking *micos* and *ukus* among the more egalitarian Choctaws, Creeks, and Cherokees. In contrast, war leaders normally achieved their positions on the basis of personal accomplishment. They also tended to be active and assertive personalities and younger, by about a generation, than the hereditary or "peace" chiefs.

The complementarity of peace chiefs and war leaders and the occurrence of competitive activities between neighbouring groups—including ball games, hunting contests, and trading expeditions—imbued traditional social structures with a characteristic dualism. The peace chief held sway in the village, whereas the war leader was ascendant in areas external to the village; he had authority in the village itself only when it was under the threat of imminent attack. Young men adjusted their behaviour according to the context of war or peace; they also prepared for the psychological and physical rigours of battle through extensive rituals in which war and peace were symbolically represented by the colours red and white, respectively.

Dualism was also expressed in the organization of clans, subtribes, and villages into complementary pairs, which, in turn, were sometimes characterized as red or white. Member towns of the Creek Confederacy were sometimes ranked in terms of their tribal affiliations or on the basis of outcomes of lacrosselike ball games between towns. The Caddos were said to have ranked their clans on the basis of the reputed strength of the totemic animal ancestor, creating a symbolic pecking order.

Social stratification was highly developed in some parts of the Southeast and insignificant in others. Although much has been written about the so-called caste systems among the tribes of the lower Mississippi, the Chitimachas appear to have been the only society to have possessed true castes in the sense of ranked groups that practiced strict endogamy, or marriage within the group. While not a caste system in the strict sense of the term, social stratification was nonetheless highly elaborated among the aboriginal inhabitants of Florida. Among the Timucuas, for instance, the "king" enjoyed an elevated status considerably above that of his followers and was sometimes carried about in a litter. The Natchez social hierarchy included strict rules for marriage and social status. In other tribes, such as the Cherokees, stratification was relatively unimportant, although certain clans might possess special ceremonial prerogatives and recruitment to certain offices might be determined on the basis of clan.

KINSHIP AND MARRIAGE

Among Southeastern peoples, descent was almost universally matrilineal, or reckoned through the mother. Many societies further organized kinship through matrilineal lineages or clans—extended families in which all members could claim descent from a particular ancestor or totem. For those groups that had them, clans were usually dispersed throughout a tribe or nation rather than limited to a particular village or tribelet. This arrangement provided a kind of social adhesive that crosscut and bound together the larger body politic. For instance, clan members were generally expected to offer hospitality to clan kin from other villages. Certain ritual knowledge and ceremonial privileges were also customarily passed down along clan lines. In addition, clans were important as mechanisms of social control, as vengeance for serious crimes was frequently a clan responsibility.

Marriage was often marked by a symbolic ceremonial exchange whereby the groom presented the bride with game and the bride reciprocated with plant food. Residence after marriage was normally established in the wife's natal household; the husband was expected to contribute to the economic maintenance of his wife's family as a form of bride service and to prove his abilities as a provider. After a few years the couple might leave to form their own household. Most tribes permitted (and some encouraged) premarital sexual intimacy. After marriage, however, adultery—especially on the part of the wife—could be severely punished. In contrast, divorce seems to have been a frequent and almost casual event. Polygyny, a form of marriage in which wives share a husband, was permitted in most groups; usually new partners could not join the marriage without the consent of all the extant partners. The levirate, a custom by which a widow marries her deceased husband's brother, was fairly common. Because it was a method for ensuring that each woman and her children had a male provider, levirate marriages increased with the heightened male mortality that resulted when tribes resisted colonial conquest.

The French described the elaborate rank system of the Natchez as being considerably entwined with marriage and kin customs. Natchez social hierarchy was divided into four groups: three upper classes composed hierarchically of the suns, the nobles, and the honoured people, and a lower class of commoners (whom the early French sources refer to as "stinkards"). Members of the upper classes were required to marry members of the commoner class; many commoners also married other commoners. The offspring of upper-class men would assume a rank one step below that of their fathers; for example, the child of a sun father and commoner mother would become a member of the noble class. The children of upper-class women, however, retained the rank of their mothers. Interestingly, the system described by the French would have been unstable, as all women would have been born into the upper classes after several generations. Many explanations have been advanced to explain this "Natchez paradox," but the problem probably originated in the inaccuracies or incompleteness of the original French sources.

SOCIALIZATION AND EDUCATION

Late in a woman's pregnancy, both she and the father were generally subject to various dietary taboos and restrictions on their activities. Children were nursed for several years, until they self-weaned or the mother again became pregnant. Responsibility for the child's early education was vested in the mother. As they grew older, girls were trained in duties such as the growing, preserving, and storing of food, receiving instruction from their mothers and other female relatives. Boys received instruction from their fathers and their mother's brothers; in many systems the mother's eldest brother, as the senior male in the matrilineage, assumed considerable importance as a disciplinarian, tutor, and sponsor for his sister's son.

Behaviour considered proper was reinforced with praise and encouragement, as when a boy killed his first deer or a girl completed her first basket. Behaviour considered improper was usually greeted mildly; preferred responses ranged from gentle ribbings, rebukes, and ridicule to shame. Children were rarely subjected to physical punishment. In those few instances in which corporal punishment was deemed necessary, it was generally meted out by someone other than the parents. A popular method of chastisement throughout the Southeast was the raking of the skin with briars or a special pointed scratching instrument, but generally such action was regarded as strengthening or toughening the child rather than as delivering direct retribution for misdeeds. Boys enjoyed considerable permissiveness and spent much of their time with their peers; common activities included wrestling, playing games imitative of adult activities, and stalking rabbits, squirrels, and birds with blowguns or scaled-down bows and arrows. Girls, in contrast, were subject to close surveillance and assumed household responsibilities from an early age.

Puberty rituals were either absent or relatively undeveloped in the Southeast. Girls were secluded at menarche, but this event occasioned no public celebration; all women were provided with a few days of seclusion and rest during menstruation. Similarly, no special rituals attended the transition from boyhood to manhood. A boy might receive instructions from tribal elders in esoteric lore or in preparation for special ritual offices, but the completion of such training was seldom marked by a formal commencement. A young man's first participation in a war party and the achievement of military honours were, however, given public recognition. Probably the clearest markers of the passage from adolescence to adulthood were marriage and the birth of one's first child.

BELIEF SYSTEMS

The delicate relationship between humans and the natural world is well expressed in what is known of traditional Southeast religions and worldviews. These emphasized animism, a perspective in which humans share the world with a proliferation of spiritual essences of animals, plants, and natural objects or phenomena.

The peoples of this region believed that animals possessed souls. Slain animals sought vengeance against humanity through the agency of their "species chief," a supernatural animal with great power. The Deer Chief, for instance, was able to exact revenge on humans who dishonoured his people—the deer—during the hunt. Hunting thus became a sacred act and was much imbued with taboo, ritual, and sacrifice. Most disease was attributed to failures in placating the souls of slain animals.

The plant world was considered friendly to humans, and the Cherokees thought that every animal-sent disease could be cured by a corresponding plant antidote. The economic significance of corn was memorialized by the near universality of the Green Corn ceremony, or Busk, throughout the Southeast. This was a major ceremonial suffused with an ethos of annual renewal. The sacred fire was rekindled, and often the hearth fires of each home were as well. Old debts and grudges were forgiven and forgotten, old clothing and stored food were discarded, and a sense of community was regenerated.

Spiritual power could reside in objects other than plants and animals. Medicine men possessed sacred stones, quartz crystals, and other mystically endowed paraphernalia. Other objects were consecrated to symbolize the collective solidarity of the group. The Cherokees made use of a palanquin or litter within which were placed revered objects, the Tukabahchee Creeks possessed sacred embossed copper plates, and the temples of several Lower Mississippi tribes contained an assortment of idols and icons. Natural objects could be infused with sacred power in a variety of ways, including contact with thunder, as in lightning-struck wood; immersion in a rapidly flowing stream; and exposure to the smoke of the sacred fire or of ritually prepared tobacco.

The outlines of a formal theology can be discerned from early accounts of some of the stratified societies and from those tribes that survived the immediate ravages of European contact. Most groups possessed origin myths, often involving a primal deluge into which prototypical beings plunged to secure a portion of mud that magically expanded to create the Earth, which was often viewed as an island. The subsequent course of mythological history was frequently related in terms of a cosmic struggle between a celestial culture hero who bestowed boons on humankind and an underworld antihero who became the source of the fatality and misfortune inherent in the human condition. Southeastern myths and folktales are populated by a myriad of nature spirits, monsters, tricksters, giants, and little people.

Among many tribes, evidence survives that suggests belief in a supreme being, sometimes depicted as the master of breath. This ultimate divinity was frequently associated with the sun and its earthly aspect, fire. In addition, the world was viewed as quadrisected by the cardinal directions. Each direction had a presiding spirit and appropriate colour symbolism. Concern with the remote supreme being seems to have rested more with the priesthood than with the everyday activities of the average individual. The life of the latter was more intimately tied up with the proximal spiritual beings who were felt to intervene more directly in human affairs.

In some of the wealthier stratified societies, priests were given specialized training and became full-time religious practitioners responsible for the spiritual health of the community. Priests also assumed the responsibility of conducting the major collective religious rituals that punctuated the calendrical cycle. Complementary to the priesthood were various individual magico-medical practitioners, such as sorcerers, conjurors, diviners, herbalists, and healers, who were generally part-time specialists and catered to individual needs and crises, especially the treatment of illness. Medical therapy was intricately enmeshed in the spiritual view of the world and might include such practical procedures as isolation, sweating, bathing, bloodletting, sucking, the inducement of vomiting, the internal and external application of herbal medicines, and the recitation of ritual chants.

The frequent elaboration of funerary practices, including interring the chiefly dead with great quantities of freshwater pearls and other rare materials, indicates that most groups believed in an afterlife. It was generally thought that the souls of the recently deceased would hover around the community and try to induce close friends and relatives to join them in their journey to eternity; thus, the elaborate funerary rites and the extensive taboos associated with death were as much a protection for the living as a commemoration of the dead. This was especially the case because death was never considered a natural event but was always the result of malevolent animal spirits, witches, or the deadly machinations of sorcerers. If a death had been caused by human agents, the soul of the deceased would never rest until vengeance had been secured by its living relatives. Once appeased, the soul moved to a final resting place, the location of which varied from group to group; typically, this was either in the direction of the setting sun, in the celestial firmament, or in a non-hellish part of the underworld.

CULTURAL CONTINUITY AND CHANGE

Permanent colonial settlements were not established in the Southeast until 1565, when the Spanish founded Saint Augustine in present-day Florida. Yet the peoples of the Southeast suffered greatly throughout the 16th century, essentially from the time of first contact.

THE 16TH CENTURY: EUROPEAN EXPLORATION AND CONQUEST

The earliest expeditions, by Juan Ponce de Léon (1513, 1521) and Pánfilo de Narváez (1528; best known for the narrative produced by Álvar Núñez Cabeza de Vaca), were short-lived but exposed indigenous peoples to the devastating effects of European diseases to which they had not been previously exposed. Epidemics soon decimated the native population; mortality rates for these nonimmune populations are estimated to have been as high as 50 to 90 percent (these rates generally combine deaths due directly to disease with those resulting from subsidiary causes, such as famine).

Hernando de Soto, who had proved instrumental in the conquest of the Inca (1532), was eventually commissioned by Spain to conquer La Florida; from 1539 to 1543 his expedition traveled through what are now the states of Florida, Georgia, South Carolina, North Carolina, Tennessee, Alabama, Mississippi, Arkansas, and Louisiana. Some Southeastern tribes greeted de Soto as they would a paramount chief, offering food, tribute of pearls and copper, sexual access to women, and porters. Other towns in de Soto's path attacked the expedition. However, as the Spanish group included some 600 to 700 heavily armed professional soldiers, the conquistadors' counteroffenses left few settlements intact.

By the close of the 16th century, several factors had combined to disrupt traditional life in the Southeast. Thousands of individuals were killed during direct warfare with explorers. European diseases caused thousands more deaths. The subsidiary effects of these losses further devastated the Southeast: Groups with too few people to plant and hunt were forced into starvation or refugee status; much practical and ritual knowledge was lost; and indigenous political structures were weakened. The final and perhaps least well-known factor was the trade in indigenous slaves, who were generally captured by rival triblets and sold to the Spanish for export to New England, the Caribbean, and elsewhere. Many groups on the coast and in the piedmont lost their political or social viability during this period; their surviving members generally became part of larger, more powerful tribes such as the Choctaw, Cherokee, or various member tribes of the Creek Confederacy.

THE 17TH CENTURY: MISSIONIZATION

During the 17th century, trade, particularly in deerskins, grew tremendously, as did indigenous reliance on European firearms and ammunition. European exploration of the inland Southeast generally ceased, and colonial settlement began in earnest on the coasts. The most important development in this century, however, was the establishment of missions and the propagation of Roman Catholicism among native peoples. Jesuits attempted to missionize coastal Georgia and South Carolina in 1565–66 but abandoned those areas after several friars were killed. Spain replaced the Jesuits with Franciscans in 1573. By 1700, more than 100 missions had been established in northern Florida and southern Georgia, particularly among the Timucua, Guale, and Apalachee peoples. Reports to Spain describe these groups as almost entirely Christianized by 1670.

The Southeastern missions drew (or were assigned) fewer Spanish soldiers and civilians than missions in other areas; their absence allowed the friars to proceed with their work unhindered by the rapes, kidnappings, and beatings that such individuals commonly visited upon native peoples elsewhere. The indigenous power structures of the region had been weakened, and the surviving hereditary chiefs and war leaders had proved incapable of ending the losses caused by disease, warfare, and slavery. As they were accustomed to accepting leadership that combined religion and politics, many people realized that allying themselves with the Franciscans would afford a measure of protection against further military and slaving raids. They may have also hoped that the presence of a new deity would bring some relief from disease. Finally, the friars themselves were careful to limit their mandate to those aspects of culture that were overtly religious, such as baptism and attendance at mass. Other aspects were left alone and might incorporate Christianity (or not) depending upon the wishes of a given community. Among the Apalachee, for instance, the late-summer Busk quickly incorporated celebrations of the feast day of San Luis Rey, which occurred at the same time of year.

In 1706 the last missions were abandoned because of the conflicts that were arising between Europe's imperial powers. However, the friars' work was enduring; during the 20th century, many indigenous groups from the Southeast persisted in practicing more or less syncretic religions that combined indigenous and Catholic practices, as well as preparing the ground for later conversion to Protestant sects.

THE 18TH CENTURY: INTERNATIONAL TURMOIL

By the late 17th century the indigenous peoples of the Southeast (and the Northeast) found themselves increasingly drawn into foreign struggles over the control of Europe and North America. Local theatres of war and their instigating European conflicts included King William's War (1689–97) and Europe's War of the Grand Alliance (1689–97); Queen Anne's War (1702–13) and the War of the Spanish Succession (1701–14); King George's War (1744–48) and the War of the Austrian Succession (1740–48); and the French and Indian War (1754–63) and the Seven Years' War (1756–63). The American Revolution (1775–83), in which France, Spain, and The Netherlands supported the colonies in their fight against England, was yet another conflict with at least some origins in European politics.

By the early 18th century many smaller indigenous groups had merged with larger tribes, and especially with major groups such as the Creeks, Chickasaws, Choctaws, and Cherokees. Each of these large polities engaged in alliances with the European powers, and they often found themselves pitted against one another. Indigenous communities soon realized that trade and diplomatic relations with Spain, France, and England were intertwined and could be manipulated to their advantage; the Creeks found it especially profitable to set the three imperial powers against one another.

By mid-century, however, the Southeastern Indians' ascendancy in trade, military might, and diplomacy was being overshadowed by an increasing mass of European immigrants. Many were fleeing homelands torn by war; some were fleeing religious persecution;

and others sought to escape depressed economies or were transported as punishment for petty crimes. The colonizing population in the Southeast alone had grown from perhaps 50,000 Europeans in 1690 to approximately 1 million individuals by 1790; the enslaved African population in the region grew from about 3,000 to 500,000 during the same period.

Previous colonizers had built most of their settlements near the swampy, malarial wetlands of the Atlantic and Gulf coasts; most Southeastern peoples found these locations relatively undesirable. As coastal locales could not support the enormous increase in European and African populations, an inland development boom ensued. This ultimately proved more dangerous to the Southeastern tribes than epidemics or war.

THE EARLY 19TH CENTURY: FORCED REMOVAL

During the first 300 years of colonization, the Southeastern peoples had adopted what new practices they found useful without completely altering their traditional cultures. This was a very successful strategy, and they often became the owners of large, prosperous farms and plantations. As the pressure to cede land to settlers increased, the tribes opted to negotiate with the nascent United States in the belief that treaties and other agreements would be enforced by this government, as they had by Spain, England, and France.

The land hunger of the burgeoning Euro-American population was fierce. Tensions were heightened by the envy that those building new farms had for those with established operations; the latter were almost all members of the Creek, Cherokee, Choctaw, or Chickasaw tribes, who with the Seminoles became known as the Five Civilized Tribes. The Seminoles were a multiethnic group that included Creek and other native refugees who had fled the mid-18th-century conflicts, as well as Africans and African Americans who had escaped slavery.

The settlers' desire for more land and their envy at indigenous prosperity caused them to agitate for oppressive Indian policies. Violence eventually erupted in the form of the Seminole Wars. The first war (1817–18) was fought in part to defend individuals of African descent from capture and a return to enslavement. American forces led by Andrew Jackson invaded northern Florida, kidnapped a few individuals, and destroyed many Seminole settlements. In response, the tribe moved south and rebuilt their society.

The Cherokees preferred to use legal strategies to maintain their property and the political independence guaranteed them by treaty. Sequoyah's 1821 invention of a syllable-based writing system for the Cherokee language enabled the wide circulation of a draft Cherokee constitution; tribal members voted to adopt the new constitution in 1827. At the same time, settler agitation regarding the primacy of state versus tribal sovereignty was accelerated by the discovery of gold within the Cherokee Nation lands, and the Georgia legislature, in turn, passed a law extending state authority to tribal lands. Many Euro-Americans felt that tribes should not be allowed to maintain separate governments within state boundaries. Instead, they proposed that tribal members choose between regular citizenship or tribal sovereignty. Indians could either give up the protections provided by treaty agreements or remove themselves to territories outside the states. The Cherokees saw this as a vacuous argument, as their sovereign status was very clearly delineated in the treaties they had negotiated with the federal government. They chose to file suit against the state in federal court.

While the Cherokee lawsuit moved through the judicial system, the United States Congress passed the Indian Removal Act (1830). This enabled the government to designate as Indian Territory land in the trans-Mississippi West. This created a process through which land in the new territory would be exchanged for tribal land in the East and provided funds for the transportation of tribes to the new domain.

The native peoples of the Southeast responded in different ways to the realpolitik of this event. The Choctaw agreed to removal relatively quickly, hoping to leave the conflict behind them. Federal corruption and incompetence ensured that their journey was poorly

Massacre of the Whites by the Indians and Blacks in Florida, woodcut from An Authentic Narrative of the Seminole War, *by Daniel F. Blanchard, 1836*. Library of Congress, Washington, D.C.

provisioned, however; inadequate food, sanitation, shelter, and transport caused many deaths.

In the meantime, *Cherokee Nation* v. *Georgia* had made its way to the United States Supreme Court. In 1831 the court decided that indigenous peoples living within the United States were no longer independent nations and that as a domestic sovereign nation—in other words, one that depended upon the United States to uphold its political independence—the Cherokees had no right to sue in the federal court system.

A related suit, *Worcester* v. *Georgia*, involved a Euro-American missionary who refused to take a state loyalty oath and visited native property without the necessary state permit. The Supreme Court decision, made in 1832, stated that

the right to regulate tribal affairs was exclusive to the federal government—states had no similar right to extend their laws to the tribes. President Andrew Jackson refused to enforce the *Worcester* decision. This allowed the states to enact further legislation damaging to the tribes. Notably, these two cases have formed the basis for most subsequent Indian law in the United States.

The Creeks agreed to removal in 1832, but delays in their departure resulted in great hardship on their journey westward. A few Seminole leaders signed an agreement of removal in 1832, but the majority of tribal members declared that the agreement was not binding and refused to go; this provoked the Second Seminole War (1835–42), a conflict that the Seminoles eventually lost, with many being forcibly removed to the west.

Learning of the hardships suffered by other indigenous groups, most of the Chickasaw tribelets took matters into their own hands. Many of these groups sold their land at a profit and moved west in the late 1830s. Having for the most part planned, provisioned, and paid for the journey themselves, they fared better than other tribes. Their journey was difficult nonetheless, and they suffered many casualties from smallpox and malnourishment.

Most Cherokees refused to depart, and many were forced from their homes at gunpoint beginning in 1837. In the most infamous of the forced relocations conducted under the Removal Act, some 15,000 Cherokee were evicted and marched westward on a harrowing journey causing the deaths of some 4,000 of their people.

The Removal Act was enforced throughout the "Eastern Woodlands" region, and very few native individuals remained there after 1840, with some notable exceptions: groups of Seminoles in Florida; the Eastern band of Cherokees in North Carolina; some Catawbas and many Lumbees in the piedmont area of North and South Carolina; the Poarch Creeks in eastern Alabama; the Mississippi Choctaws; the Tunicas and Chitimachas of Louisiana; small remnant groups in the coastal Carolinas; and, scattered throughout the Southeast, innumerable unrecognized groups claiming Indian descent. In all, historical demographers estimate that some 100,000 people from the so-called Eastern Woodlands were forced from their homelands and that some 15,000 died while on what has become known as the Trail of Tears.

THE LATE 19TH CENTURY AND BEYOND: FIGHTING TO REGAIN SOVEREIGNTY

Once in Indian Territory (present-day Oklahoma), the Five Civilized Tribes worked to rebuild their economies. Most individuals focused on farming, with some providing other services such as blacksmithing. Economic revitalization was very successful, but it was later interrupted by the Civil War. Surrounded by states committed to the war, Indian Territory became a crossroads of conflict. Many residents suffered at the hands of the Union and Confederate armies. People were assaulted, farms and outbuildings burned, and crops and livestock stolen, destroyed, or dispersed. After the war, the tribes worked to rebuild their communities yet again. The United States, having allowed indigenous owners to retain slaves during removal, now insisted that all former slaves be freed and recognized as official members of the tribes of their owners. Known as freedmen, this population experienced various phases of acceptance and rejection from others in the Native American community, and their status remained controversial in the early 21st century.

During Reconstruction (1865–77), conflicts in the West resulted in the movement of a large number of displaced Plains tribes and others from their traditional homelands to Indian Territory. The United States took land assigned to groups already resident in the territory and transferred it to the newcomers. By the 1890s, continued Euro-American land hunger had resulted in allotment, a federal policy under which land held in common by tribes was divided into parcels and dispersed. Each indigenous head of household was assigned a parcel, as were orphans and a few other categories of individuals. The remaining land was made available to settlers, railroads, and others for development. Although the Five Civilized Tribes were immune from the initial enforcement of the new policy because they held clear title to their property, an act of Congress brought them under allotment jurisdiction in 1898. Like the other indigenous residents of the territory, they lost tens of thousands of acres.

Under policies initiated in 1906, indigenous peoples lost the right to elect their own tribal governments, which were replaced by federally appointed chiefs and tribal councils. The administration of schools and other institutions formerly managed by the tribes of Indian Territory also devolved to the United States. With allotment, these policies paved the way for Euro-American settlement of the territory and thus for statehood. In 1907 Indian Territory and Oklahoma Territory combined to become the new state of Oklahoma.

These and other pressures on traditional culture were clear abrogations of tribal sovereignty, but tribes from the Southeast culture area saw just as clearly that fighting them head-on would prove unproductive. As a result, many engaged in passive resistance. Families refused to sign up for or receive their allotments; former tribal council members revitalized traditional governance and ritual activities away from the geographic seats of power; and children were schooled at home. Ironically, the United States' efforts to complete the assimilation of the Southeastern peoples had resulted in a grassroots movement that strengthened traditional cultures considerably.

During the remainder of the 20th century, Southeastern peoples were affected by a number of events of global importance, such as the oil boom of the 1920s; the Great Depression; the World Wars and the Korean, Vietnam, and Gulf wars; and the advent of the civil rights and counterculture eras of the 1960s. In 1968 three Southeastern groups that had long been in bureaucratic limbo allied themselves to gain greater traction with the federal government. They included groups that had escaped removal—Cherokee communities in North Carolina and Seminole groups in Florida—as well as a tribelet of Choctaw that had traveled only as far as the state of Mississippi during removal. Having avoided removal and undertaken efforts to escape governmental scrutiny, they had seen many of their rights as native peoples abridged;

their efforts eventually led to federal recognition of their status as tribes.

During the 1970s the federal government relinquished the right to appoint tribal governments. The Southeastern tribes quickly reinstated their constitutions and held elections. From that point into the early 21st century, the Southeast nations emphasized economic development, the revenues of which were used to support programs ranging from education to health care to cultural preservation. For instance, Chickasaw Nation Industries and Choctaw Management Services Enterprise, each owned by its constituent tribe, included firms providing construction, information technology services, and professional recruiting. The Florida Seminole instituted ecotourism programs that acquainted visitors with the state's wetlands. Many tribes also turned to casino-based gaming; these operations often included hotel and restaurant facilities that generated income and provided employment to tribal members. Casino revenue, sometimes referred to as "the new buffalo," lifted many tribes above the poverty line and encouraged a revival of traditional cultural practices.

CHAPTER 7

NATIVE AMERICAN ART

The visual arts of the aboriginal inhabitants of the Americas is also called Indian art, or American Indian art. All of these terms are problematic at some level. The very use of the word *art* suggests one of the basic differences between European or European-derived and American Indian concepts.

THE ROLE OF THE ARTIST

Not only did few Indian groups allow art to become a major way of life, as in the West, but many Native American languages even lack a term meaning "art" or "artist." If one wished to refer to a beautiful basket or a well-carved sculpture, it was usually necessary to rely upon such terms as "well-done," "effective," or perhaps "powerful" (in the magical sense). And the concept of an artist was largely of a person who was simply better at the job than was another. Generally, artists were accorded special significance only where wealth was a major factor in the culture. The elite of many cultures, whether wealthy in their own right or (more commonly) by having attained a high religious office, supported groups of artists who produced memorial and religious art. Although Indian people may not have considered artistic skill in terms of a vocation, the difference between a well-woven basket and a careless piece of work or a particularly well-designed carving and a crudely made example did not go unnoticed. Fine workmanship commanded a premium long before European contact, and with the advent of the monetary system, it was even more highly prized.

The basic role of the American Indian artist is the same as that of the artist in any culture—to arouse an emotional response in his audience. In Native American cultures, the artist's ability to communicate successfully depended largely upon the recognition of the force of tradition. The social organization of the various tribes allowed less latitude for experimentation than Western cultures and usually compelled the artist to work in familiar channels. Yet, within this rigid framework of tradition, there was sometimes a surprising degree of freedom of expression. There are recorded instances of individuals having made considerable changes in the art (and the economy) of their tribes. In North America, perhaps the most striking have been the careers of Nampeyó (1859?–1942), the famed Hopi potter, and María Martínez (1881?–1980) and Julián Martínez (1897–1943), of San Ildefonso pueblo. Through sheer individual talent these people achieved a personal triumph by developing a style that not only was copied by other artists but in time also was regarded as "traditional" in that particular village. Although there is no way of knowing how often this happened in the past, there are suggestions that it occurred at Mimbres, among the Haida slate carvers, and quite possibly in some areas of the so-called Mound Builder cultures of the Southeast.

ORIGINS OF DESIGNS

The origins of most Native American decorative designs cannot be traced accurately today; most of them are lost in antiquity. Many obviously came from natural forms, while others are simple developments of geometric or lineal motifs. Some have become so interwoven with alien concepts—Western, after the advent of the European, for example—that it is impossible to completely unravel their sources. There is evidence, however, that some of the original forms were creations of individual artists and were often the result of a vision quest. To the Indian, the world of the vision quest is mysterious, a place where the soul can leave the body, participate in many strange activities, and see many unusual sights. Since many of the designs seen or creatures encountered during the vision quest are regarded as protective forms or spirit-beings, these would be carefully re-created during waking hours. Non-artists would occasionally describe their dream creatures to a designated artist so that they could be recorded on hide, in wood, or in stone. But since these supernatural visions were extremely personal, they were usually recorded by the individual himself; hence they vary tremendously in aesthetic quality.

Because art designs were regarded as personal property, an artist could buy a design or receive it as a gift from its creator, but to appropriate and use it for his own purposes was taboo.

VISION QUEST

Vision quests are supernatural experiences in which an individual seeks to interact with a guardian spirit, usually an anthropomorphized animal, to obtain advice or protection. They are most typical among the native peoples of North and South America.

The specific techniques for attaining visions varied from tribe to tribe, as did the age at which the first quest was to be undertaken, its length and intensity, and the expected form of the guardian spirit's presence or sign. In some tribes nearly all young people traditionally engaged in some form of vision quest, as participation in the experience was one of the rituals marking an individual's transition from childhood to adulthood. In other groups vision questing was undertaken only by males, with menarche and childbirth as the analogous experiences for females. Some groups, notably in South America, limited vision quests and guardian spirits to shamans (religious personages with powers of healing and psychic transformation).

Usually an individual's first vision quest was preceded by a period of preparation with a religious specialist. The quest itself typically involved going to an isolated location and engaging in prayer while forgoing food and drink for a period of up to several days. Some cultures augmented fasting and prayer with hallucinogens. In some traditions the participant would watch for an animal that behaved in a significant or unusual way. In others, the participant discovered an object (often a stone) that resembled some animal. In the predominant form, the initiate had a dream (the vision) in which a spirit-being appeared. Upon receiving a sign or vision, the participant returned home and sought help in interpreting the experience. Not all vision quests were successful; religious specialists generally advised individuals to abandon a given attempt if a vision was not received within a prescribed period of time.

The techniques of the vision quest were fundamental to every visionary experience in Native American culture, whether undertaken by ordinary people seeking contact with and advice from a guardian or by great prophets and shamans. It was not unusual for vision quests to be integral parts of more elaborate rituals such as the Sun Dance of the Plains Indians.

Despite having been heavily discouraged by Christian missionaries and even outlawed by colonial governments during the 19th and 20th centuries, vision quest participation continued as an important cultural practice for many indigenous peoples into the early 21st century.

THE FUNCTION OF ART

Many Indian art objects are basically intended to perform a service—for example, to act as a container or provide a means of worship. The particular utilitarian form that Native American arts take often reflects the social organization of the cultures involved. Political and military societies seem to have found their major art forms in the world of weaponry, regalia, and panoply. This is most pronounced in the Plains, Aztec, and Inca civilizations, all of which reflect the dominant warrior culture in their arts. Those cultures in which life was heavily governed by religion tended toward a greater degree of ceremonial art than those in which life was less ritualized. All of the aesthetic expressions that have come down from the Maya, for example, obviously reflect the considerable weight of theocracy that existed in their world.

Generally, but not necessarily, the best of Indian artwork was applied to those objects intended to please a deity, soothe the angry gods, placate or frighten the evil spirits, and honour the newly born or recently deceased. Through such means, Native Americans sought to control the environment and the human or supernatural beings that surrounded or threatened them.

Some specific articles were reserved solely for religious uses, and some were for secular needs alone. Decoration does not always provide a clue as to these uses. Some of the most highly revered religious articles are completely devoid of ornamentation—in fact, they may be rather ugly—while others are highly embellished. Some peoples used plainware bowls for food preparation, while others used polychrome bowls for the same purpose. Many objects served a dual function. Normally, they were used for everyday household purposes, yet under a different set of circumstances they could fulfill a religious function.

Beneath the surface, there was a magic at work, and, in initiated hands, a mundane article might release its supernatural power, calling upon unseen forces to aid its owner. This power might be visually evident in the form, shape, or decoration of the object or might simply be believed in no matter what the physical state or appearance of the object might be. A Crow warrior's rawhide shield, for example, might be embellished with a symbolic drawing, as well as with such materials as sacred eagle feathers and a crane's head, in order to imbue him with such qualities as invulnerability and supernatural swiftness and strength.

The aim of the Indian artist was not merely to set down realistic records but to create the semi-magical designs so common in the art of non-Western cultures. He quickly realized that he could not draw a tree as perfectly as it could be made by the Creator; so, with common sense, he did not try. Instead, he sought the spirit or essence of the tree and represented this in his design. Carvings, paintings, effigies, or realistic portraits are not simply pictures of people or objects; they embody the essence of that particular subject as well. This semi-magical character of Native American art is difficult for the Western mind to understand. Not infrequently, the non-Indian will ask, "What does that design mean?" Native Americans often attach names to designs, largely for convenience. Viewers may be confused when an Indian calls a given design a "leaf," or an "arrowhead," when what he actually means is that the design is "leaflike," or "leaf-shaped," and so on. But the non-Indian immediately translates this to mean that the design signifies a leaf or an arrowhead and tries to impart a narrative to the overall visual concept that is not relevant to the original artist's work.

Ritual was often interwoven into the very process of creating Indian art. Western assessment of Native American art often centres on the product rather than the process; Indian artists, however, give exacting attention to the creative process and interact with their materials at all stages of creation. The Iroquois False Face mask, for example, must be carved from the trunk of a living tree—hence the term *live mask*. The tree is ritually addressed before the carver begins, and the mask and the tree are "fed" tobacco before the two are separated. Such prescribed ritual is of equal, if not more, importance than the artistic skill employed in the production of the work. If the ceremonial acts were ignored, the article would lose its efficacy—and might even prove dangerously counteractive. This ritual aspect, which permeates most of the ceremonial paraphernalia, is extremely complex and must be considered throughout the creation of the work of art.

Not all Indian art, however, was religious or political. There was also a considerable amount of mundane, humorous, and even profane art produced by most cultures. Although much of the eroticism has disappeared in the Puritan fires that continue to burn the Westerner, sufficient examples remain from prehistoric and recent times to indicate a wholly relaxed freedom of expression reflecting a healthy, naturalistic outlook.

MATERIALS

Working in the materials natural to their respective homelands, the various Native American cultures produced art that reflected their environment. Those peoples living in heavily forested regions, for example, inevitably became gifted sculptors in wood; those for whom clay was a major resource became skillful potters; and those living in the grasslands became fine basket weavers. There is virtually no natural medium that has not been explored and mastered by the Indian: jade, turquoise, shell, metals, stone, milkweed fibre, birch bark, porcupine quills, deer hair, llama dung, sea lion whiskers—all were used by the artist to lend colour or texture to the finished product.

In many instances, such materials became desired commodities in themselves, to be traded over great distances, for certain objects were not regarded as "official" unless they were manufactured from a prescribed material. A substitute could not be tolerated, especially when the materials were to be used for religious purposes. Often, in such cases, the materials achieved a standard value within the economy, with ready acceptance as a medium of exchange wherever they were in vogue.

The relationship between material and design in Indian art was quite different from that in the Western tradition.

Iroquois shoulder bag made of buckskin and decorated with porcupine quills and deer hair, c. 1750; in the Linden-Museum für Völkerkunde, Stuttgart, Ger. By courtesy of the Linden-Museum für Völkerkunde, Stuttgart, Germany

Cree birch bark container with scraped-surface motifs, c. 1870. Height about 7.5 inches (19 cm). Courtesy of the Denver Art Museum

The Western painter usually imposed a design on the artificially limited surface of a flat, rectangular canvas; and the sculptor, following predetermined spatial arrangements, imposed a shape on his material. On the other hand, the Indian painter and sculptor were less likely to force their materials to conform to a preconceived design. They tended instead to adapt their design to the natural outlines of their materials, which often happened to be a complete and therefore irregular buffalo hide, a tree branch, or a stone. This naturalism is one of the most pleasing aspects of Indian art and often demonstrates the artist's remarkable ability to incorporate the natural form into his composition.

REGIONAL STYLES OF AMERICAN INDIAN VISUAL ARTS

The term *Native American art* covers an extremely broad category, encompassing all art expressions of the original inhabitants of the Americas and their cognate descendants. It thus includes not only varied and completely disparate cultures, but also spans great time sequences—from the early 21st century back to prehistoric times. (Surviving artifacts clearly demonstrate that ancient man was already possessed of considerable aesthetic ability; flint, for example, was carefully flaked into attractive, well-balanced forms, and stone carving and pottery were capably handled.)

Although the dissimilarities between the artistic expressions of different cultures and different times are great, there are also similarities, for the borrowing of art forms from distant and occasionally alien peoples was a common practice. Objects in museum collections reveal, for example, that ornamental materials such as feathers, shells, jade, and turquoise were traded or transported thousands of miles. This far-flung trade expanded the limits of tribal styles, for new ideas were diffused as well as materials. In time, new designs and motifs became part of the stylistic concepts and traditions of people to whom they had been introduced. Intertribal marriage, too, affected regional styles. While in some tribes marriage within the group was required, in others it was forbidden. In the latter case, artistic traditions could spread to the new group, into which they were subsequently incorporated.

It is becoming increasingly evident that there were common forces at work in the art of various groups, even if widespread in time and space. There are certain symbols that are widely encountered, and some would seem to have had similar significance over a wide area. It is likely that trade routes or political hegemony levied the major influences upon this phenomenon. In Middle America, for example, the so-called Plumed Serpent motif is to be found in one form or another in almost every culture, and this motif extends even into the United States, where it is encountered in visual form as well as in legend. Certain customs also have enjoyed wide acceptance; for example, the role of trophy heads, the use of masked personations, and winter solstice New Fire ceremonies. And each of these customs was accompanied by related visual art expressions.

Despite the similarities between the art forms of different cultural groups and different times, one cannot speak of Indian art as though it were a single concept. Just as there were several hundred native languages, dialects, and speech forms, so were there an equal number of tribal styles, motifs, and design forms. In trying to establish a common aesthetic bond, the well-schooled researcher generally finds as many differences as he does similarities.

When two completely different peoples move into a common area, such as occurred with the migration of the Athabaskan Navajo into the Pueblo Southwest, the eventual result may be a melding of cultures, the loss of certain ancient individualities—since each contributes to the new expression—and the emergence of new aesthetic qualities. It is not certain just how skilled the Navajo weavers were when they arrived in the

Classic Navajo blanket, c. 1855–65; in the Newark Museum, New Jersey. About 43 × 61 inches (110 × 156 cm). Collection of the Newark Museum, New Jersey

Southwest, but the Pueblo people, particularly the Hopi, were highly developed in that art. Subsequently, the Navajo not only learned new weaving techniques and designs but, in time, also improved upon the acquired Pueblo methods, transferred the gender role of the weaver from male to female, and matured as far more sophisticated artisans.

On the other hand, under the same circumstances, surprising differences can sometimes be found. For example, while the Hopi and Zuni people live almost side by side and under similar cultural conditions, it is quite possible to identify the art products of both groups without great difficulty. This is equally true of cultures in ancient times, such as the Aztec and Mayan or, in another time and another region, the Sioux and the Crow.

It is in those tribes or cultural entities that at one time were part of a whole but have subsequently split off that one most often finds common themes, art elements, and cultural patterns so similar as to be confusing.

The aesthetic products of North American prehistory are perhaps the least well known to the non-Indian public. This is partly because these early people left few spectacular architectural ruins as compared with their Latin American cousins. This is not to say that architectural monuments did not exist. Spanish accounts report that great temple mounds were in use in the Southeast at the time of the first European entry, in the mid-16th century. But most of these structures were of perishable wood and have long since disappeared—as have most examples of the great use of colour and the tremendous range of textiles. So many materials were perishable that scholars have little by which to judge their arts and must, in effect, draw conclusions about a people by only a small proportion of their achievement.

SOUTHWEST

In the Southwest, the monumental stone cliff dwellings that remain are eloquent

NAVAJO WEAVING

Traditional Navajo rug, c. 1900; Taylor Collection, Hastings, Eng. Richard Erdoes/ Alpha

The Navajo, formerly a seminomadic tribe, settled in the southwestern United States in the 10th and 11th centuries and were well established by 1500. With a new life as a sedentary and agricultural people, the tribe began to practice weaving, which had been virtually unknown to them, learning from the Hopi how to build looms and construct fabrics on a large scale. The introduction of domestic sheep by Europeans revolution-ized weaving by making a steady supply of wool available, and the Navajo began to raise sheep for wool.

The Hopi had limited their designs to striped patterns, but the Navajo introduced geometric shapes, diamonds, lozenges, and zigzags. Symbolic representations of such phenomena as the elements, the seasons, and the times of day did not develop until about 1820. Mexican design influenced Navajo weaving.

Before 1800, Navajo blankets were largely made of natural-coloured wool—black, white, and a mixture of the two that produced gray; a limited amount of dyeing was done, with roots, herbs, and minerals from the rich soil of the area, primarily producing dark colours, like those of the Hopi. Shortly after the turn of the 19th century, however, red bayeta cloth purchased from the Spaniards was unraveled and the thread used to make Navajo textiles. The introduction of aniline dyes in the late 19th cen-tury led to a period in Navajo weaving characterized by bright and even gaudy designs. Vividly coloured yarns were used to weave into the rugs and blankets a broad range of decora-tive motifs based on commonplace modern objects; representations of automobiles, bottles, tomato cans, and airplanes, for example, found their way into the formerly dignified and restrained fabrics.

More traditional, geometric designs subsequently regained their popularity and are once again the dominant patterns. Blankets and rugs made by the Navajo are thought to be some of the most colourful and best-made textiles produced by North American Indians. Weaving remains a vital aspect of contemporary Navajo community life and of its economy.

testimony to the culture that existed there. Progressing from a simple pit house through aboveground homes, these people moved out onto the plateau regions of what are now Arizona and New Mexico and built remarkable multistoried structures, some—such as Pueblo Bonito in New Mexico—sheltering hundreds of families in more than 400 rooms.

These apartment houses were well suited for the demands of their environment; their walls were of stone or clay and sand mixed as an adobe. The thick stone walls provided excellent insulation, being warm in winter and cool in summer. Heights reached to seven stories, although most villages were of three or four levels.

Major divisions of these early Southwestern Indians include the Hohokam of southern Arizona, the Ancestral Pueblo (Anasazi) of northern Arizona–New Mexico, and the Mogollon of southwestern New Mexico. In addition to these groups—each of which produced a style of its own, distinct from all others—were dozens of lesser subgroups that archaeologists have been studying for decades in an effort to assemble the pieces of this giant jigsaw puzzle.

The people living in the pueblos produced some of the most successful artwork. They were masters of weaving, painting, and particularly of pottery making. Their weaving techniques long antedated the arrival of Spanish sheep; a native cotton provided ample fibre for intricate weaves coloured with native dyes. Mineral and vegetable pigments provided colourful decorations when applied with a fibre brush to wood or clay or to white-plastered walls in a fresco technique. Fortunately, abundant kaolin deposits yielded high-quality clay for the creation of excellent pottery forms. Although small stone effigies have been found, sculpture was not a highly developed art form. Pueblo art is essentially linear or geometric in design and reveals a preference for applied decoration. The large underground kivas (rooms used for religious purposes) were decorated with murals executed in brilliant mineral-pigment colours.

Pueblo art became a strongly conventionalized art, held to relatively rigid forms. This characteristic was determined, no doubt, by the closely knit communal nature of a culture that depended upon close cooperation for survival. At its best, early Southwestern art is marked by technical competence and fine control of line and form; but it reflected little experimentation, tending more to rework established patterns in many intricate designs.

In the Southwest the arts flourished and are still active forces in the lives of the peoples who practice them. Almost all of the crafts practiced in prehistoric times are still practiced today, along with some newly introduced expressions. The early trade routes brought new ideas to the Pueblos, encouraging the development of new creations and the strengthening of new markets. Yet, because of its essential conservatism, Pueblo art, like the culture in which

it thrives, remain[...]
ancient antecede[...]

Along the s[...]
invading tribes f[...]
ticularly the Na[...]
subsequently se[...]
and in time sur[...]
certain arts that [...]
upon, and made [...]
versmithing an[...]
Pueblo weavers [...]
tile field, the w[...]
inventive Navajo [...]
sought after in [...]
Silversmithing, [...]
art, is more recen[...]
the first Navajo s[...]
his craft, but w[...]
Navajo jewelry ar[...]
wide appreciatio[...]

As in the prehistoric era, south-western sculpture has failed to develop as a major art form. The most active sculptural work in the Southwest is reflected in the carved and painted cottonwood kachina (*katsina*) dolls of the Hopi and Zuni, which have enjoyed wide popularity as collectors' items. Many variations of these wood carvings are also found in altar and shrine figurines, which are not produced for commercial consumption.

The crafts of basketry and pottery are moderately active, but very little pottery is made for native use. It is largely intended for the outside market. Although both pottery and basketry are produced in much smaller quantities than they were after first European contact, the quality of contemporary work is consistently high.

Wooden Hopi kachina doll, c. 1925; in the George Gustav Heye Center of the National Museum of the American Indian, New York City. Height 25 inches (64 cm). By courtesy of the Museum of the American Indian, Heye Foundation, New York.

Specialization has long been a factor in Southwestern art and has become increasingly so in recent years. Certain tribes produce almost all of the small carved fetishes, or tiny drilled shell and stone beads. The Zuni favour intricately worked silver jewelry with tiny turquoise settings, while the Navajo make use of massive silver castings with heavy turquoise sets. The Navajo also make most of the heavy rugs and textiles, while the Hopi supply lightweight ceremonial kilts, sashes, and similar costume fabrics.

Another art form that may have been brought from the north, but that was more likely adopted from Pueblo culture, is sand painting (more accurately termed dry painting). The use of a variety of finely ground mineral pigments, which are allowed to trickle through the fingers to form a variety of complicated patterns, has become uniquely Navajo. These designs provide a focus for curing ceremonies.

MIDWEST AND GREAT PLAINS

The existence of rich textile art in the prehistoric Middle West is known, but its range and development are lost in hundreds of years of history from which few examples survive. Examples of basketry and wood are similarly rare. Enough of these perishable items have survived to indicate that these arts had been mastered, but not enough examples remain to enable scholars to judge their aesthetic development. What has survived in profusion is stone, worked skillfully and in many ways. Pottery, too, though not of highest quality, and copper and mica ornaments have been found.

Of the relatively perishable substances, finely carved and incised shell is common, which, along with bone, indicates the artistic range of these early peoples. The quantity of objects found is impressive. Numerically significant groups, the peoples of the region were active in the production of materials and implements with which to meet the challenge of their environment. Scholars cannot determine the function of all the recovered examples of stonework, but it is known that much of the archaeological wealth was ceremonial in nature, indicating a highly organized civilization.

Ritual structures existed, such as the so-called effigy mounds—great piles of earth fashioned to represent a variety of animals. The Serpent Mound in Ohio is an example of this custom. Truncated pyramids served as large bases for wooden temples, now long vanished but still in use when Spanish explorers first entered the region. Monks Mound, dominating the Cahokia Mounds, near Collinsville, Ill., is the largest prehistoric earthen construction in the New World.

Major cultural expressions from this region included those of the Adena, Hopewell, Oneota, and Old Copper culture peoples. Their art was extensive, making great use of sculptured stone pipes, polished ornaments of both stone and copper, and incised shell decorations.

The later Great Plains region is the area most familiar to the average non-Indian, for this is the world of the Buffalo Bill shows, television and movie programs, and fiction. From it came the buckskin and beadwork costumes, feathered warbonnets, colourful porcupine quill decoration, and painted shields that

SAND PAINTING

Sometimes known as dry painting, sand painting is a type of art that exists in highly developed forms among the Navajo and Pueblo Indians of the American Southwest and in simpler forms among several Plains and California Indian tribes. Although sand painting can be considered an art form in the aesthetic sense, it is valued among Native Americans primarily for religious reasons. Its main function is in connection with healing ceremonies.

Sand paintings are stylized, symbolic pictures prepared by trickling small quantities of crushed, coloured sandstone, charcoal, pollen, or other dry materials in white, blue, yellow, black, and red hues on a background of clean, smoothed sand. About 600 different pictures are known, consisting of various representations of deities, animals, lightning, rainbows, plants, and other symbols described in the chants that accompany various rites. In healing, the choice of the particular painting is left to the curer. Upon completion of the picture, the patient sits on the centre of the painting, and sand from the painting is applied to parts of his body. When the ritual is completed, the painting is destroyed.

For years the Indians would not allow permanent, exact copies of sand paintings to be made. When the designs were copied in rugs, an error was deliberately made so that the original design would retain its unique power. Today many of the paintings have been copied both to preserve the art and for the record.

personify the American Indian in the minds of most people.

Yet, there was no monolithic culture. The arts of the Plains Indian varied considerably from tribe to tribe; some peoples seem to have had superior aesthetic taste, demonstrated by their sensitive and inventive developments in the arts.

Very little woodcarving was produced here in proportion to the other arts, yet a respectable body of wooden bowls, clubs, effigies, figurines, and similar objects indicates that the Plains artist did not ignore this medium. Even less pottery and basketry was produced, for containers were primarily made from buffalo hide.

A great deal of Plains art served both decorative and spiritual ends. A given design might appear to be primarily a colourful decoration, yet to the initiated it was also the guardian spirit of the owner.

Colour was originally achieved by mineral pigments or vegetable dyes. In time, these were supplanted by commercial dyes and trade colours. Porcupine quilling—the use of small quills of the North American porcupine (*Erethizon dorsatum*), which are flattened, dyed, and then applied to the surface of animal hides or textile materials—is an art produced nowhere else in the world. For a time quill art was replaced by the use of glass trade beads, which were not only technically similar in their application to

Painted buffalo hide depicting the Battle of the Little Bighorn, by a Cheyenne artist, c. 1878; in the George Gustav Heye Center of the National Museum of the American Indian, New York City. About 36 × 34 inches (116 × 87 cm). Courtesy of the Museum of the American Indian, Heye Foundation, New York

quill art but did not fade and gave a richness of colour unobtainable in any other way. But in the late 20th century, the art of quill art experienced a resurgence.

The art forms themselves range from realistic to extremely abstract and symbolic. Often they are narrative in content, as with the Winter Counts, those painted records that recounted tribal history by means of annual symbols, and the personal history paintings on hide that recount the exploits of the owner.

Not only did the Plains Indian decorate his home but also his person, with carefully coiffured hair, facial painting, and clothing enhancement. And he devoted the same aesthetic attention to his horse as he did to himself, creating beautifully decorated gear for special occasions. Statically displayed in a museum exhibit, much of this ornamentation loses the grace of motion. When worn as intended, the motion of the wearer and the wafting of the Plains breeze gave the feathered regalia or the fringed buckskin a lively grace and colour.

Middle Mississippian diorite bowl in the shape of a crested wood duck, from Moundville, Ala., U.S., c. AD 1500; in the George Gustav Heye Center of the National Museum of the American Indian, New York City. Length 10 inches (25.4 cm). Courtesy of the Museum of the American Indian, Heye Foundation, New York

Far West, Northeast, Central South, and Southeast

In prehistoric times, the central south and southeast were part of the most artistically exciting region of the North American continent. This land of temples, mounds, and monuments was an amazing world, and one can truly understand the legends that grew up around the riches that were evident when the Spanish arrived and that are still found in archaeological excavations. Testifying to the highly developed civilizations that existed are the beautifully carved shells, incised gorgets, and intricately decorated clothing ornaments; the carved stone effigies of ancestor figures or deities, which suggest a strong affinity with ancient Mexico; and the many bird and animal pipes in museums throughout the country. Had the Middle Mississippian culture diorite bowl found at Moundville, Ala., been the only masterpiece to survive, however, no other proof of the artistic brilliance of these peoples would be required.

Wood was used in profusion, although little of it has been preserved in anything resembling its original condition. A quantity of textiles, albeit in fragments, has also survived. Other perishables include decorative freshwater pearls, featherwork, bone, and animal hides.

But it is in the claywork that the greatest vitality seems to have been expressed. While much of the clay used was of inferior quality, the results were astonishing. Exuberant forms, delicately traced surface lines, and strong, powerful designs were all executed with a confidence and grace that still attracts contemporary art students. A tremendous assortment of vessel designs was created in the Southeast: floral, geometric, clay

EFFIGY MOUNDS

Effigy mounds are earthen mounds in the form of an animal or bird found throughout the north-central United States. Prehistoric Native Americans built a variety of earth-berm structures in addition to effigy mounds, including conical, linear, and flat-topped mounds.

Although other mound forms preceded them in time, the first effigy mounds were built about AD 300; in some places people continued to build them as late as the mid-1600s. During his voyage of 1539–42, the explorer Hernando de Soto recorded that flat-topped mounds in the southeastern United States served as earthen platforms on which the native people built their temples and sometimes the houses of their chiefs.

People of the Hopewell and Adena cultures were responsible for a great proliferation of mound building in the Ohio River Valley, including hundreds of conical burial mounds in which

Conical burial mound built by the Adena culture c. 50 BC, in the Grave Creek Mound Archaeology Complex, Moundsville, W.Va. Michael Keller/WV Division of Culture and History

large numbers of artifacts, especially effigy pipes and gorgets (ornamental collars), have been found. Although it is known that most effigy mounds are burial sites, some are not, and their significance remains a mystery. For those in which human burials are found, grave offerings are seldom present.

Many effigy mounds are in the form of birds, but other animal forms—such as those of bears, deer, turtles, buffalo, and snakes—are common. The largest bird effigy mound has a wingspan of 624 feet (190 m) and is located near Madison, Wis. Many other effigy mounds are found in southern and southwestern Wisconsin and in some adjacent areas of Minnesota, Iowa, and Illinois. The largest effigy mound is located in southern Ohio. In the form of an uncoiling snake holding an egg-shaped object in its mouth, the mound is more than 1,300 feet (400 m) long and 2.5 to 3 feet (75 to 90 cm) high.

appliqué, delicate polished water bottles and huge burial jars, as well as many lovely vessels created to hallow a shrine, decorate a temple, or do homage to a god—all providing evidence of the imagination, skill, and sheer love of clay for its own sake that these early potters must have felt. Enough of the remarkably large output has survived to give an excellent idea of the aesthetic heights that were attained.

With the coming of European settlers, this creativity was ended or diverted. Tribes were killed off or dispersed by battle, disease, and slavery, or their social organization was so disrupted that normal pursuits were destroyed and their energies were spent on survival. While the introduction of new and better tools allowed greater technical proficiency, the economic stability that had formerly allowed time to express a strong creative impetus was no longer present. Artists had lost their old markets—purchasers who understood what they were buying—and instead served a customer more concerned with external appearance than with the function of the object. The result was what is disparagingly known as tourist art—ostentatious elaboration that had little to do with the integrity of the product.

Today almost all of the aboriginal arts of the Southeast have been lost or are much less actively pursued. The great stone sculpture for which it was so famous has entirely disappeared, although excellent wood sculpture is a continuing art. Pottery is quite different from the earlier styles. The most active art, and probably the most successful, is basketry, in which the present-day artists are in every way equal to, or better than, their predecessors.

The great art of the California Indians was basketry; no other people in the world has produced such a wide variety of superb basketry. The Pomo, Hupa, Yurok, and Karok peoples of the north developed basketry to its ultimate

Karok twined basket, c. 1890. Height 6 inches (15.5 cm). Courtesy of the Denver Art Museum, Colorado

with weaves so tightly composed as to provide a watertight container, baskets so small that they measure less than ⅛ inch (3 millimetres) in diameter, huge grain-storage baskets, and delicately woven "gift" baskets with the feathers of birds interwoven that provided not only an opportunity for the weaver to demonstrate her mastery of the art but also a means whereby she could display her affection for the deceased. Elsewhere the Chumash, Mono-Paviotso, Washoe, and Panamint proved no less skilled.

The Eastern Woodlands tribes fall into three divisions: the Southeast (discussed above) and the Great Lakes and Northeast. The Great Lakes group produced various arts, including woodwork,

a style of weaving with rush and hemp, and a strong porcupine quill art, later replaced by beadwork. This style of beadwork was popular around the turn of the 19th century, when large quantities of it became available. The art depended upon a weaving frame, which allowed the manufacture of long strips, useful for necklaces, belts, panels, and headbands. Fabric, especially ribbon, appliqué is an important art in the Great Lakes region. Wood art made effective use of burls (hemispherical outgrowths on a tree), from which bowls and containers were fashioned. Pottery was almost nonexistent.

The people of the Northeast, notably the Iroquois, are famous for their False Face Society masks, quill art and beadwork, wooden bowls and ladles, and the woven wampum belts, which are important historical documents. Some pottery was produced, but not of significant quantity or quality. Woodlands basketry was common, but it was not of the quality found elsewhere. Primarily a splint-weave type, it was rarely ornamented, and when it was, the ornament consisted of stamped or painted vegetable-dye designs.

ESKIMO (INUIT)

It may seem unlikely that art would occupy very much of the attention of the inhabitants of the bleak Arctic regions; not only is there little raw material to work with, but the ever-present need to secure a food supply would seem to leave little time for craftwork. Yet, from this harsh environment came some of the most imaginative and humorous of Indian carvings. During the long winter nights, the Eskimo had ample time to work the ivory that came from the walrus and whale.

Art styles of the area favoured carving in the round, decoration by incising, and a modest amount of inlay. Since the basic material was often a tusk or a tooth,

Stylized ivory amulet from the Dorset culture, found in Labrador or Quebec, Canada. Courtesy of the Museum of the American Indian, New York City

these objects partially dictated the form, which was embellished after carving by incising or engraving. Black pigment, from charcoal fires, was rubbed into the lines for emphasis. Such prehistoric wood carving as may have existed has almost entirely disappeared, but enough has survived to indicate that it was a rich and varied art form. Ancient ivory carvings have also been excavated, revealing a sophisticated, formal style. The so-called fossil ivory from which these carvings were made is highly prized even today and, when found, is invariably turned into beautiful carvings that gain value because of the scarce, richly colourful raw material.

A predominant characteristic of Eskimo art is the warm sense of humour that is so prevalent. Sometimes it is expressed in caricature, sometimes in sequential "cartoon strip" form. Its surrealistic expression is probably a reflection of the Eskimo's awareness that, because life in the Arctic is so tenuous, humour is vital to psychological health.

Another significant feature of the art of this region is the remarkable mechanical skill that was often involved in the creative process. Part of the Eskimo's artistry was his ability to neatly piece together small parts to create a whole—and his ability to fashion the tools needed to carry out the operation, many of which were works of art themselves. This skill is evident in the region's most famous art form: the fantastic wooden masks used for various dances and social affairs. While many tribes made wooden masks

QUILL ART

Embroidery using the quills of a porcupine, or sometimes with bird feathers, is called quill art. This type of decoration was used by American Indians from Maine to Virginia and westward to the Rocky Mountains. For all practical purposes the art has died out. Quills were used on tobacco and tinder bags, knife and paintstick cases, cradles, amulets, burden straps, tunics, shirts, leggings, belts, moccasins, arm and leg bands, robes, horse trappings, and birchbark containers.

Dyes were compounded of roots, whole plants, and buds and bark of trees. The natural colour of quills was white, with red, yellow, green, blue, and black being produced by steeping in solutions of plant materials. No variegated hues were made and rarely more than one shade of a colour was used. Patterns were stenciled or drawn with a bone paintbrush, stick, or dull knife, on the skin or bark that was to be worked.

Quill art designs were made up of wide or narrow lines, each composed of a series of close stitches. The decorations put on men's garb were generally related to their work, hunting, and war, while figures worked on children's garments were usually symbolic and expressed prayers for safety, long life, and prosperity. There was considerable borrowing of designs, and figures that were sacred symbols in some tribes came to be purely ornamental in others.

and decorated them with colourful ingenuity, no North American aboriginal people developed the art of imaginative characterization to such an extreme—surrealism par excellence. These masks demonstrate a combination of realistic, imaginative, and supernatural qualities that is uniquely Eskimo.

Since about 1950, a stone art form, utilizing deposits of gray and green soapstone, or steatite, found in the vicinity of Hudson Bay, has become familiar to art collectors. Usually given an artificial colouring, these pieces of small-scale sculpture are popular examples of genre art. They reflect the inherent sculptural skills of the Eskimo and owe their origin and promotion to non-Indian agencies that have worked closely with several of the crafts groups in the region. A form of graphic art derived from Japanese printmaking techniques has also become popular in this way.

NORTHWEST COAST

It was in this region, richly endowed with tremendous cedar and spruce forests, that the Native American sculptor achieved his finest expression. It is probably here that the influence of tools upon the artist is best exemplified, for with the introduction of steel cutting knives, the Northwest Coast artist was free to demonstrate his talent in the aesthetically superb sculpture that is

Painted wooden mask of the Kuskokwim Eskimos, 1875. Height about 12 inches (31 cm).
Courtesy of the Museum of the American Indian, Heye Foundation, New York

rivalled by no other Indian people in North America.

Tall, straight cedar poles furnished the material for the huge memorial, or totem, poles, the smaller wooden figures, the masks, and the other carved objects so loved by the Northwest Coast Indian. Inlaid with abalone *Haliotis* shell and carefully painted, these products took on a quality so distinctive that they are immediately identifiable.

Another remarkable quality of the Northwest Coast artist is his skill and interest in fitting designs into forms. He excels at fitting his designs into a given area, shape, or prescribed form, yet without sacrificing the integrity of the design.

The role of the tall totem poles from this area has not been well understood by non-Indians, and many erroneous accounts have been published as to their purpose and meaning. They were not religious and were never intended to be worshipped. They were instead memorial documents, recording the social position, wealth, and relative importance of the person who had paid for the pole. Because family lineage, class status, wealth, and other social facts were thus recorded, it was possible to gain an "introduction" to the village chief or house owner by simply examining the tall pole.

The goal of most of this rich art was the exaltation of the individual—more specifically, a wealthy village chief or a great noble, for the society was based on a class system. Part of the insignia of social position was the accumulation of wealth, and objets d'art were an important part of that wealth. With the coming of the Euro-Americans, who coveted the rich furs of the region, the control of the great fishing areas and strategic position of the Northwest Coast tribes enabled them to acquire staggering wealth in an extremely brief space of time. The existence of an Indian purchasing class, with its ever-increasing need for impressive possessions, created a supplier: the professional artist. This was thus one of the very few aboriginal cultures outside Mexico that gave rise to art patrons who hired artists on a commission basis.

More surprising, the works that were commissioned were usually destined to be given away. While this may seem paradoxical, the logic was simple: the more one gave away, the greater one's prestige.

The Northwest Coast tribes were among the first American Indians to master metalcraft. While some copper came from local sources, most came from whaling ships, both as cargo brought in for trade and as scrap peeled from the hulls of wrecked ships. This metal was worked with great skill by Tlingit and Haida artists into fighting knives, masks, overlays for artworks, and the great shield-shaped *tinneh* that were so highly prized.

Among the Northwest Coast tribes, the Tlingit people of Alaska seem to have produced the most sensitive and sophisticated sculpture. The Kwakiutl, on the other hand, expressed their feeling for line and form in extremely impressive and powerful painted carvings. The designs are usually outlined in strong

Totem poles from Kitwancool Creek, B.C., Can. W.E. Ferguson/Shostal Associates

colours, there is far less subtlety of form, and the overall feeling is of a potent force at work. Between the two extremes are the Haida carvers, whose work, often less strongly painted than Kwakiutl work, is marked by precision of design, skill in execution, and strength of expression. These are the people who were responsible for the familiar black "slate carvings," which are actually made of argillite, a stone found locally only on Queen Charlotte Islands, in British Columbia.

The work of the neighbouring Northwest Coast peoples, such as the Niska, Kitksan, and Tsimshian, who lived

Haida argillite "slate carving," c. 1890, depicting a folktale in which the Bear Mother endures a cesarean birth, in the George Gustav Haye Center of the National Museum of the American Indian, New York City. Courtesy of the Museum of the American Indian, Heye Foundation, New York

upriver from the Tlingit, is perhaps slightly less well known, due largely to the smaller population and their more remote interior location. It is, however, of equal aesthetic merit, and can stand comparison on any basis with the art of the rest of the peoples of this region.

With the coming of Euro-Americans, there was a brief period of economic benefit enjoyed by the Northwest Coast people, but this soon disappeared, and the arts rapidly degenerated to curio-shop products. In time, even these provided so little income that all but a few Indian carvers and basket weavers abandoned the arts. In the late 20th and early 21st centuries, several crafts products that had all but disappeared, such as the famed handwoven Chilkat blankets, were being revived to a limited extent. Wooden masks that are often carved and painted replicas of older ones have also enjoyed a revival; but, in essence, this is a copying process, largely mechanical and lacking the creativity of the original. Argillite carving, too, is experiencing a modest renaissance, but as yet most of the products are very small, ornamental, accessory forms. In general, the exuberance and power of the earlier forms is yet to be fully realized by the gifted, determined artists of Northwest Coast Indian descent.

ARTS OF CONTEMPORARY NATIVE AMERICANS

In the contemporary art world, Native American art occupies a peripheral role.

Until the last few decades, the only strong effort to exhibit this art in galleries or museums was made by those few institutions specializing in ethnological, exotic, or art history subjects, together with the rare specialized museum devoted only to Indian materials or to those of the American West.

The most active interest in American Indian art seems to have been less in products of still-living cultures than in prehistoric arts and less in the arts of prehistoric North American peoples than in "pre-Columbian art," which is generally understood to mean the works of the so-called high civilizations—notably the Maya, Aztec, Inca, and Moche. This is to be regretted, for it not only results in an overemphasis that destroys intellectual balance but it also has relegated to the background some of the more exciting aesthetic accomplishments of the Native American. The diorite bowl representing a crested wood duck that has been called

Herding Sheep, *watercolour on paper by Allan Houser, a Chiricahua Apache, 1953; in the Denver Art Museum.* Courtesy of the Denver Art Museum, Colorado

by some "the Portland vase of America" is not an isolated instance, for there are other fine sculptures equally deserving of attention.

More active efforts to preserve American Indian art have been made in the United States than elsewhere. The first was in the 1920s, when a group of Euro-American artists located in and around Santa Fe, N.M., found excitement in the work of the Indians of the Southwest. Together with the so-called Taos colony of artists, these influential people succeeded in bringing the values of Native American art to the attention of the outside world through publications, exhibitions, and their artworks, in which Indian design often figured predominantly. In time, this group saw to the establishment of a School of Indian Art in Santa Fe. Out of this school came many of the most familiar names in Indian art. Oqwa Pi, Jack Hokeah, Awa Tsireh, Pablita Velarde, Andy Tsinajinnie, Allan Houser, Ben Quintana, Gerónima Cruz Montoya, Eva Mirabal, and Waldo Mootzka are but a very few of the students involved during this exciting period. Following an initial success, the school enjoyed a period of prosperity but then fell victim to the Great Depression.

Another surge of interest came with the enactment of the Indian Reorganization Act of 1934, by means of which the Indian Arts and Crafts Board came into existence. Sparked by John Collier, then commissioner of Indian affairs, this body is one of the few governmental organizations set up specifically to promote, encourage, and revive native arts and crafts. While intended largely as an economic device to increase Native American income, the board fortunately included members who were knowledgeable about, and sensitive to, the aesthetic and cultural strengths of Native American cultures. A program of exploration revealed surprising resilience in native crafts, and a core of still-active craftspeople who remembered older techniques was engaged to perpetuate their arts. Out of this program came a renaissance that still continues, even after the board has become less influential, as the native artist more and more finds himself in his art. What promises to become the major factor influencing Indian art is the Institute of American Indian Arts in Santa Fe, an outgrowth of the early interest of the Indian Arts and Crafts Board in assisting young Native American artists in securing needed training.

Stimulated by these developments, the interest of art museums and collectors in native art brought home to the general public the existence of a remarkable, if overlooked, art form.

Today a growing interest in Indian cultural expression is found among many North American Indians. Many Indians want to learn what they can of their past and salvage what can be preserved.

Perhaps the greatest positive force to appear in some time are the Indian tribal councils and economic development boards, many of which support the arts in their own areas, not only to augment income but also out of an awareness of the cultural value of those arts. Many tribes, particularly the Navajo, Hopi, Cherokee, and Crow, have set up funds to develop crafts areas, sales centres, and museums to promote the appreciation of their traditional arts and thereby strengthen the fabric of the tribe. Some have set up crafts schools so that the younger people will have access to the necessary training.

Painting has taken several new and positive directions. Many Native American artists are creating remarkable works in acrylic, tempera, oil, and related media, gaining recognition in the fine arts and establishing successful careers in the world at large. Reflecting their own diverse interests and identities, some prefer to paint in a completely free manner, meaning that their work will not necessarily reflect their ancestry. Others seek means whereby they can paint in "Indian style" or combine native themes and techniques with those of other cultures.

CHAPTER 8

NATIVE AMERICAN MUSIC

The Americas contain hundreds of native communities, each with its own distinctive history, language, and musical culture. These communities—although united in placing music at the centre of public life—have developed extraordinarily diverse and multifaceted performance traditions. This chapter provides a general introduction to Native American musics with treatments of the roles of music in culture, musical styles and genres, musical instruments, music history, and the study of American Indian musics.

MUSIC IN NATIVE AMERICAN CULTURE

Generalizations about the relationship between music and culture in Native American communities are gleaned from musical concepts and values, the structure of musical events, and the role of language in song texts. Musical concepts and values encompass ideas about the origins and sources of music, as well as musical ownership, creativity, transmission, and aesthetics. Each community's musical concepts and values develop over time through complex social and cultural processes. These concepts and values reflect broader ways of thinking and therefore offer important insight into general patterns of culture. Native peoples differ in the degree to which they discuss musical concepts. But even for the peoples who do not verbalize musical ideas, underlying conceptual structures exist and may be perceived by observing musical practice. Despite the great diversity of American Indian peoples, general features of Native American musical concepts and values may be summarized.

Native Americans trace the ultimate origin of their traditional music to the time of creation, when specific songs or musical repertories were given to the first people by the Creator and by spirit-beings in the mythic past. Sacred narratives describe the origins of specific musical instruments, songs, dances, and ceremonies. Some ritual repertories received at the time of creation are considered complete, so that by definition human beings cannot compose new music for them. But many occasions are suitable for new music; this music may be received in a variety of ways. For example, shamans and other individuals may experience dreams or visions in which spirit-beings teach them new songs, dances, and rituals. Many Indian communities learn new songs and repertories from their neighbours and have a long history of adopting musical practices from outsiders. Yet in every case, the music is a gift that comes from beyond the individual or community.

Some Native Americans consider songs to be property and have developed formal systems of musical ownership, inheritance, and performance rights. On the northwest coast of North America, the right to perform ancestral songs and dances is an inherited privilege, although the owner of a song can give it away. Other communities believe that specific pieces of music belong to an ensemble or to the entire community and should not be performed by outsiders without specific permission. Music has intrinsic value to individuals, ensembles, and communities, and performance rights are granted according to principles established by the group through long practice.

New music is provided each year for specific occasions in some communities. An individual may have a vision or dream in which he or she learns a new song; the song may be presented to the community or retained for personal use. More often, however, musical creativity is a collective process. Certain musical genres, such as lullabies or songs for personal enjoyment, are improvised. Where new ceremonial songs are not composed because the repertories are considered complete, individual song leaders exercise musical creativity by improvising variations on traditional melodies or lyrics within accepted parameters. The creation and performance of music are dynamic processes.

Musical transmission involves the processes of teaching and learning that preserve songs and repertories from one generation to the next. Native Americans transmit music primarily through oral tradition. Some genres, such as social dance songs, are learned informally through imitation and participation. Other genres require more formal teaching methods. Some communities have developed indigenous systems of music notation, but these are used by experienced singers as memory aids, not as teaching tools. In the 21st century, it is common for Native Americans to supplement oral tradition with the use of audio and video recordings for teaching, learning, and preserving traditional repertories.

Aesthetics, or perceptions of beauty, are among the most difficult concepts to identify in any musical culture. Native Americans tend to evaluate performances according to the feelings of connectedness they generate rather than according to specifically musical qualities. Some communities judge the success of a performance by how many people participate, because attendance demonstrates cultural vitality and active social networks. Where musical performance is meant to transcend the human realm, success is measured by apparent communication with spirit-beings. Where music and dance represent a test of physical strength and mental stamina, success is appraised by the performer's ability to complete the task with dignity and self-discipline, demonstrating commitment to family and community. Regardless of the specific criteria used to evaluate performance, musical designs that employ repetition, balance, and circularity are appreciated by American Indians because they resonate with social values that are deeply embedded in native cultures.

MUSICAL EVENTS

Native American performances integrate music, dance, spirituality, and social communion in multilayered events. Several activities may take place simultaneously, and different musicians or ensembles sometimes perform unrelated genres in close proximity. Each performance occasion has its own musical styles and genres. Although the organization of Native American performances may seem informal to outside observers, in actuality each event requires extensive planning, and preparations may extend over months or even years. Preparations include musical composition, rehearsal, instrument making or repair, and the assembling of dance regalia. The hosts or sponsors of an event must prepare the dance ground, which symbolizes concepts of sacred geography and social order in its layout. The hosts also prepare and serve food to participants and guests, and they may distribute gifts to specific individuals. In addition, participants prepare themselves spiritually in a process that may involve fasting, prayers, and other methods of purification. Native American ceremonials may last several days, but the different musical components are interconnected in various ways.

The roles of musicians, dancers, and other participants in a Native American performance are often complex and may not be apparent to an outsider. Everyone who attends the performance will participate in some way, either through active involvement in music and dance or by witnessing the event. Performances may be specific to one community or may involve several communities or even different tribes and nations. In addition, unseen spirit-beings are usually thought

RITUAL CLOWNS

The New Year festivals of various preliterate and ancient cultures throughout the world include ritual or ceremonial figures who represents a reversal of the normal order, an opening to the chaos that preceded creation. The reversal of normality that is the distinguishing mark of the clown relates him to the powerful world that existed before the present one.

In certain traditions clowning is an apotropaic (averting evil) ritual, a way of deflecting demonic attention from serious religious activities. In other contexts it serves as an initiatory ordeal in which the initiate must persevere through the jests and insults hurled at him.

Though some attempts have been made to discover the religious origins of secular clowns, fools, and jesters, it is the elaborate ritual roles of masked clown societies among such groups as the American Indians that have attracted most attention. The most famous of these are the Koyemshi, the dancing clowns of the Pueblo Indians. Their obscene and sacrilegious actions punctuate the most important religious ceremonies and serve as a sign of the presence of the powerful primordial beings and as a means of social control by their satire of the antisocial behaviour of particular individuals.

to take part. Lead singers and dancers may be political as well as spiritual leaders, who have an important voice in decision making and are influential in the community. Musicians performing in collective ceremonies do not expect to receive applause or verbal response from the audience; their role is to serve the community. Native men and women have complementary musical roles and responsibilities. In the southeastern United States, for example, men sing while women shake leg rattles.

Humour is essential to many native ceremonial events. Some ceremonies include ritual clowns, with their own songs for entering and exiting the dance arena; their antics serve the dual purpose of keeping people lighthearted while reinforcing social values by demonstrating incorrect behaviour. Certain song genres may feature humorous lyrics that poke fun at people or describe comical situations.

MUSIC AND LANGUAGE

Traditional music plays an important role in perpetuating Native American languages, some of which are no longer spoken in daily life. American Indian song texts constitute a genre of poetry in terms of structure, style, and expression. Native Americans often perform songs as part of traditional storytelling; these songs may illuminate a character's thoughts and feelings. Song texts may employ the traditional language, although words are modified by adding or eliding syllables to accommodate the music. Song texts usually refer to local flora and fauna, specific features of the landscape, natural resources such as water, or aspects of the community. Sometimes archaic words appear in ceremonial songs, and many communities use words or phrases from foreign languages. These practices tend to obscure the meaning of the text, distinguishing it from everyday language.

In certain regions, Native Americans developed lingua francas in order to facilitate trade and social interaction. In these areas, song texts may feature words from a lingua franca. Many Native American songs employ vocables, syllables that do not have referential meaning. These may be used to frame words or may be inserted among them; in some cases they constitute the entire song text. Vocables are a fixed part of a song and help define patterns of repetition and variation in the music. When used in collective dance songs, they create a sense of spirituality and social cohesion.

ASPECTS OF STYLE

The following discussion of styles and genres by region addresses a number of characteristics of music and how they are produced. It is possible to speak of musical regions because, although each Native American group has distinctive musical styles and genres, certain musical similarities exist between those who are roughly neighbours. However, musical boundaries continually shift and change as people from different cultures exchange musical ideas, repertories, and instruments.

Generally, in each regional category a description of the music encompasses vocal style, melody, rhythm, phrase structure, use of text, typical instruments, and occasions for music. Vocal style may be said to be tense (requiring greater muscular effort) or relaxed to varying degrees, depending on the use of the throat, tongue, mouth, and breath. Higher notes for a particular voice type often sound more tense than notes in the middle of a singer's vocal range. The sound may be nasal or not. Men especially may use falsetto voice, for a higher timbre than is available using full voice. Vibrato is a rapid, slight variation in pitch that may be ornamental and is often part of the aesthetic of musical performance.

When people sing together, they may perform the same melodies in very nearly the same way (blended unison) or without attempting to sing exactly together (unblended unison). Choral singing may also entail the simultaneous performance of separate musical lines (polyphony). Scales may be described by the number of discrete pitches used, as well as by the intervals between those pitches. Melodies form contours as they move higher or lower in pitch, proceeding by relatively large or small intervals.

Rhythm encompasses the underlying musical pulses and how they are organized (i.e., metre)—often into groups of two or three (i.e., duple or triple metre)—as well as how the melody relates to that structure with its varying durations of notes and syncopations that contradict the regularity of the beats. Melodic and rhythmic units organize into larger phrases and then into phrase patterns that involve repetition, variation, and contrast. Meaningful text and vocables may be sung in varying combinations.

Each region uses characteristic musical instruments, sometimes without voices, and each uses music in identifiable ways—e.g., private and public, social and ritual, or as pure song and as accompaniment to dance.

REGIONAL STYLES

North American Indians emphasize singing, accompanied by percussion instruments such as rattles or drums, rather than purely instrumental music. North American musical genres include lullabies, songs given to individuals by their guardian spirits, curing songs, songs performed during stories, songs to accompany games, ceremonial and social dance songs, and songs to accompany work or daily activities. Music, dance, and spirituality are tightly interwoven in a worldview that perceives little separation between sacred and secular. Six musical style areas—which differ somewhat from anthropologists' designations—exist in Native North America: Northeast and Southeast (in musicology often called Eastern Woodlands), Plains, Great Basin, Southwest, Northwest Coast, and Arctic.

NORTHEAST AND SOUTHEAST INDIANS

In terms of musical characteristics, the Northeast and Southeast culture areas stretch from New Brunswick, Canada, south to the Gulf of Mexico and from the Mississippi River east to the Atlantic Ocean. The large area was the traditional home of a diverse array of peoples, including the Iroquois, Huron, and Ojibwa to the north and the Choctaw, Chickasaw, Creek, Cherokee, and Seminole to the south. The singers of the Northeast and Southeast use a relatively relaxed vocal style and emphasize the middle part of their range. In some songs singers use special vocal techniques, including rapid vibrato and yodeling, which enhance the expressive quality of the music. Most scales involve four, five, or six tones, usually with notes at roughly equidistant intervals. Melodies tend to undulate and often feature a descending inflection; rhythmic characteristics include frequent changes of metre and the use of syncopation.

The most distinctive style element of Northeast and Southeast music is the use of call and response in many dance songs; the leader sings a short melody as a solo and is answered by the dancers in unison. The alternation between leader and dancers creates an antiphonal texture that is otherwise rare among

North American Indians. Songs of the Northeast and Southeast feature strophic forms, in which the music repeats; sectional forms, in which the music changes in blocks; and iterative forms, in which there may be short sections with repetition. Song texts employ vocables or words framed by vocables. Musical instruments from this region include rattles, drums, and a few flutes used primarily for ritual purposes. Northeast and Southeast peoples perform traditional musics to accompany ceremonial dances, such as the Green Corn ceremony of the Southeast or Iroquois Longhouse events of the Northeast. In addition, traditional songs accompany individual curing rituals, recreational social dances, and public folkloric dance demonstrations.

PLAINS

The Plains area extends from Texas north to south-central Canada and from the Rocky Mountains east to the Mississippi River. Peoples from this area include the Blackfoot and Sioux of the northern plains, the Kiowa and Comanche of the southern plains, and the Ho-Chunk (Winnebago), Sauk, and Fox of the prairie. The most distinctive stylistic feature of this area is the tense, nasal vocal quality cultivated by Plains singers. Musicians from the northern Plains emphasize the high part of their range, while southern Plains singers use a somewhat lower range. Most scales employ four or five tones with equidistant intervals. Plains songs feature a cascading melodic contour that starts high and descends by steps, ending on the lowest pitch at the end of the strophe. In powwow dance songs, the tempo used by the singers differs slightly from the tempo of the drumbeat, which adds rhythmic complexity to the music.

Singers perform in unblended unison, and most songs use a kind of strophic form that is repeated four times. Song texts may be composed entirely of vocables or may include a combination of words and vocables. Instruments from this region include the single-headed hand drum, the large bass drum used simultaneously by multiple performers to accompany powwow songs, and the end-blown flute or flageolet, played as a solo instrument for courtship music. Music is performed for collective ceremonies such as the Sun Dance, men's warrior society dances, rituals associated with sacred objects such as medicine bundles, and recreational events such as hand games (e.g., guessing which hand holds an object).

GREAT BASIN

Tribes such as the Shoshone, Paiute, Washoe, and Ute live in the Great Basin area, which reaches from the Colorado River Basin north to the Fraser River in British Columbia, Canada, and from the Rocky Mountains west to the Sierra Nevada and Cascade Range. Musicians from this region emphasize the middle part of the vocal range and sing with a relaxed and open quality; special vocal techniques include subtle aspirations at the start and end of musical phrases. Scales feature four or five tones with mostly equidistant intervals. Melodic contours undulate, sometimes with a descending inflection, and singers achieve rhythmic complexity through special breathing techniques they use to vary durational values.

Singers perform collective dance songs in moderately blended unison, and some dance songs are unaccompanied, which is unusual among Indians in North America. The most distinctive style element of Great Basin music is the form used in seasonal round dances, in which each line of text and music repeats and alternates with one or two other lines; scholars refer to this form as paired-phrase structure (e.g., AA BB AA BB and so on). Great Basin song texts combine words and vocables, employing intricate and subtle imagery that refers to the local environment and natural forces. In the past, shamans from this area accompanied certain curing rituals with a musical bow; other distinctive musical instruments include notched rasps played with a basket resonator, strung rattles made of deer hooves, and striking sticks used to accompany hand-game songs. Important performance contexts include life-cycle events such as the Washoe Girl's Puberty ceremony, seasonal first fruits celebrations such as the Ute Bear Dance, and storytelling.

SOUTHWEST

The Southwest region, which includes New Mexico, Arizona, and southern California, is home to traditionally sedentary Pueblo Indians, such as the Hopi and Zuni, as well as to tribes that were traditionally transhumant (seasonally moving), such as the Navajo and Apache. Pueblo singers prefer an open, relaxed vocal style emphasizing the lower range and perform communal dance songs in blended unison. Pueblo scales employ five, six, or seven tones with equidistant intervals, and their ceremonial dance songs feature a five-part form with lengthy and detailed poetry. Pueblo melodic contours often involve an upward leap at the beginning of a phrase, followed by an undulating descent, and Pueblo songs feature some of the most complex rhythmic structures in North America, including patterned pauses and frequently changing metres. Their most distinctive musical instrument is a large, brightly painted double-headed barrel drum made from cottonwood.

Pueblo musical contexts include seasonal agricultural ceremonies such as kachina (*katsina*) dances, Catholic feast day dances, and other community celebrations. Navajo and Apache singers use a tense, nasal vocal quality covering a wide range, and Navajo singers use falsetto voice in certain genres. They sing in unblended unison, and their songs use strophic forms as well as complex sectional forms with many short interwoven melodic motifs. Navajo and Apache songs employ a wide range of melodic contours, which involve dramatic leaps and cascading descents in certain genres. Some of these groups' songs feature rapid tempos and use a variety of durational values. Most of the song texts combine words with vocables. Navajo and Apache instruments include many kinds of drums and what is known as the Apache violin, a traditional one- or two-stringed solo instrument. Important contexts for Navajo and Apache musics include life-cycle ceremonials, such as the Girl's Puberty ceremony, and elaborate curing ceremonies that include many components and last for several days.

Northwest Coast

The Northwest Coast area covers a thin strip about 100 miles (160 km) wide between the Pacific Ocean and the coastal mountains of the United States and Canada, extending from northern California to the Alaska panhandle. Some peoples of this area are the Haida, Kwakiutl, Tsimshian, and Bella Coola. Northwest Coast singers prefer a moderately relaxed and open vocal style that emphasizes the lower range, but they also use a variety of ornaments and special vocal techniques for expressive purposes. Scales range from four to six tones and sometimes include half-step intervals, which is a distinctive style element in music of this area. Most melodies feature stepwise motion and undulate with a descending inflection. Rhythmic structures in this area are highly complex; there are frequent changes of metre, various durational values, and intentional tempo displacements between the singers and the drum.

Singers perform in moderately blended unison, although some part-singing may also be traditional in this region. The songs employ strophic and sectional forms with intricately detailed phrase designs. Some Northwest Coast songs alternate a stanza of poetic text with a vocable refrain, while other genres, such as songs performed in the course of storytelling, consist primarily of vocables. Peoples of the Northwest Coast use a wide variety of musical instruments, many of which are beautifully carved and painted to represent mythical beings. Performance contexts include potlatch feasts, initiation rituals, seasonal dance ceremonies, shamanic rituals, and gambling events.

Arctic

Many independent but related communities occupy the Arctic region, which reaches from Alaska across northern Canada to Greenland. Inuit or Eskimo peoples such as the Netsilik, Copper, Iglulik, and Baffin Islanders inhabit the Arctic area. In this region, singers use a moderately tense and nasal vocal style, emphasizing the middle range and ornamenting the melody with grace notes, vocal pulsations, and special breathing techniques. Songs feature four- or five-note scales, and melodies employ a relatively narrow range. Rhythmic structures include intentional tempo displacement between the voice and drum as well as the use of ties (notes that hold over several beats), cross-rhythms (complex combinations of values, especially simultaneous two- and three-note groupings), syncopations, and frequently changing metres.

Most choral songs are performed in moderately blended unison, although part-singing in parallel intervals is also performed in some Inuit communities. Songs from this area tend to be relatively short but display a variety of strophic and through-composed (i.e., not based on a repeated pattern) forms. In addition, some songs contain recitative-like sections in which passages of text are recited rhythmically on a single pitch. Song texts combine vocables with words, and many genres are humorous. Distinctive musical instruments of this area include dance gloves, which are decorated with small objects that rattle as the dancer moves, and the box drum, which is a rectangular wooden box open at the top and bottom and suspended from a ceiling pole or tripod during performance. Performance contexts include shamanic rituals, storytelling, song contests, traditional games, and sacred dances performed at events such as the Bladder Festival or the Messenger Feast.

MUSICAL INSTRUMENTS

Musical instruments are important throughout the Americas. A few indigenous instruments can be made in an hour or two by virtually anyone in the community from materials readily available in the natural environment. Other instruments require weeks or even months to make by a specially trained craftsman using materials prepared by different individuals. Many musical instruments carry symbolic significance, which appears in the ways instruments are used, decorated, named, or handled before and after use. The names of instruments may reflect ideas about social relationships; for example, Anishnabe water drums come in two sizes, called "grandfather" and "little boy." Decorations often have spiritual significance or refer to sacred narratives. Some instruments are thought to be sentient and require respectful treatment.

Each tribe has its own approach to instrument classification, based on traditional ways of organizing knowledge. To compare musical instruments across cultures, scholars have developed a system of classifying them into four categories: idiophones, membranophones, aerophones, and chordophones. (A fifth category, electrophones, is often added to characterize electric and electronic instruments.) These designations derive from the method through which each instrument produces sound and are based upon physical descriptions.

IDIOPHONES

Idiophones produce musical sound by vibrating when the body of the

Kwakiutl man in traditional dress, holding a ceremonial staff and a shaman's rattle; photograph by Edward S. Curtis, c. 1914. Edward S. Curtis Collection/Library of Congress, Washington, D.C. (neg. no. LC-USZ62-52212)

instrument itself is struck, stamped, shaken, scraped, rubbed, or plucked. By far the largest category of musical instruments in Native American musics, idiophones appear in many shapes and sizes and are made of extraordinarily diverse materials, from beetle wings to sections of plastic pipe. Concussion instruments, which consist of two similar elements that are clapped together, include striking sticks (Choctaw, Mi'kmaq [Micmac], and others). Struck instruments with a solid body include plank or foot drums (Pomo and Maidu). Some examples of struck instruments with a hollow body are box drums (Arctic and Mixtec) and basket drums (Pueblo).

Native Americans use many shaken instruments, including container rattles, strung rattles, and jingle rattles. Container rattles consist of a receptacle with small objects inside, such as pebbles, clay pellets, beads, seeds, dried corn kernels or beans, fruit pits, or buckshot. Containers are made from natural materials, including dried gourds, calabashes, turtle shells, cocoons, wood, bark, sections of animal horn, hide pouches, coconut shells, and woven fibres. Native Americans also make container rattles from manufactured materials, such as tin cans or hollow metal tubes. Container rattles can be made with or without wooden handles; some are clustered and attached to leggings worn by dancers. Native peoples from the southeastern United States make leg rattles from turtle shells or evaporated milk cans filled with small pebbles and attached in rows to a piece of leather. Female dancers use these rattles to provide rhythmic accompaniment for ceremonial dances. In addition to container rattles, Native Americans make rattles from small objects strung together in clusters; these objects include deer hooves, seashells, seeds, seed pods, nuts, fruit pits, brass shotgun shells, and bottle caps. Strung rattles may be played by hand, suspended down a dancer's back, or worn by a dancer on the knees, ankles, or wrists. Jingle rattles are made from metal or wooden disks that slide up and down on a post or stem. In addition, many American Indian dancers attach bells or other tinkling objects to their dance regalia; these objects are set into motion when the dancer moves, adding another layer of sound to the performance.

Other idiophones include scrapers, friction idiophones, and plucked idiophones. Scrapers or rasps are serrated objects that are scraped with a stick or other implement. Rasps are used as musical instruments throughout the Americas and are made from various materials, including notched sticks, dried alligator skin, armadillo shells, gourds, food graters, and sections of corrugated tin. Unlike rasps, friction idiophones consist of a solid or hollow body with a smooth surface rubbed with a stick or other implement. Plucked idiophones consist of a flexible tongue or lamella that is fixed to a frame and plucked with the finger or thumb; these are not widespread among American Indians.

Native Americans often decorate idiophones with intricate and colourful

MUSICAL BOW

The stringed musical instrument known as the musical bow is found in most ancient cultures, as well as in many in the present day. It consists of a flexible stick 1.5 to 10 feet (0.5 to 3 m) long, strung end to end with a taut cord that the player plucks or taps to produce a weak fundamental note. The player may produce other notes by stopping the string with finger and thumb; by lightly touching the string to produce faint-sounding overtones; by tying the string to the stick to form two taut segments; or, on a mouth bow, by using the mouth as a resonator, varying its cavity in order to isolate overtones. In a gourd bow a truncated gourd attached to the stick serves as a resonator. Other musical bows may have separate resonators, such as a gourd or pot.

patterns or images. Peoples from the Northwest Coast are known for their skillfully carved wooden container rattles, some of which represent mythological beings. Some idiophones have special meaning to native peoples. For certain peoples of the Northeast, the Southeast, and the Great Lakes, the sound of a gourd rattle symbolizes the sound of Creation. Among tribes of the Northwest Coast, rattles represent voices from the spirit world.

MEMBRANOPHONES

Membranophones are instruments that have a skin or membrane stretched over a frame; musical sound is produced by striking or rubbing the membrane or by setting the membrane into motion with sound waves (as with a kazoo). Drums are the largest subcategory of membranophones. Native Americans make drums in many sizes from a wide variety of natural and manufactured materials. Three basic kinds of drums exist among indigenous groups: single-headed drums, double-headed drums, and kettledrums.

Single-headed drums consist of one drum head stretched across a frame. Shallow hand drums of this type are widespread in North America. For example, Plains peoples use a single-headed drum to accompany hand games, personal songs, or curing songs. The drum frame is made from a strip of wood about 2 inches (5 cm) deep that has been soaked and bent into a circle about 13 to 20 inches (33 to 50 cm) in diameter. The drum head, made of deer hide, is stretched across the frame and fastened with thongs or thumb tacks. Thongs are also stretched across the open side of the drum to form a handle. The singer usually holds the drum in his left hand and strikes the head with a stick held in his right hand. Some Plains hand drums have snares, or short sticks attached to the head by a thong, which create a buzzing sound when the drum is struck. Inuit peoples also use single-headed hand drums to accompany ceremonial dances. The Inuit drum may be as much as 39 inches (1 m) in diameter and has a wooden handle attached to the frame; the head is made from caribou hide, and the drum is played by striking the edge of the rim rather than the head itself.

Double-headed drums come in many sizes and shapes. Pueblo peoples accompany certain ceremonial dances with a cylindrical drum about 30 inches (75 cm) high and 15 inches (38 cm) in diameter. Made from cottonwood, the shell is scraped to a thickness of about 0.5 inch (about 15 mm). The heads are stretched across each open end and laced together with strips of hide. Two small wooden objects are placed inside the drum shell— a ball symbolizing the earth and a cylinder representing the universe. These objects bounce when the drum is played, adding complexity to its sound. An Ojibwa double-headed dance drum is made from a wooden washtub or barrel. The bottom of the tub is partly cut out to enhance the drum's resonance. The drum measures about 25 inches (65 cm) in diameter at the top and about 22 inches (56 cm) at the bottom and is about 13 inches (33 cm) tall. The drum is suspended from stakes while it is played in order to help it resonate, and it is decorated with a cloth skirt, a beaded belt and tabs, fur strips, and additional pendants and tassels. Some Native Americans attach snares to double-headed drums; the Mississippi Choctaw use a double-headed snare drum to accompany

processions and to generate enthusiasm during ball-game performances.

Kettledrums can be made from wooden, ceramic, or metal containers covered with hide or with rubber from an inner tube. Sometimes this kind of drum is partially filled with water, which affects the instrument's tone quality. Kettledrums are widespread. They usually accompany ceremonial dances or shamanic rituals. Musicians of the Eastern Woodlands make kettledrums from small wood or ceramic pots covered with a hide and partially filled with water; the drummer may place a lump of charcoal, healing herbs, a potsherd, or other materials inside the pot to symbolize natural elements and forces.

Among Native Americans, ceremonial drums are treated with great care and respect. North American powwow drums are placed on a blanket or stand during performance and are covered when not in use. They are smudged with tobacco in a special sunrise ceremony before the public powwow events, and neither drugs nor alcohol may be used near the drums. In addition, paraphernalia such as drumsticks, stands, or medicine bags may belong to a particular drum. The Ojibwa dance drum is regarded as a living being, and great care is taken with its construction and decoration. The sound of the drum conveys symbolic meaning for many Native Americans. A rapid drumbeat in certain songs from the Northwest Coast signifies the transformation of a Thunderbird into a human state.

Aerophones

Aerophones require an airstream to produce sound. They may be whirled through the air (bull-roarer) or blown into by a player (flutes, whistles, reed instruments, and horns). Bull-roarers, made of a wooden slab tied to a string or rawhide thong, are whirled in the air to create sound. They are significant in some native healing and conjuring practices. Arctic peoples used bull-roarers as part of a ritual to harden snow, making travel easier, while the Tohono O'odham people of the southwestern United States used a bull-roarer in earlier times to imitate the sound of rain in rituals calling for rain.

Flutes and whistles are tubular or globular vessels with an edge against which the player blows. Native American flutes and whistles come in many shapes and sizes and are made from various materials, including wood, bone, cane, clay, and bamboo. The number and position of finger holes, specific design of the mouth hole, and number of pipes involved are all features that differentiate various kinds of flutes. In the Americas, end-blown or vertical flutes are most common. These are played by blowing air directly over the rim of the mouth hole. The mouth hole may be plain (cut straight across), notched, or connected to an internal duct.

Duct flutes are also widespread. These have an internal block that forces the airstream against the beveled edge of an air hole. (The recorder is a European duct flute.) Indigenous duct flutes are played throughout the Americas, but the best-known example is the Plains courting flute, made popular by contemporary performers such as Carlos Nakai. In addition to end-blown flutes, some Native Americans also play side-blown or horizontal flutes, which have a lateral mouth hole.

Whistles are essentially a simple form of end-blown flute that produce one or two pitches. These are used throughout the Americas for ritual purposes.

Horns produce musical sound when the player vibrates his lips against the mouth hole. Most Native American horns are end-blown, have a cylindrical bore, and are made from bamboo, wood, bark, bone, clay, or calabash. End-blown conch-shell horns with a spiral bore are fairly widespread among Native Americans, who use them primarily for signaling purposes. The Cayuga of what is now central New York play a conch-shell horn to announce Longhouse ceremonial events.

In sacred traditions throughout the Americas, wind is associated with spirit-beings as well as with breath, the essence of life. For this reason, Native American aerophones are imbued with special meaning and are strongly associated with shamanism and sacred ceremonies. North American Indian flutes may be incised with symbolic designs or decorated with feathers and carved fetishes. Many native peoples use wind instruments to communicate with spirits; for example, peoples of the Northwest Coast use a small wooden whistle to signal the presence of spirit-beings at ceremonials.

CHORDOPHONES

Chordophones have one or more stretchable strings attached to a frame or sound box. Sound is produced by plucking, rubbing, striking, or bowing the string. The musical bow is a kind of chordophone indigenous to the Americas. Musical bows consist of a string stretched between the two ends of a curved stick. The string may be struck, plucked, or rubbed to create musical sound. This instrument rarely appears in contemporary Native American musics, but it has existed among peoples of the Southwest, the Great Basin, and the Atlantic Coast.

After contact with Europeans, American Indians developed many other chordophones based on construction and playing techniques of European prototypes. However, native peoples modified and adapted these instruments to suit their own aesthetic values, musical styles, and performance contexts. Thus, over the centuries, these instruments have become indigenous. Some chordophones developed by Native Americans in the early postcontact period include the harp, guitar, and fiddle. Particularly popular in North America is the fiddle. As a class of chordophones, fiddles are similar to guitars except that the strings are bowed rather than plucked. Many Native communities have developed indigenous fiddles, which they may prefer to call

violins. The Apache of the Southwest make a one- or two-string instrument called *tsii'edo'a'tl* (which they term a *violin* in English) from the hollow stalk of an agave plant; the instrument can be played in social and ceremonial contexts as well as for personal enjoyment.

Over time, American Indians have altered and adapted the materials used in constructing musical instruments. In the early 20th century, some Northeast and Southeast peoples made water drums from maple syrup buckets, while others used wooden kegs. Peoples from the Northwest Coast have used metal gun barrels to create end-blown flutes. By the late 20th century, many North American Indians used sections of plastic pipe as drum frames. In addition, for centuries American Indians have adopted and adapted the musical instruments and repertories of Europeans. These kinds of musical interaction and exchange illustrate the dynamic nature of native musical traditions and cultural processes.

MUSIC HISTORY OF THE NATIVE AMERICANS

The early history of American Indian musics may be gleaned from native methods of recounting history, traditional narratives, archaeology, iconography, and linguistics. Methods of recounting history existed among peoples such as the Inca and the Aztec. The Inca had a genre of historical songs, while the Aztec carved symbolic pictures onto some instruments indicating how, when, where, and by whom they were played. Traditional narratives as well as linguistics reveal that Native Americans have extensive histories of regional interaction; over time this has enriched and broadened their musical lives. Reciprocal participation in collective ceremonies has been a part of life among peoples of the Eastern Woodlands for centuries, with the result that a complex network of musical exchange has developed, extending from Florida to Ontario, Canada. Archaeology reveals extensive information about the history of musical instruments, and the study of ancient sculpture, paintings, and other visual materials suggests something about instrumental performance techniques and ceremonial contexts.

COLONIAL MIXTURES

Descriptions of native musics written by early European travelers and missionaries provide additional information on indigenous music history, but these accounts must be read with a critical eye, because they often explain as much about the writers' prejudices as they do about music. Some of the most important literature on indigenous music history has been provided by writers who were themselves American Indians. Francis La Flesche, of mixed Omaha, Ponca, and French ancestry, was the first North American Indian to become an anthropologist; he was the author or coauthor of several early 20th-century publications on indigenous music that continue to be relevant a century later.

From the 1500s through the 1700s, Native Americans borrowed and adapted many European musical instruments and genres through creative processes of musical interaction. Soon after contact, Europeans began teaching American Indians to read, perform, and compose European music and to build European instruments. Contact with European musics has had a lasting impact on Native Americans. Spanish colonists taught Pueblo peoples of the Southwest to perform the *matachines* dance, a pantomime accompanied by violin and guitar; the Pueblos blended this dance with their own spiritual practices, and it now occupies a central role in their traditional ceremonialism. The colonists also transported Africans to the Western Hemisphere, and the Africans, in turn, influenced American Indians. Africans introduced new drums and other instruments to indigenous peoples from the southeastern United States to Suriname. The disastrous consequence of contact was that millions of native peoples died from European epidemics, enslavement, warfare, and outright massacre; in some cases entire cultures became extinct.

INDIGENOUS TRENDS FROM 1800

New indigenous musical trends emerged in the 1800s as native communities began to develop their own hymn repertories, fiddle traditions, and marching bands. American Indians began publishing their own hymnals for use in Christian worship during the first half of the 19th century. Some of these books—such as *Indian Melodies*, published in 1845 by the Narragansett composer Thomas Commuck—present hymn tunes composed in European notation by Native American musicians with texts in English. Other sources provide hymn texts in an Indian language, sometimes in a newly created writing system. The Cherokee published a hymnal using the syllabary completed in 1821 by Sequoyah. This kind of hymnal does not include musical notation; rather, the congregants learn the melodies through oral tradition. In the 21st century, Christian hymns in Indian languages constitute an important repertory of traditional music throughout the Americas, and indigenous peoples also perform hymns and gospel songs in English. Indian-language hymns tend to be sung from memory without instrumental accompaniment, whereas hymns in English feature piano or organ accompaniment.

Native Americans began playing European fiddle music by the 1800s, and those repertories are considered traditional in the 21st century. The Mi'kmaq fiddler Lee Cremo is well known among the First Nations of Canada, while the Coushatta fiddler Deo Langley won a regional Cajun music contest in Louisiana during the 1980s. By the 1860s, the Tohono O'odham fiddlers were playing music for the mazurka, schottische, and polka at public dances in Tucson, Ariz.; they developed a repertory known as *waila* that has become an important traditional music. A similar history unfolded among Indian marching bands, which began performing in the mid-1800s for parades, fairs, and exhibitions, attracting both native and nonnative audiences.

Other musical innovations of the 1800s were associated with the development of new belief systems such as the Indian Shaker Church, the Ghost Dance, and the Native American Church. The Indian Shaker Church developed in about 1882 among the Squaxin people of the Northwest Coast under the leadership of John Slocum and Mary Slocum, who combined indigenous healing practices with a church-centred form of worship. Their sacred music includes Indian-language hymns accompanied by foot stomping and handbells. Two successive incarnations of the Ghost Dance were fostered by Great Basin prophets who experienced millenarian visions involving the imminent return of the dead (hence "ghost"), the retreat of settlers, and the restoration of Indian lands, food supplies, and ways of life. These ends, it was believed, would be hastened by the dances and songs revealed to the prophets and also by strict observance of a moral code that emphasized harmony, hard work, and sobriety and that forbade war against Indians or Euro-Americans. The Ghost Dance involved collective singing and dancing without instrumental accompaniment; the songs followed the general musical style associated with the area, using paired-phrase structure, moderate tempos, narrow melodic ranges, and blended unison. In 1890 the U.S. government banned the Ghost Dance, but some adherents continued to perform it in private into the late 20th century.

The Native American Church, based on native spiritual traditions from northern Mexico, was introduced to the Apache in the 1700s, expanded throughout North America during the 1800s, and became an organized religion during the 1900s. This syncretic belief system combines rituals and beliefs of traditional indigenous religions with Christianity; prayer meetings involve the ingestion of peyote, a traditional medicine that has hallucinogenic properties. The songs performed during prayer meetings have a distinctive style unlike any other North American Indian music. These songs are accompanied by a water drum and rattle; they feature a kind of strophic form, a fast tempo, and a somewhat tense and nasal vocal quality. Since they represent a form of prayer, the songs are performed in a quiet and reflective manner.

The most significant innovation in Native American music during the 1900s was the development of the powwow, a collective celebration involving music and dance performed throughout North America. The term *powwow* derives from a word in the Algonquian language referring to healing rituals. In the early 20th century, the term was used in reference to traditional gatherings, and it later became associated with a specific kind of event based on aspects of Plains cultures. Powwows differ from one another

in terms of length (one or more days), details of organization, and sponsorship, but each event generally begins with the Grand Entry of the colour guard and dancers into the arena, followed by a welcome speech. Then most powwows include performances in various categories of dance, such as Men's Traditional, Women's Traditional, Men's Fancy Dance, Women's Fancy Shawl, Grass Dance (male), and Jingle Dress Dance (female). The exact number and names of dances differ somewhat across North America.

Many powwows involve dance competitions, with prizes awarded in each category. Powwow songs often reflect the style of music from the Plains area. The singers accompany themselves on a large bass drum, and the ensemble as a whole is known as a Drum. Each Drum includes three or more singers. Like many other aspects of 21st-century Native American life, powwows generally promote indigenous culture, spirituality, and social unity. Most powwows are open to the public; they offer an excellent opportunity for non-Indians to experience Native American music and dance.

Other significant 20th-century developments were the rise of Native American popular music and the nearly simultaneous renaissance of indigenous musics. Some Native Americans became involved in popular music early on. Yet not until the 1960s did Native American popular music come of age. Native American musicians participate in many genres, including jazz, rock and roll, blues, country, folk, gospel, rap, hip-hop, new age, *norteño*, and reggae. Their lyrics express native issues and concerns in both English and native languages, and the music is appreciated by Indians and non-Indians alike. Some of the best-known Native North American popular musicians are Buffy Sainte-Marie (Cree), Philippe McKenzie (Innu [Montagnais]), Joanne Shenandoah (Oneida), Joy Harjo (Creek), Geraldine Barney (Navajo), Robert Mirabal (Taos Pueblo), and Jim Pepper (Kaw and Creek). Some well-known Native North American groups include Redbone, XIT, and Ulali. Movements to revive and restore Native American musical repertories had begun by the 1950s and were common throughout the hemisphere by the 1990s.

PARTICIPATION IN ART MUSIC

American Indians have been active for centuries as composers of European art music. The first published Native North American composer of European art music was Thomas Commuck, whose hymnal, as mentioned above, appeared in 1845. Native North American composers of the 20th century have produced symphonies, ballets, chamber music, choral music, film scores, and more; these include Carl Fischer (Cherokee), Jack Kilpatrick (Cherokee), Louis Ballard (Cherokee-Quapaw), and Brent Michael Davids (Mohican).

European and European American composers have long been influenced by American Indian musics. The first European composer to quote an Indian melody in a piece of art music appears to have been the French missionary Gabriel Sagard-Théodat, who in 1636 published a Mi'kmaq song arranged in four-part harmony. In the 1700s, European composers such as Carl Heinrich Graun, James Hewitt, and Louis-Emmanuel Jadin produced operas based on aspects of native peoples, without incorporating indigenous melodies or style elements.

Serious efforts to develop American musical nationalism began during the late 1800s, when composers such as Edward MacDowell (United States) began to quote indigenous melodies in their operas, symphonic music, and short piano pieces. Interest in American musical nationalism peaked in the first half of the 20th century, when composers throughout the Western Hemisphere, including Arthur Farwell (United States), participated in the Indianist movement, using indigenous melodies, rhythms, and musical instruments. Interest in Indianism had declined by the mid-20th century, although a few composers continued to refer to native peoples in their music.

THE STUDY OF AMERICAN INDIAN MUSICS

The study of American Indian musics began in the late 1800s with the emergence of a scholarly discipline called comparative musicology, which later became known as ethnomusicology. The first ethnomusicological study was a book on Native American music published in 1882 by Theodore Baker. His research methods included interviewing Indian musicians, observing performances of indigenous music and dance, and transcribing the melodies in European staff notation. In 1890 scholars began to document native musics through sound recordings, which have remained central to ethnomusicological research.

After more than a century of study, thousands of sound recordings, musical transcriptions, and publications exist on American Indian musics. At first, native music research focused on documenting musical cultures that were thought to be vanishing. But these musics did not disappear, and 21st-century research thus emphasizes documenting current musical practices, repatriating archival materials, and supporting community-based preservation and transmission initiatives. Some major archives for American Indian musics include the Archive of Folk Culture of the Library of Congress (Washington, D.C.), the Archives of Traditional Music at Indiana University (Bloomington), and the Phonograph Archive (Berlin).

Authenticity is an issue in the understanding and appreciation of American Indian music. Indigenous people define authenticity according to their own musical concepts and values, which sometimes differ from the criteria applied by outsiders. Some non-Indians think that musical instruments constructed from manufactured materials, such as plastic pipes, lack authenticity and are therefore inferior to instruments made from natural materials. However, Native American musicians define authenticity through construction methods, sound quality, and use rather than by outward appearance. Similarly, non-Indians sometimes devalue certain kinds of native performance, including ceremonial dances recontextualized for public folkloric demonstrations or newer styles such as hymns or fiddle music. Yet for Native Americans, these performance styles and contexts provide opportunities to reaffirm core cultural values, to celebrate identity, and to maintain connections to the past. Music and tradition in Indian communities are continually renewed through creative processes and play an integral role in the ongoing reproduction of culture.

CHAPTER 9

NATIVE AMERICAN DANCE

The treatment of Native American dance in this chapter is meant to focus first on certain general features of dance and their manifestation in a number of areas. The diversities existing within this larger framework then become apparent through consideration of the dances of the several culture areas or tribal groupings.

Among the essential factors in an overall picture of Native American dance are the diverse types of dance, the organization of the dances in terms of participation, and the relations of human and deity expressed in the dances. In addition, a variety of other stylistic considerations are relevant, as are the foreign influences that have been absorbed.

EXTENT OF DANCE FORMS

Many themes, typically the celebrations of life transitions, developed in the Americas during millennia of residence, migration, and exchange. These were most prominent in the marginal cultures, such as those of western North America (particularly in what is now California). Mortuary rites were prominent in the northland and the deserts. War and hunt dances have had different degrees of prominence, their greatest development being among the hunters in the Great Plains of North America. So-called animal dances varied according to the local fauna, a tiger mime belonging to tropical peoples and a bear cult reaching across the northern part of North America and into Siberia.

Religious magic, or shamanism, practiced by societies or individual priests, is somewhat similar to some practices among Siberian peoples. Variously practiced and used for healing the sick and communication with the spirit world, shamanism is most potent and most trance-oriented among the Arctic peoples.

PATTERNS OF PARTICIPATION

A distinction between performer and spectator has long existed in American Indian dance, though it is not the artificial separation that characterizes much of Western stage dancing. This latter condition has occurred only with the performance, largely in North America, of dances for tourists and during indigenous participation in folk dance festivals or regional powwow gatherings.

Spirit impersonations, including maskings and noise, were used in widely separated areas to frighten nondancers. Specific instances of such practice included the puberty rites of the Kwakiutl Kusiut of British Columbia in Canada, among whom ceremonies were held in dance houses with a definite performing area. Except for a few specialized rites like the eagle and False Face dances, the change of roles among spectators, dancers, and musicians is characteristic of the sacred ceremonies of the Iroquois longhouses of the Northeast Indians of North America. Outsiders are welcomed, especially into such dances for the Creator as the great feather and drum dances; and all, from the aged to mothers with babies in arms, are expected to join in.

Among the Pueblos of the U.S. Southwest, the dancers remain separate because they require special rehearsals and ritual blessings. When they emerge from their sanctuaries, or kivas, onto the dancing plaza, they dance to invoke rain, health, and other blessings for the people from the supernatural spirits. After the ceremony, they often join in less-formal social dances that unite all participants and observers. Though these dances have religious connotations, as among the Iroquois, they are secular, and anyone may enter or drop out at will.

SOCIALLY DETERMINED ROLES IN DANCE

Visitors may not perceive the patterns of social organization reflected in the dances. It is clear that men or women alone begin some dances and the other sex may then join in and that men monopolize some dances, women others. Less clear are the relations, especially complex in the longhouse dances of the Iroquois, between the moieties, the complementary divisions of the tribe based either on kinship or on ceremonial function. In all Iroquois dances, specific traditions decree the nature and degree of male and female participation and whether they dance simultaneously but separately or in pairs or other combinations. The leader of the dance and song and his helper, however, must be of different moieties, whether they lead from the floor or from the sidelines. When women enter a dance line, singly or with another, they must pair with a moiety opposite, or "cousin."

The Iroquois moiety pattern is crossed by another comprising various public or secret societies whose members are bound together for life, often joining the society during illness or other catastrophe. These societies perform such dances as the False Face curative rites, the female mortuary dances known as *ohgiwe*, and the dances of the sexually integrated Bear and Buffalo medicine societies. Elsewhere, religious dance societies were based on age grades, as in the male warrior societies of the northern Plains.

RELIGIOUS EXPRESSION IN DANCE

Religious symbolism is significant even in the human interactions of the dance. Men often symbolize phallic, aggressive supernatural beings and rain-bringing deities, whereas women symbolize actual fertility. In Iroquois ceremonies, women represent the Three Life-Giving Sisters— i.e., the spirits of corn (maize), beans, and squash, with no mimetic representation. Similarly, Pueblo women promote plant and human fertility by their symbolic dancing.

With no mimetic elements, the basket dance of the Tewa Pueblo rites includes invocations for plant growth and for the transmission of the gift of human life. The ceremony symbolizes the woman's central role in sustaining the life of the pueblo.

In the animal realm there are also separate roles for men and women. Ottawa and Ho-Chunk women imitate the winged flight of wild swans and geese, whereas the Iroquois and Pueblo men represent eagles. Both men and women join in the mime of supernatural bears and buffalo in ceremonies of the latter tribes, more realistically in Iroquois dances. In the Southwest, especially in the New Mexican pueblos, male representations of supernatural deer show gradations of stylization ranging from the naturalistic portrayals in Taos Pueblo to the semistylization in Santa Clara, San Ildefonso, Cochiti, and San Felipe pueblos, in which sticks replace forepaws, to the abstract upright deer dancers of San Juan Pueblo and masked, unreal deer in the kachina (*katsina*) dance of the Hopi. The solo deer dancer of the Arizona and Sonora (Mexico) Yaqui, always a man, is relatively realistic, with mime of the hunt and killing.

On the whole, in both Americas, agricultural dances tend to be abstract, and animal dances are usually decidedly mimetic. The animal maskers of British Columbia are terrifying portrayals of supernatural beings.

Here and there the human-deity relationship is expressed in hand gestures. The Kwakiutl of northwest North America evolved codified ceremonial

Yaqui deer dancer from Sonora, Mexico. Miguel Salgado

sign languages, as did the Pueblos, Aztecs, and Maya. In San Juan Pueblo of New Mexico, the appearance of the rain gods is heralded by two ceremonial clowns using traditional gestures. Looking for the rain gods in the clouds, one of the clowns claps ashes from his hands, representing a cloud. He looks upward, shading his eyes to indicate his attempt to see into the distance. This gesture is always used whenever the clown speaks of what he "sees." The clowns repeat this action toward the four points of the compass, continuing to see the approaching rain gods, who bring with them the rain cloud. Similar performers may appear in the pueblo's plaza, outside the kiva. Dancing, unmasked clowns enact motions of luring rain, of sowing seeds, of digging, and of gathering the plants as they rise from the ground.

Clowns also appear in the men's spring dances and in the summer corn dances. After their entrance with a large group of male and female dancers, the corn dance singers station themselves in an arc near the drummers. They fit gestures to tunes and texts that are composed for each occasion but follow a traditional pattern and trend of ideas, beckoning to the rain gods in their cloud homes in the north, west, south, and east.

Invocations to the directions survive among the peoples originally from the Great Plains and Great Lakes areas, especially in the pipe dance. A solitary man offers a pipe to the thunderbird in the east, south, west, and north, moving clockwise, then to the deities of the sky and earth.

PATTERNS AND BODY MOVEMENT

This religious, nature-oriented concept of space differs from that of Western folk and art dance, which has only geometrical or emotional significance. The geometric ground plans, however, show similarities with Western practices. The circling dances are sunwise in areas of former hunting people and countersunwise, or widdershins, among agriculturalists. Serpentine line dances also prevail among agriculturalists, notably among the Iroquois and Pueblo peoples. Among the Iroquois, many round dances are open, with a leader, coincidentally resembling dances of the Balkans of southeastern Europe.

Characteristic of Indian dancers is a slightly forward-tilted posture, forward raising of the knee, flat-footed stamp or toe-heel action, and tendencies toward muscular relaxation and restraint in gesture. This basic style of body movement varies not only from area to area or from tribe to tribe but also from dance to dance and even from one individual to another. The agricultural dances generally are performed with an upright posture and an easy manner. Male war dances may include complex gyrations and flexion of the torso, as do animal dances. Vision and clown dances may induce bodily distortion.

Posture, however, varies with sex. Women tend to be more erect than men, to lift their feet and knees less, and in general to perform in a more restrained manner. Except for the war dances, women use the same steps as men, within the stylistic restrictions. In the woodlands of eastern North America, everyone proceeds with the stomp step, a flat-footed trot. In the Pueblo area, where men and women use a similar step, the dancers also specialize in a foot lift and solid stamp. In certain dances, especially clown, animal, and war dances and in some social round dances, individuals often invent variants of the basic steps. Sometimes the innovators borrow American ballroom steps such as those of the Charleston, though they adapt them to their own styles. The steps and formations of the Indian dance, as well as the overall structure of a dance or ceremony, follow the music closely.

FOREIGN INFLUENCES AND REGIONAL DANCE STYLES

Among the influences from the Old World, the dances of northern Europe and the Euro-American dances have found little acceptance. The longhouse Iroquois reject all Euro-American dances. Among the few influences are some Oklahoma jazzlike, war-dance steps, an Indian two-step danced by couples, and a waltz in a Pueblo social dance.

The most distinctive tribal dance customs originated in response to animistic religious beliefs—i.e., that all objects and living things have living souls. The customs changed with prehistoric and historic migrations, with intertribal contact, and, since European contact, with upheavals in the way of life and thought. Although many dances became extinct, some survived European influences; others are amazing hybrids or new creations of the period after European colonization.

To give an accurate understanding of the role of dance in traditional Indian society, it is necessary to examine both dances that became extinct as European influences weakened tribal customs and dances that have survived, with or without European modification.

ESKIMO (INUIT)

In some places the traditional shamanistic exhibitions and masked animal rites persist alongside Western-style square dances. The most prominent ritual figure in the former was the *angakok*, the shaman who communed with spirits by the rhythm of a single-headed drum and by ecstatic dancing, usually inside an igloo.

Formerly, Eskimos held elaborate outdoor ceremonies for whale catches and similar events. In Alaska, preliminaries included the rhythmic mime of a successful whale catch, with a woman in the role of the whale. A sprinkling of ashes on the ice drove away evil spirits, and there were incantations and songs when leaving shore, when sighting the whale, and before throwing the spear, all of them songs that the "great *kashak* (priest)" sang when he created the whale. As the whale was towed in, Fox Islands men and boys danced, naked except for wooden masks that reached to their shoulders. At Cape Prince of Wales on the Bering Strait, the whaler's wife came to meet the boat in ceremonial dress, dancing and singing, and boys and girls performed gesture dances on the beach. Then, inside a circle of large whale ribs, the whaler's wife and children performed a dance of rejoicing. In what is now Nunavut on the west coast of Hudson Bay in Canada, communal feasting, dancing, singing, games, and shamanistic performances took place within a circle of bones or one of stones. The men's motions consisted of vigorous and angular arm jerking and jumping, the women's of curving gestures and swaying with the torso and arms, in a seated or standing posture.

NORTHEAST AND SOUTHEAST INDIANS

In the area from the Atlantic coast to about the Mississippi River and across

Detail of Ojibwa birch-bark scroll showing ceremonial dance in a moiety-determined pattern, c. 1875; in the Denver Art Museum, Colorado. Courtesy of the Denver Art Museum, Denver, Colorado

the Great Lakes and the St. Lawrence River, dream, medicine, plant, war, calumet (ceremonial peace pipe), and animal dances predominate. Among the Northeast Indians, mortuary and hunting rites are dominant; among Southeast Indians, corn, bean, and squash rites are most frequent. The recurrent dance pattern is a counterclockwise circling by large groups, with a running step or stomp to antiphonal singing (alternation of two groups or of a leader and a group). Medicine rites are often exclusively for female or male members of a society, but dances for hunting or agriculture admit men, women, and children. During the winter and in war or hunting ceremonies, men are the organizers and leaders; during the summer and in agricultural ceremonies, women are featured performers.

The Iroquois continue to maintain their ancient ceremonies and a large repertory of dances and songs, including rites for crises of life and for animals and plants. They also have acquired steps and dances from other tribes, especially those of formations in two straight lines. The Iroquois bear dance combines former hunting associations both with a clan-origin legend and with a curative society. When the bear spirit is displeased, he causes neurotic spasms in a person and must be appeased in a ritual at midwinter or in private summer ceremonies. The focal personnel consist of the patient and paired conductors, dance leaders, and singers from opposite moieties.

Ceremonial songs and ritual offerings are followed by group dancing in which visitors and society members participate.

Although the Cherokee of the Smoky Mountains in North Carolina and Tennessee speak an Iroquoian language and have animal dances, they emphasize corn dance ceremonies. The Creek, Yuchi, Seminole, and other tribes of the southeastern United States greatly emphasize the summer green corn harvest ceremony, or Busk. Before the removal of many of those tribes to reservations in Oklahoma, they acquired a few dances outside their own traditions. They carried the stomp circling to its utmost development by winding the line of dancers into a spiral or even into four spirals at the four corners of the dance ground.

Among tribes of the large Algonquian family, the stomp dances performed until a few decades ago by the Penobscot of Maine and the Narraganset of Rhode Island have experienced a strong revival. Algonquian tribes around the Great Lakes share many of the medicine and animal dance ceremonies known to the Iroquois, and the more southerly groups hold corn dances. The Ojibwa (Chippewa) in the Upper Peninsula of Michigan and the Menominee and Ho-Chunk of Wisconsin have maintained a hunting dance and a special wild-rice ceremonial danced in September when this crop is harvested. These groups show the influence of the adjoining Great Plains tribes in some of the circle dances, men's war dances, and buffalo dances.

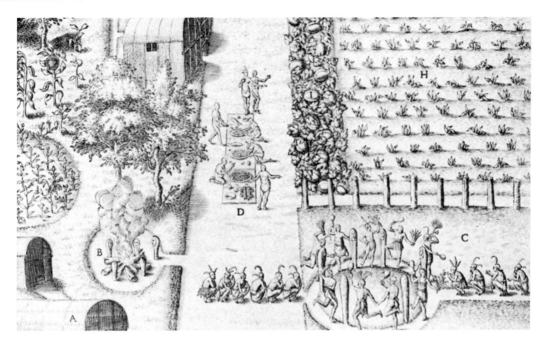

Crop fertility dance of an Algonquian tribe in Virginia, detail of an engraving by Theodor de Bry after a watercolour by John White, 1590; in the collection of the Thomas Gilcrease Institute of American History and Art, Tulsa, Okla. Courtesy of the Thomas Gilcrease Institute of American History and Art, Tulsa, Oklahoma

THE GREAT PLAINS

In the area extending from the Mississippi River to the Rocky Mountains and from Texas and Oklahoma into Canada, the dream dance ritual becomes part of a visionary cult associated with boys' puberty and with a votive Sun Dance ceremony. During the one to four days' duration of the Sun Dance, usually held during the summer solstice, the participants abstain from food and drink. Dancers paint their bodies in symbolic colours and carry an eagle-wing bone whistle in their mouths. To the beating of a large drum and the singing of special songs, they circle in procession and salute the sun with lamentation. They dance in place facing the sun and continue until falling unconscious or achieving a vision.

The calumet (peace pipe) and peace dance originated in the tobacco rite of such northern Plains tribes as the Crow, Dakota, and other Siouan-speaking groups. Its most elaborate development, however, was in the central Plains ritual of the Pawnee and the neighbouring Omaha,

Bull Dance, Mandan O-kee-pa Ceremony, *oil painting by George Catlin, 1832; in the Smithsonian American Art Museum, Washington, D.C.* National Museum of American Art, Washington, D.C.

Iowa, Ponca, and Osage. The war dance is organized into male war societies. Women, in turn, have a variety of societies emphasizing fertility and also perform a scalp dance. Animals are associated as tutelaries, or guardian spirits, in the vision, war, and fertility cults. The most spectacular hunting ceremonies, such as the bull dance of the Mandans, developed from the economic significance of the buffalo herds. Buffalo rites merged with sun, war, and fertility ceremonies and spread to tribes in other areas. The individual warrior, his prowess, and dancing skill were extolled as women progressed clockwise in a closed circle, with a sideward shuffle

or bounce unlike the running step of the woodlands Indians.

THE NORTHWEST COAST

Indian tribes along the Pacific coasts of Washington and British Columbia developed masked medicine dances and elaborate fishing ceremonies, such as that performed for a bountiful salmon catch. Their two most striking types of ceremonies are the potlatch, a feast and a dance for display and distribution of the host's wealth, and the midwinter initiation ceremony. Lasting several months in a special dance house, this rite initiates

SUN DANCE

The most important religious ceremony of the Plains Indians of North America is the Sun Dance. Traditionally, a Sun Dance was held by each tribe once a year in late spring or early summer, when the buffalo congregated after the long Plains winters. The large herds provided a plentiful food source for the hundreds of individuals in attendance.

The origin of the Sun Dance is unclear. Most tribal traditions attribute its conventions to a time deep in the past. By the end of the 19th century it had spread to include most of the tribes from the Saulteaux in Saskatchewan, Canada, south to the Kiowa in Texas.

The most elaborate versions of the Sun Dance required up to a year's preparation by those pledging to dance. Typically the pledges' spiritual mentors and extended families were heavily involved in the preparations, as they were obligated to provide most of the necessary supplies—payments or gifts to mentors and ritual leaders, often in the form of elaborately decorated clothing, horses, food, and other goods.

As the community gathered, specific individuals—usually members of a particular religious society—erected a dance structure with a central pole that symbolized a connection to the divine, as embodied by the sun. Preliminary dances by a variety of community members often preceded the rigours of the Sun Dance itself, encouraging supplicants and ritually preparing the dance grounds. One such preliminary was the Buffalo Bull Dance, which preceded the Sun Dance during the complex Okipa ritual of the Mandan people.

Those who had pledged to endure the Sun Dance generally did so in fulfillment of a vow or as a way of seeking spiritual power or insight. Supplicants began dancing at an appointed hour and continued intermittently for several days and nights; during this time they neither ate nor drank. In some tribes supplicants also endured ritual self-mortification beyond fasting and exertion; in others such practices were thought to be self-aggrandizing. When practiced, self-mortification was generally accomplished through piercing: Mentors or ritual leaders inserted two or more slim skewers or piercing needles through a small fold of the supplicant's skin on the upper chest or upper back; the mentor then used long leather thongs to tie a heavy object such as a buffalo skull to the skewers. A dancer would drag the object along the ground until he succumbed to exhaustion or his skin tore free. Among some tribes the thongs were tied to the centre pole, and the supplicant either hung from or pulled on them until free. Piercing was endured by only the most committed individuals, and, as with the rest of the ritual, it was done to ensure tribal well-being as well as to fulfill the supplicant's individual vow.

In 1883 the U.S. Secretary of the Interior criminalized the Sun Dance and a variety of other indigenous religious practices. Despite government efforts, the original forms of the Sun Dance were never completely repressed, and in the early 21st century sun dancing remained a significant religious ritual among many Plains peoples.

young men into a ceremonial society and includes many highly individual masked enactments of totemic spirits.

The Great Basin, the Plateau, and California

Great Basin Indians, such as the Havasupai of the Grand Canyon and the related Yumans, developed agricultural dances. The Yuman Mojave (Mohave) stress cremation processions and ceremonies, but, like the Navajo, they also have curative and animal dances with long song cycles. In this area the vision quest ceremony is at its peak, and in southern California the Diegueño and Luiseño aided the vision by means of a narcotic, *Datura*. Some tribes, such as the Paiute and the Coast Salish, individually danced themselves into trances. In this area arose the Ghost Dance, a religious movement whose rituals included a hypnotic circle dance that spread to the Great Plains in the 19th century. The ceremonies are frequently addressed to the spirits of the dead. There are also many two-line dances, especially among the Ute and southern Paiute. The innumerable small tribes of California shared some of the preoccupations with vision, cure, and death, as well as the seed and root gathering economy of the tribes adjoining them on the east. They specialized in elaborate masked ceremonies for the initiation of boys and less elaborate circle dances for girls' puberty rites. The more northerly groups also stressed exhibition of dexterity and costuming.

The Southwest

The semiarid desert country from the Rio Grande west to the Mojave Desert of southern California and into northern Mexico and the southern Rocky Mountains is subdivided into three tribal areas: the Pueblo farmers along the Upper Rio Grande, the Zuni of New Mexico, and the Hopi of northern Arizona; the Navajo nomads, now turned shepherds; and the desert tribes that include agriculturists such as the Pima, Tohono O'odham, Yaqui, and former nomads, such as the Apache. The pueblo dwellers of New Mexico and Arizona perform medicine rites and many winter animal and fertility dances. But the cycle of summer corn ceremonies and continuous prayers for rain form the core of their ceremonialism. The dances, organized by a male priesthood, are mostly well-practiced collective performances. Summer and winter clan or moiety groupings dominate ceremonies in alternation rather than through interaction as among the Iroquois. The most characteristic step is a stamp followed by a foot lift in a stationary line. This predominates especially in the very sacred dances held in the kivas, or sanctuaries. Semisacred dances in the village plaza add other steps and formations such as double lines, circles, and interweavings.

The most spectacular public dances of the Pueblos are the corn dances, or *tablita* dances, named for the women's tablet crowns with cloud symbols. They recur at various times during the spring and summer, with most pageantry after Easter and on the pueblo's saint's day. The people pay homage to the patron saint in an early morning mass and a procession to the plaza carrying the saint's image, followed in the evening by a recessional to the church. By tradition each performance of the corn dance includes a slow and a fast dance. In the slow dance for entering the plaza, a chorus of 7 to 70 older men shuffles across the plaza, singing and invoking the rain gods. A banner bearer leads a double file of 12 to 200 dancers, with a pair of men always ahead of a pair of women. For 10 minutes they trot counterclockwise around the plaza. Following a pause, the singers form an arc, and the dancers line up face-to-face in two or four long files. They cross over, circle, and interweave in elaborate formations. Clowns meander in and out among the lines. The entire set is repeated at the other end of the plaza, and the group retires. The two moieties make alternate appearances. On the last appearance

Hopi Snake Dance, *watercolour by Awa Tsireh, c. 1920; in the Denver Art Museum, Colorado.* Courtesy of the Denver Art Museum, Denver, Colorado

they combine, with the two choruses singing simultaneously.

One of the most famous ceremonies is the snake-antelope dance of the Hopi in Arizona, a rite in which snakes are released in the four directions to seek rain. It includes swaying dancing to rattles and guttural chant, circling of the plaza with snakes, and ceremonial sprinkling of corn meal on the principal dancers by women of the snake clan. Masked dancers are a striking feature of Pueblo ceremonialism. The kachina dancers are sacred and represent the rain gods. Clowns with various names represent an ancient ritual heritage; in their black-and-white striped disguise of paint, they are eerie and also comical. Pueblo masking influenced neighbouring tribal dances such as the curative *yeibichai* of the Navajo. Curative ceremonies, with long song cycles, are emphasized by the Navajo, along with circular social dances, recalling those of the Great Plains tribes. The Apache have developed a spectacular masked dance, called the *gahan*, to obtain cures but chiefly to celebrate a girl's coming of age. They also have rites for vision and divination, sometimes with the aid of a vision-inducing communal drinking ceremony. The male dance style is strong, angular, even acrobatic, while the women's style is subdued.

STUDY AND EVALUATION

The secular dances of native North America, such as the Oklahoma dances, the round and war dances of Plains tribes,

and the stomps of Southeastern tribes, all have spread from coast to coast in modern times. The most copious and reliable materials on these and other aboriginal dances are strewn through the works of anthropologists, folklorists, and a few musicians. General descriptions are often incorporated into anthropological studies and into notes on earlier observations by colonists, missionaries, and 19th-century scholars. Essential to all such studies is an examination of the arts in their cultural context. It is equally important to recognize the dance as an expressive art, to learn and analyze the movements, and to present them in dance notation alongside musical scores. Such presentation facilitates intertribal and intercontinental comparisons. The materials must stem from fieldwork, but they can be supplemented by the many motion pictures in college archives and museums and in repositories such as the Wenner-Gren Foundation and the American Philosophical Society.

CONCLUSION

For Native Americans the period between first contact with Europeans and the present day was, for the most part, bloody and painful. This circumstance intensified after 1776 and the formation of the new republic. Whereas the Indians had earlier dealt with representatives of Europe-based empires seeking only access to selected resources from a distant continent, now they faced a resident, united people yearly swelling in numbers, determined to make every acre of the West their own and culturally convinced of their absolute title under the laws of God and history. There was no room for compromise. Even before 1776, each step toward American independence reduced the Indians' control over their own future.

For armed resistance to have had any hope of success, unity would be required between all the Indians from the Appalachians to the Mississippi. This unity simply could not be achieved. The Shawnee leaders known as Tenskwatawa, or the Prophet, and his brother Tecumseh attempted this kind of rallying movement in the first decade of the 19th century, much as Pontiac had done some 40 years earlier, with equal lack of success.

The outbreak of the War of 1812 sparked renewed Indian hopes of protection by the crown, should the British win. Tecumseh himself was actually commissioned as a general in the royal forces, but at the Battle of the Thames in 1813, he was killed, and his dismembered body parts, according to legend, were divided between his conquerors as gruesome souvenirs.

In 1814 U.S. Gen. Andrew Jackson defeated the British-supported Creeks in the Southwest in the Battle of Horseshoe Bend. The war itself ended in a draw that left American territory intact. Thereafter, with minor exceptions, there was no major Indian resistance east of the Mississippi. After the lusty first quarter century of American nationhood, all roads left open to Native Americans ran downhill.

In the East, centuries of coexistence with whites has led to some degree of intermarriage and assimilation and to various patterns of stable adjustment. In the West, the hasty expansion of agricultural settlement crowded the Native Americans into reservations, where federal policy has vacillated between efforts at assimilation and the desire to preserve tribal cultural identity, with unhappy consequences. The Native American population has risen from its low point of 235,000 in 1900 to 2.5 million at the turn of the 21st century.

The reservations are often enclaves of deep poverty and social distress, although in some instances the casinos operated on Native American land have created great wealth. The physical and social isolation of the reservation prompted many Native Americans to migrate to large cities, but by the end of the 20th century, a modest repopulation occurred in rural counties of the Great Plains. In the latter half of the 20th century, intertribal organizations were founded to give Native Americans a unified, national presence. Although their battle for reparations of stolen sacred objects was difficult, the tide of personal opinion was turning in the 21st century and many museums had begun to repatriate these materials. Moreover, in 2008, Canadian Prime Minister Stephen Harper apologized to indigenous Canadians for the abuses that occurred in the Indian Residential Schools. Further battles remained to be fought.

GLOSSARY

aboriginal Being the first or the earliest of its kind in a particular region.

acculturation The process of changes in customs and beliefs from one culture to another, either voluntarily or as the result of being vanquished.

aerophone A class of musical instruments that make sound when encountering a vibrating air mass.

animism The belief that all things—animate or otherwise—had a living essence and were capable or either harming or helping human beings.

apotropaic Possessing the ability to ward off evil spirits.

breechcloth A soft leather strip drawn between the legs and held in place by securing at the waist with a belt.

calumet A ceremonial tobacco pipe, known colloquially as a "peace pipe."

chordophone A class of musical instrument that sounds when its strings are plucked.

circumlocution The unnecessary use of many words to describe an object or concept.

consanguineous Having the same familial relationships; blood relatives.

cosmogony Creation theory.

culture area The anthropological term for a geographic region in which the inhabitants share many societal traits.

dugout A boat made from a single hollowed-out log.

effigy mounds Large earthen berm in the shape of a bird or other animal that may be tied to Native American burials.

idiophone A class of musical instrument, made from solid material, which depends on vibrations to make sound.

joking relationship A humour-filled, exceedingly open, and occasionally ribald bond between two individuals or groups of people.

kashim A large subterranean house inhabited by Yupik men; also used for ceremonial circumstances.

levirate A custom in which a man wed his dead brother's widow and took on the responsibility of providing for her and her children.

membranophone A class of musical instrument that produces sound when a stretched membrane is struck, such as a drum.

moiety A tribal subdivision that has a complementary counterpart.

petroglyphs Drawings etched into rock by ancient peoples as a form of communication or record.

plebiscite A tribal, regional, or country-wide vote to decide whether a proposal that affects all should be carried.

polyandry Being married to more than one man at the same time.

potlatch A ceremony marking a special occasion where the social status of members of Northwest native tribes was established or announced by the giving of gifts.

shaman A man or woman who has shown an exceptionally strong affinity with the spirit world. Shamans also are considered healers and are thought to be adept at divination.

sororate A custom practiced among some Plains tribes where a woman married the widower of her deceased sister.

subsistence The minimum of food and shelter necessary to support life.

taiga A biome where the land is covered by conifers and lichen, and the climate is harsh and cold.

transnationalism Extending beyond national boundaries.

travois A mode of transport used by Native Americans, created by two joined poles and a platform of some sort that is attached to both and draped between them.

tribe A large group that shares traditions, lineage, language, or ideology. Native American tribes are made up of smaller groups, called bands, that share some of these features.

vision quest A supernatural experience in which an individual seeks to interact with a guardian spirit, usually an anthropomorphized animal, to obtain advice or protection.

wampum Beaded strings or belts made from polished shells, to which some Native Americans ascribed monetary value.

wickiup A dome-shaped form of lodging favoured by Northeastern Native American peoples, constructed by draping bent saplings with rushes or bark.

BIBLIOGRAPHY

ARCTIC AND SUBARCTIC

William C. Sturtevant (ed.), *Handbook of North American Indians*, vol. 5, *Arctic*, ed. by David Damas (1984), is by far the single-most important and comprehensive source on Arctic peoples, with more than 50 articles covering environment, prehistory, physique, language, and the ethnography of specific groups from Greenland to the far western Aleutian Islands and Siberia. William S. Laughlin and Albert B. Harper (eds.), *The First Americans: Origins, Affinities, and Adaptations* (1979), explores physical anthropology of American Indians, with a heavy focus on Arctic peoples, including Eskimo and Aleuts. Robert McGhee, *Ancient People of the Arctic* (1996), presents the earliest history of the Canadian Eskimo, from the Arctic Small Tool tradition to the Thule culture. J. Louis Giddings, *Ancient Men of the Arctic* (1967, reissued 1985), is an archaeological study of the major progression of prehistoric cultures in the Bering Strait region. Wendell H. Oswalt, *Eskimos and Explorers* (1979), recounts the earliest known contacts with Eskimo groups by Europeans, from Greenland to western Alaska, excluding the Aleutian Islands and Siberia, and provides fairly standard, if sometimes arguable, early population estimates.

With some 20 books, the most prolific scholar of the American Arctic during the late 20th and early 21st century may be Ann Fienup-Riordan; much of her work features Yupik collaborators or translations of Yupik-language folklore and history. A sample includes Ann Fienup-Riordan, *The Nelson Island Eskimo: Social Structure and Ritual Distribution* (1983), her first book; *Eskimo Essays: Yupik Lives and How We See Them* (1990); *Hunting Tradition in a Changing World: Yup'ik Lives in Alaska Today* (2000); and *Yuungnaqpiallerput/ The Way We Genuinely Live: Masterworks of Yup'ik Science and Survival* (2007).

A number of classic syntheses of the traditional cultures of the American subarctic exist: Frederick Johnson (ed.), *Man in Northeastern North America* (1946, reprinted 1980), brings together authoritative papers on geography, physical anthropology, linguistics, mythology, psychological characteristics, and culture in general; William C. Sturtevant (ed.), *Handbook of North American Indians*, vol. 6, *Subarctic*, ed. by June Helm (1981), includes a series of topical essays on the region's peoples, cultures, and history; and Keith J. Crowe, *A History of the Original Peoples of Northern Canada*, rev. ed. (1991), is a useful textbook.

NORTHWEST COAST AND CALIFORNIA

Classic syntheses of the traditional cultures of the Northwest Coast include

Philip Drucker, *Indians of the Northwest Coast* (1955, reissued 1963) and *Cultures of the North Pacific Coast* (1965), the former emphasizing material culture, technology, and art and the latter emphasizing social and ceremonial organization; Norman Bancroft-Hunt and Werner Forman, *People of the Totem: The Indians of the Pacific Northwest* (1979); Robert H. Ruby and John A. Brown, *Indians of the Pacific Northwest: A History* (1981), and *A Guide to the Indian Tribes of the Pacific Northwest*, rev. ed. (1992), including North American Plateau peoples; Maximilien Bruggman and Peter R. Gerber, *Indians of the Northwest Coast* (1989; originally published in German, 1987); William C. Sturtevant (ed.), *Handbook of North American Indians*, vol. 7, *Northwest Coast*, ed. by Wayne Suttles (1990); and R.G. Matson, Gary Coupland, and Quentin Mackie (eds.), *Emerging from the Mist: Studies in Northwest Coast Culture History* (2003).

The histories of indigenous Northwest Coast peoples include Robert Boyd, *The Coming of the Spirit of Pestilence: Introduced Infectious Diseases and Population Decline Among Northwest Coast Indians, 1774–1874* (1999). Indigenous activism is addressed in a number of volumes, including Alexandra Harmon, *Indians in the Making: Ethnic Relations and Indian Identities Around Puget Sound* (1998). Local court records, mobility patterns, and methods for conflict resolution are analyzed in Brad Asher, *Beyond the Reservation: Indians, Settlers, and the Law in Washington Territory, 1853–1889* (1999); a consideration of the ways that methods of conflict resolution differ among a group of ethnically similar communities may be found in Bruce G. Miller, *The Problem of Justice: Tradition and Law in the Coast Salish World* (2001); and treaty making, the legal system, and regional economics are discussed in Roberta Ulrich, *Empty Nets: Indians, Dams, and the Columbia River*, 2nd ed. (2007).

Classic syntheses of the traditional cultures of the California Indians include A.L. Kroeber, *Handbook of the Indians of California* (1925, reprinted 1975); Robert F. Heizer and M.A. Whipple (compilers and eds.), *The California Indians: A Source Book*, 2nd ed., rev. and enlarged (1971); Lowell John Bean and Thomas C. Blackburn (eds.), *Native Californians: A Theoretical Retrospective* (1976); William C. Sturtevant (ed.), *Handbook of North American Indians*, vol. 8, *California*, ed. by Robert F. Heizer (1978); Robert F. Heizer and Albert B. Elsasser, *The Natural World of the California Indians* (1980); and Jack D. Forbes, *Native Americans of California and Nevada*, rev. ed. (1982).

PLATEAU AND GREAT BASIN

Although there is no broad synthesis of traditional Plateau cultures, essays considering the cultures and history of the region may be found in William C. Sturtevant (ed.), *Handbook of North American Indians*, vol. 12, *Plateau*, ed. by Deward E. Walker, Jr. (1998). Classic texts on the archaeology of the region include Earl H. Swanson, *The Emergence of Plateau Culture* (1962); and B. Robert Butler, *The Old Cordilleran Culture in the Pacific Northwest* (1961).

There is no general monograph on all Great Basin Indians, but William C. Sturtevant (ed.), *Handbook of the North American Indians*, vol. 11, *Great Basin*, ed. by Warren L. d'Azevedo (1986), provides summary articles on various groups and aspects of Great Basin anthropology; it also updates the approximately 6,500 references listed in Catherine S. Fowler (compiler), *Great Basin Anthropology: A Bibliography* (1970).

SOUTHWEST AND PLAINS

Regional syntheses of the traditional cultures of the Southwest include William C. Sturtevant (ed.), *Handbook of North American Indians*, vol. 9 and 10, *Southwest*, ed. by Alfonso Ortiz (1979–83); Linda S. Cordell, *Prehistory of the Southwest* (1984); and Trudy Griffin-Pierce, *Native Peoples of the Southwest* (2000), and *The Columbia Guide to American Indians of the Southwest* (2007).

Regional syntheses of the traditional cultures of the Plains include Robert H. Lowie, *Indians of the Plains* (1954, reprinted 1982), a classic work; W. Raymond Wood and Margot Liberty (eds.), *Anthropology on the Great Plains* (1980), a collection of topical essays; Peter Iverson (ed.), *The Plains Indians of the Twentieth Century* (1985); William C. Sturtevant (ed.), *Handbook of North*

American Indians, vol. 13, *Plains*, ed. by Raymond J. DeMallie, 2 vol. (2001); and Loretta Fowler, *The Columbia Guide to American Indians of the Great Plains* (2003). Patricia Albers and Beatrice Medicine, *The Hidden Half: Studies of Plains Indian Women* (1983), is one of the first scholarly collections written about and by Native American women.

The artistic and material traditions of the Plains are discussed in a number of richly illustrated volumes, such as George C. Frison, *Prehistoric Hunters of the High Plains*, 2nd ed. (1991); Evan M. Maurer, *Visions of the People: A Pictorial History of Plains Indian Life* (1992); Candace S. Greene and Russell Thornton (eds.), *The Year the Stars Fell: Lakota Winter Counts at the Smithsonian* (2007); and Michael Bad Hand Terry, *Daily Life in a Plains Indian Village, 1868* (1999), a volume that includes photos of rare items such as 19th-century sunglasses. The description, development, and symbolism of the earth lodge are the focus of the essays in Donna C. Roper and Elizabeth P. Pauls (eds.), *Plains Earthlodges: Ethnographic and Archaeological Perspectives* (2005); prehistoric and early historic material culture are the focus of Stanley A. Ahler and Marvin Kay (eds.), *Plains Village Archaeology: Bison Hunting Farmers in the Central and Northern Plains* (2007).

NORTHEAST AND SOUTHEAST

Regional syntheses of the traditional cultures of the Northeast are in Robert E.

Ritzenthaler and Pat Ritzenthaler, *The Woodland Indians of the Western Great Lakes* (1970, reissued 1991); Howard S. Russell, *Indian New England Before the Mayflower* (1980); Bruce G. Trigger, *Natives and Newcomers: Canada's "Heroic Age" Reconsidered* (1985), covering the period from 9000 bc to the mid-19th century; William C. Sturtevant (ed.), *Handbook of North American Indians*, vol. 15, *Northeast*, ed. by Bruce Trigger (1978); and Kathleen J. Bragdon, *The Columbia Guide to American Indians of the Northeast* (2001).

Regional syntheses of the traditional cultures of the Southeast are in John R. Swanton, *The Indians of the Southeastern United States* (1946, reprinted 1979); Fred B. Kniffen, Hiram F. Gregory, and George A. Stokes, *The Historic Indian Tribes of Louisiana: From 1542 to the Present* (1987); Charles Hudson, *The Southeastern Indians* (1976, reissued 1992); Theda Perdue and Michael D. Green, *The Columbia Guide to American Indians of the Southeast* (2001); and Raymond D. Fogelson (ed.), *Southeast* (2004), vol. 14 of *Handbook of North American Indians*, ed. by William C. Sturtevant.

The profound impact of removal on the Southeastern tribes is illuminated in a variety of works, including Grant Foreman, *The Five Civilized Tribes* (1934, reissued 1989), and *Indian Removal: The Emigration of the Five Civilized Tribes of Indians*, new ed. (1972, reissued 1989); Angie Debo, *And Still the Waters Run* (1940, reprinted 1984); Walter L. Williams (ed.), *Southeastern Indians Since the Removal Era* (1979); J. Leitch Wright, Jr., *The Only Land They Knew: The Tragic Story of the American Indians in the Old South* (1981); Samuel J. Wells and Roseanna Tubby (eds.), *After Removal: The Choctaw in Mississippi* (1986); James H. Howard and Willie Lena, *Oklahoma Seminoles: Medicines, Magic, and Religion* (1984); Thurman Wilkins, *Cherokee Tragedy*, 2nd ed. rev. (1986); and William L. Anderson (ed.), *Cherokee Removal: Before and After* (1991), a collection of interdisciplinary essays.

NATIVE AMERICAN ART

Overviews are found in Frederic H. Douglas and Rene d'Harnoncourt, *Indian Art of the United States* (1941, reprinted 1969); Wolfgang Haberland, *The Art of North America*, rev. ed. (1968); Peter T. Furst and Jill L. Furst, *North American Indian Art* (1982), a wide-ranging study with illustrations; Edwin L. Wade and Carol Haralson (eds.), *The Arts of the North American Indian: Native Traditions in Evolution* (1986); Ralph T. Coe, *Lost and Found Traditions: Native American Art, 1965–1985* (1986), a treatment of the contemporary development of the native tradition; Jerry Jacka and Lois Essary Jacka, *Beyond Tradition: Contemporary Indian Art and Its Evolution* (1988); Christine Mather, *Native America: Arts, Traditions, and Celebrations* (1990); Christian F. Feest, *Native Arts of North America*, updated ed. (1992); David W. Penney and George C. Longfish, *Native American Art* (1994); and Jeremy Schmidt and Laine Thom, *In the Spirit of Mother Earth: Nature in Native American Art* (1994).

NATIVE AMERICAN MUSIC

A broad survey of North American Indian music appears in Marcia Herndon, *Native American Music* (1980), by a Cherokee author. Information on the music of several different tribes, written in most cases by Native American musicians, is offered by Charlotte Heth (ed.), *Native American Dance: Ceremonies and Social Traditions* (1992). An overview of North American Indian music, followed by articles on regions, instruments, 20th-century developments, and other topics, is provided by Ellen Koskoff (ed.), *The Garland Encyclopedia of World Music*, vol. 3, *The United States and Canada* (2001). Another useful general source is Tara Browner (ed.), *Music of the First Nations: Tradition and Innovation in Native North America* (2009).

Books on Native North American musical instruments include Beverley Diamond, M. Sam Cronk, and Franziska von Rosen, *Visions of Sound: Musical Instruments of First Nations Communities in Northeastern America* (1994), a groundbreaking study of Native American instruments based on indigenous concepts and classification systems; and Thomas Vennum, Jr., *The Ojibwa Dance Drum: Its History and Construction* (1982), which offers detailed information on making and decorating a ceremonial drum.

Detailed information on the powwow is provided by Tara Browner, *Heartbeat of the People: Music and Dance of the Northern Pow-wow* (2002), the first full-length book on the topic by a Native American (Choctaw) scholar and pow-wow dancer; Luke E. Lassiter, *The Power of Kiowa Song* (1998), which offers insight into the southern style; and William K. Powers, *War Dance: Plains Indian Musical Performance* (1990), a compilation of articles.

The representation of Native North American musics in European music notation is explored in Victoria Lindsay Levine (ed.), *Writing American Indian Music: Historic Transcriptions, Notations, and Arrangements* (2002), which includes examples of indigenous music notation systems, as well as work by scholars and composers who are themselves Native Americans.

NATIVE AMERICAN DANCE

Several suitable references on dance are found in the section on music above. Additional titles of interest are Erna Fergusson, *Dancing Gods* (1931, reissued 1988), an evaluation of ceremonial dances of the indigenous peoples of the Southwest; Curt Sachs, *World History of the Dance* (1937, reissued 1965; originally published in German, 1933), including several sections on various tribal dance performances; Bernard S. Mason, *Dances and Stories of the American Indian* (1944), a well-illustrated work almost entirely concerned with North American Indian dance steps, forms, and costumes; John L. Squires and Robert E. McLean, *American Indian Dances* (1963), a volume intended primarily for hobbyist readers; Reginald Laubin and Gladys Laubin, *Indian Dances of North America: Their Importance to Indian Life* (1977, reissued 1989), highlighting dance of the Plains area, with discussion of the music, costumes, and religious meaning; and Charlotte Heth (ed.), *Native American Dance: Ceremonies and Social Traditions* (1992), a valuable collection of essays on the history and meaning of dance of North, Central, and South American tribes.

Choreography is a major theme in Julia M. Buttree (Julia M. Seton), *The Rhythm of the Red Man* (1930), containing choreographies and some music; Bessie Evans and May G. Evans, *American Indian Dance Steps* (1931, reprinted 1975), descriptions of steps, six choreographies, and music; William N. Fenton and Gertrude P. Kurath, *The Iroquois Eagle Dance: An Offshoot of the Calumet Dance* (1953, reprinted 1991), history, choreographies, music, analysis, photographs, and bibliography; and Gertrude P. Kurath, *Michigan Indian Festivals* (1966), history, choreography, music, photographs, and bibliography.

INDEX